Unaccompanied Migrant Children

Unaccompanied Migrant Children

Social, Legal, and Ethical Perspectives

Edited by
Hille Haker and Molly Greening

LEXINGTON BOOKS
Lanham • Boulder • New York • London

Published by Lexington Books
An imprint of The Rowman & Littlefield Publishing Group, Inc.
4501 Forbes Boulevard, Suite 200, Lanham, Maryland 20706
www.rowman.com

6 Tinworth Street, London SE11 5AL, United Kingdom

British Library Cataloguing in Publication Information Available

Library of Congress Cataloging-in-Publication Data Is Available

ISBN: 978-1-4985-7452-5 (cloth: alk. paper)
ISBN: 978-1-4985-7453-2 (electronic)

∞™ The paper used in this publication meets the minimum requirements of American National Standard for Information Sciences—Permanence of Paper for Printed Library Materials, ANSI/NISO Z39.48-1992.

Printed in the United States of America

Contents

Acknowledgments

This book would not have been possible without the help and insights of many individuals and Loyola University Chicago. We are very grateful to the Center for the Human Rights of Children at Loyola University Chicago for their support, beginning with our initial stages of research and continuing till the final compilation of this book. The Department of Theology at Loyola University Chicago provided us the much-needed resources necessary for creating an edited volume. A special thanks to Jacob Torbeck for generously offering his time and technical skills for last-minute issues.

Sarah Craig and Julia Torres from Lexington Books were most helpful to get the manuscripts ready for publication, and Michael Gibson and Mikayla Mislak for taking over during the final stages of producing the book.

Our deepest gratitude goes to each one of our contributors who have worked on an expedited time frame amidst all kinds of life circumstances so that the book would be ready as soon as possible. They agreed with us that the topic did not bear any delay.

We are especially grateful for the many people who are working nonstop to create a better life for unaccompanied migrant children. For those who have ever been classified as an unaccompanied migrant child: we honor your courage in the face of countless obstacles. We hope that this book does justice to your experiences and pushes the public conversation toward immigration policies that recognize your human dignity.

Introduction

Molly Greening and Hille Haker

Child migration is not a new phenomenon. However, over the last years, when civil wars, regional wars, violence, climate change, and poverty have forced many people to leave their homes, increasingly large numbers of children take buses, cross deserts, and board rubber boats, heading to the United States of America or to Europe in search of a better life. The term "migration crisis" and "refugee crisis" have come to describe the high numbers of migrants over the last years. They approach the border between Mexico and the United States, and millions of people have fled Afghanistan, Syria, and several African countries since 2015. Many of them seek asylum in the European Union, among them were almost 100,000 unaccompanied migrant children in 2015 and still more than 60,000 in 2016.[1] Yet, statistics show that the most common destinations for refugees are bordering countries, and migration within national borders is more common than international migration.

At the border to the United States, many unaccompanied migrant children try to cross multiple times. Often, when they are caught, they will try again, and again. Death is always a possible outcome. But for these children, there is a promise on the other side—maybe a false one, but risking one's life may still be better than enduring the likewise life-threatening circumstances at home. The stakes are high; there may be family on the other side, or maybe not. Maybe "family" itself is caught in the in-between. Some travel to the United States or to Europe to reunite with their parents who made the journey themselves, months or years before. Others are chosen by their family to embark on a dangerous journey in order to support those whom they leave behind. Some are truly alone, with no family support, neither at home nor in the destination country. Some are separated from their parents or family members during the journey itself, while some are separated from their parents by officials once they reach the border: the "zero tolerance" policy introduced by the Trump administration in April 2018 provoked a public outcry because it meant that every child who was separated at the border from their families was now considered an "unaccompanied alien child," put in the custody of the Office of Refugee Resettlement. Though this policy was as quickly revoked as it was implemented, only two months after it was launched, it remains to be seen how the next steps of the new policies will play out.

The people who, at some point in their lives, fall under the category of unaccompanied migrant children can have as many differences as they have similarities, but, through their creativity and perseverance, often needed in order just to survive, they all have learned to be what Gloria Anzaldúa calls *nepantleras*, border crossers.[2] *Nepantleras* are the ones whose home is in-between worlds, regardless of whether they make it to their intended destination or whether they are deported back to where they started. The borders that unaccompanied migrant children cross are not just geographical, they are also cultural. Coming across a variety of customs, dialects, and landscapes that may differ considerably from the ones in their home culture requires a level of adaptability and street smarts most Western notions of childhood would never expect (or demand) a young person to acquire. The first encounter with the new culture is the border, and more often than not, immigration or asylum procedures dehumanize unaccompanied migrant children. They are met by a security system that is institutionalized and reinforced with helicopters, border patrol agents, the barrel of a gun, attack dogs, drones, and ever-more sophisticated forms of surveillance technologies and identification measures. Unaccompanied migrant children, like all undocumented immigrants and people seeking asylum, are "welcomed" with the full force of a border security system that seems to have one overall purpose: to prevent people from crossing the border. Media reports show two sides of the same distorting caricature of unaccompanied migrant children: the overly helpless child versus the violent adolescent. This dichotomy reverberates out of judge's stands, checkpoint booths of the US Department of Homeland Security, TV speakers, or photo captions, and it becomes engrained in the public perception.

How do the children respond to the challenges they face in their home countries, in transit, and in their destined countries where they are resettled? How can nations, societies, and citizens uphold the dignity and rights of migrant infants, children, and adolescents? The institutions set up to protect and care for unaccompanied migrant children are increasingly failing them. In order to restore the humanity of those who survived the risks of drowning in the Mediterranean Sea or the heat of the Sonoran desert, and to "unlock the human dignity[3]" of those who grow up in immigrant detention or refugee camps, we, the editors of this book, wanted to listen and attend to unaccompanied migrant children's experiences, take the insights from those working with and for them, and reflect the contexts in empirical studies and legal analyses before entering into the ethical evaluations. The scholars of this book provide numerous answers how to practically proceed, whether this concerns nongovernmental work, Church-led initiatives, political and legal advocacy, or the social work that accompanies children and youth in their education and professional formation.

This book counters many of the myths around migration, asylum, and refuge. The chapters in this volume offer insights from those professionals who work with and for migrant children in Central America, the United States, and Europe; they draw attention to the effect on children of being "uprooted"; and they explain the immigration procedures children currently face in the United States and, in one case, in a European Union member state. Building upon these and other empirical studies on child migration, several experts of migration ethics, child ethics, and human rights ethics engage in the ethical reflections concerning unaccompanied migrant children. The book explicitly engages with one ethical tradition in particular, namely Catholic social ethics. Representatives and organizations of the Catholic Church as well as other Christian organizations regularly contribute to the current debates on migration, often advocating for those whom they encounter in the desert, on the Sea, in the shelters, detention centers, or communities. The Catholic Migration and Refugee services in particular have established an indispensable support system for many migrants, refugees, or asylum seekers, especially in the United States. In fact, church advocates are highly visible in their public critique of the current migration policies. The US Conference of Catholic Bishops has urged the Obama administration as well as the Trump administration, for example, to end the policies of detention; furthermore, it has long argued that it is morally imperative to keep families together or, when separated, to reunify the members as fast as possible. This advocacy and the work of countless groups can only be applauded. But the *ethics* of *child* migration has rarely been examined, and the scholarship on children's rights in the context of migration is not on par with this practical work. In order to fill this gap, we asked several theologians to explore the theoretical framework of Catholic social ethics more thoroughly. The chapters in this part offer therefore important insights into a Catholic and Christian approach to the ethics of migration, centered on unaccompanied migrant children. On the one hand, these chapters contribute to the discussion within Catholic and Christian ethics, and on the other hand, they entail important arguments for any ethics of child migration.

Given the complexity of child migration, the volume is certainly limited in its scope: we mostly engage with current US policies, and in a smaller part with Europe, too, because the ethical issues concerning unaccompanied migrant children are confronted with similar debates and practices in the

United States and in Europe. Strikingly, only a few decades after the Berlin Wall was torn down resulting in the more or less free migration between the Western and Eastern European countries, new walls are being erected at the external border; a new symbolic "wall" is meant to protect Europe from the "invasion" of refugees, migrants, and asylum seekers from non-European countries. Likewise, for Donald Trump, the "wall" has become the symbol of his border politics. In both cases, ethical arguments invoking human rights and Christian principles seem to be too weak to remove the almost unsurpassable obstacles for those who claim to have a right to human dignity and rights, which is, after all, the normative basis of the United Nations. In contrast to the political failure of meeting the obligations toward children and minors, the authors of this volume all place the unaccompanied migrant children and minors—their needs, rights, and desires as well as the obstacles they confront when "going it alone"—at the center of the discussion.

Part 1 offers insights into the personal experiences of unaccompanied migrant children, told from the first-person perspective as well as from the perspective of social workers from several countries. The chapters in this part look at the ways unaccompanied migrant children experience their life as border crossers, how they are accompanied in the transition, and how they *should* be accompanied if their developmental needs were taken seriously.

Chapter 1 opens the book with a poem by Javier Zamora. He crossed the border alone when he was nine years old and offers glimpses into the emotional world of a child adjusting in his new home in the United States, and as an adult still torn between his life in El Salvador and his life in the United States Zamora's introduction to the poem is written in 2018, nineteen years after he came to the United States. The Trump administration has recently revoked the Temporary Protected Status (TPS) for Salvadorans, Haitians, and Hondurans, among others, to the effect that many of those who fled their countries decades ago are now faced with deportation. Javier Zamora's desperation is echoed in many analyses of this book, shedding light on the recent policy changes primarily in the United States. Many of the children who, like Javier Zamora, traveled alone to reunite with family members under these protections will once again have their lives turned upside down. The poem reminds readers of what is at stake for an ethics of child migration: it is the dignity of every individual person who immigrates into another country. But likewise, a moral society is defined by the humane—or inhumane—responses to the most vulnerable people in their midst.

In chapter 2, Maria Vidal, Celeste Sanchez, and Adam Avrushin provide insights from a cross-cultural empirical study carried out with social workers, lawyers, and several other professionals working with unaccompanied migrant children in Tegucigalpa, Honduras, Guatemala City, Guatemala, and Chicago, Illinois. Their experiences of working with migrating and immigrating children and youth correct the projections of children as merely passive addressees of help, or of overly independent actors. The study also demonstrates the anger and despair professionals feel regarding the social and political responses to the structural violence many of the unaccompanied migrant children encounter. Their work sets a counterpoint to the indifference or, worse, denigration that unaccompanied migrant children fight against in the receiving countries, and they show ways how to support children and youth professionally in order to create spaces of social belonging.

In chapter 3, Stephanie Arel picks up on the necessity of belonging, focusing on the psychological development and the impact of traumatic experiences on children and youth. Attachment theory especially demonstrates how important it is for the maintenance or restoration of unaccompanied migrant children's psychological well-being to find attachment figures during and after the migration journey. Arel's chapter offers some important insights for trauma-informed social services and the important role that community organizations can play in the receiving countries by providing community, social connection, and role models that all help children and youths to recreate a sense of belonging.

In chapter 4, Philip M. Anderson shares his experiences working with unaccompanied youth in the vocational training programs that are offered in Bavaria, Germany. He highlights the variety of experiences youth bring to the classroom, how they navigate cultural differences, and how they, like all adolescents, search for their own individual identity. Anderson emphasizes, among other things, that social service professionals working in integration or resettlement programs must be sensitive to their own biases in order to support the youth in acquiring the cultural competencies they need to socially belong.

Immigration and asylum laws determine the policies and institutional frameworks that border control, resettlement agencies, and social work programs implement for unaccompanied migrant children. The second part takes up the human rights of children in the international rights framework, confronting it with particular case studies from the United States and Sweden. They highlight the legal complexities, showing how laws that are purported to protect minors may actually violate their basic human and legal rights. No ethics of child migration can ignore these realities.

In chapter 5, Katherine Kaufka Walts provides an overview of the systems that unaccompanied migrant children navigate when they are apprehended by the US Customs and Border Patrol. With a focus on children's human rights, US immigration law, and the impact of the child's "best interests standard," Kaufka Walts walks the reader through the multiple barriers young people face when traversing complex and continuously changing legal systems alone. These become particularly dramatic when policies are changed without any regard for the children's and their families' rights and well-being. One striking example Kaufka Walts turns to is how the best interests standard is used to legitimize the recent decision to separate parents and children at the border.

In chapter 6, Susan Terrio examines the contested case of "Jane Doe," an unaccompanied youth who, while in the custody the US Office of Refugee Settlement (ORR), was denied access to abortion services due to recent policy changes. Following up on her interviews with multiple actors in this case and an in-depth analysis of some of the newest policies, Terrio highlights the contradictions of this case.

As necessary as the legal enforcement of children's rights is, which these studies clearly demonstrate, reducing human rights to legal rights may still be problematic. In chapter 7, Elena Namli and Linde Lindkvist exemplify the security-driven policies that unaccompanied migrant children confront. Since the treatment of children differs from that of adults, the Swedish immigration services have begun to use X-rays of the knee joint and dental examinations to determine the age of refugees who may enter the country without sufficient paperwork and are suspected to pose as children beyond the age of eighteen. Namli and Lindkvist elucidate how this practice creates a tension between legal rights and human dignity.

Part 3 takes up many of the insights of the preceding studies in order to envision a Catholic social ethics of child migration, centered on the unaccompanied migrant children. In chapter 8, Cristina Traina gives an account of unaccompanied migrant children as vulnerable agents. Emphasizing the agency and remarkable resilience of children, Traina also offers an original interpretation of the Christian trope of the Holy Family. In her ethical analysis that draws on the biblical story of the childhood of Jesus of Nazareth, she shows that families sometimes must make dramatic decisions in order to survive.

Political narratives often reduce migration causes to individual choices and stories, ignoring the structural causes for the poverty, violence, and instability in the home countries and regions. How can ethics, and Christian ethics in particular, counter the narratives that discard the responsibility for the conditions that force children to flee or migrate in the first place? What narratives are to be put in place? Two authors turn to these questions, analyzing the historical political connection between Central American countries and the United States, and exploring ways how Christian ethics may spell out the responsibility in the context of child migration.

In chapter 9, Kristin Heyer recalls the recent US immigration history, drawing attention specifically to the US military presence in in the Northern Triangle. Instead of seeing migration almost entirely through the lens of the politics of border control and "law and order," Heyer argues that the United States must acknowledge its own responsibility for the crisis. Furthermore,

Heyer points to the recent increase of privatized shelters and detention centers, turning immigration enforcement into a growth industry and blurring the lines between immigration policies and incarceration. This move criminalizes those who bear the consequences of failed policies both in their home countries and in the United States. In her ethical interpretation of Catholic Social Teaching, Heyer turns to the concepts of social sin, solidarity with the poor, the common good, and conscientization as a path toward conversion.

In chapter 10, Tisha M. Rajendra introduces her approach of "justice as responsibility to relationships." Using Guatemala and El Salvador as case studies, she specifically focuses on the responsibilities of US citizens toward unaccompanied migrant children and youth seeking asylum from gang violence in their countries of origin. Rajendra's ethical approach offers a social and political ethics as an alternative to the mere reference to the universal rights framework as well as to the call to benevolence through charitable hospitality.

In the concluding chapter, Hille Haker examines the recent shift in US and European migration, asylum, and refugee policies toward a particular nationalist populism that threatens not only the human rights of millions of people but also defies the global human rights *regime*. Haker argues for a political ethics of child migration that embraces a cosmopolitan framework of human rights. Haker demands to prioritize human dignity and the human rights of children, and over against the instrumentalization of Christianity in the US and European nationalist anti-migration movements, she emphasizes the Christian notion of hospitality to strangers as a core commandment of Christian ethics.

Undoubtedly, for migrant children to "go it alone" is a time of crisis that will shape them for the rest of their lives. Likewise, there is no question that the sheer numbers of global migrants and refugees have caused a political crisis in the West. We contest, however, that unaccompanied migrant children seeking asylum in the United States or Europe are a threat to these countries' national security, and we also reject the myth that they cause a crisis for their cultural identities. Instead, this book demonstrates that the real—and often unacknowledged— crisis is in fact a moral crisis: it is a crisis of refused responsibility and lack of care for the most vulnerable group of migrants and refugees, namely children.

NOTES

1. Eurostat News release, "Asylum applicants considered to be unaccompanied minors. 63 300 unaccompanied minors among asylum seekers registered in the EU in 2016," May 11, 2017, https://www.google.com/url?sa=t&rct=j&q=&esrc=s&source=

web&cd=1&ved=0ahUKEwjlzrnQ_4PbAhVV1IMKHSH_BrAQFggpMAA&url=http%3A%2F%2Fwww.europeanmigrationlaw.eu%2Fdocuments%2FAsylum%2520applicants%2520considered%2520to%2520be%2520unaccompanied%2520minors.pdf&usg=AOvVaw1ce_iae4k72oJP9fbSXxH5.

2. Gloria Anzaldúa, "Preface: (Un)natural Bridges, (Un)safe Spaces," in *This Bridge We Call Home: Radical Visions for Transformation*, eds. Gloria Anzaldúa and AnaLouise Keating (New York: Routledge, 2002).

BIBLIOGRAPHY

Anzaldúa, Gloria. "Preface: (Un)natural Bridges, (Un)safe Spaces." In *This Bridge We Call Home: Radical Visions for Transformation,* edited by Gloria Anzaldúa and AnaLouise Keating, New York: Routledge, 2002.

Eurostat News release. "Asylum applicants considered to be unaccompanied minors. 63 300 unaccompanied minors among asylum seekers registered in the EU in 2016." May 11, 2017, https://www.google.com/url?sa=t&rct=j&q=&esrc=s&source=web&cd=1&ved=0ahUKEwjlzrnQ_4PbAhVV1IMKHSH_BrAQFggpMAA&url=http%3A%2F%2Fwww.europeanmigrationlaw.eu%2Fdocuments%2FAsylum%2520applicants%2520considered%2520to%2520be%2520unaccompanied%2520minors.pdf&usg=AOvVaw1ce_iae4k72oJP9fbSXxH5.

United States Conference of Catholic Bishops/Migration and Refugee Services/ The Center for Migration Studies. "Unlocking Human Dignity: A Plan to Transform the U.S. Immigrant Detention System." Washington, DC, 2015.

Part I

GOING IT ALONE: EXPERIENCES AND SOCIAL RESPONSES

Chapter 1

Unaccompanied

Javier Zamora

May 8, 2018

I write this after going to the USCIS field office in San Francisco. I'm trying to return to my country to interview for my already approved EB-1 Visa. If I leave the country with my current status, I forfeit it. An Advance Parole permit was what I was asking for. The regional person there could not understand my request and it was not granted.

I was really hoping to obtain my green card on June 4, 2018; almost exactly nineteen years before I first entered this country in June 10, 1999. When the events depicted in *June 10, 1999* happened. I like this title because as you can tell, even nineteen years after, I have to try to jump through immigration's bureaucratic hoops in order to say, "I exist, I matter. Look at all I've done. Aren't I extraordinary?"

The poem, I think, is pretty self-explanatory. The metaphor is the repetition. Again and again I'm reminded of my status. Of my trauma. Of my second-class citizenship or lack of citizenship in this country, or anywhere else. I hope my situation gets resolved in time to obtain my visa.

I hope my humanity is fully recognized soon. Oh so very soon. Rest assured, I'll keep trying.

June 10, 1999[1]

i.

first day inside a plane I sat by the window
like when I ride the bus
correction when I rode buses
below the border I sat by the window attention
to dogs under a mango
trash under parked cars
drunks passed out

I sat by plane window
same afternoon I crossed
desert the third time
was not nervous at white
people at terminal all those questions
did not cry did not stop
looking out the window
for Statue of Liberty Golden
Gate Disneyland Miami

i.

we were lost and didn't know which star
was north what was east west we all
dropped out of the van too soon to remember
someone said the sun rose east we circled
so much we had no maps and the guide we paid
twisted his ankle was slowing us down

we couldn't leave him *why*
asked the ones who walked ahead
whispered they'd heard coyotes fake they're hurt
circle and circle so much they make it seem they tried
but all they did was steal money

I don't know
his ankle *was* swollen he *was* feverish
it's true
the sun's heat *was* a reptile but I know
if we hadn't left him we'd still be
run-over toads

i.

I didn't recognize Dad
different from pictures

he remembers the smell
shit piss dust in your hair
he says now
crying

Mom had a bag with Nikes
Levi's *Star Wars*
Episode One shirt

I left my ripped clothes
inside a Ross fitting room

I'm tired of writing *the fence the desert*
the van picked us up
took me to parents
I'm tired it's always that

even now outside United Airlines 18F
I see clouds first like quilt
then like cheese
melting in a plastic bag
under *creosotes*
next to those *empty*
gallons of water

i.

Mom didn't know
Dad didn't know
even if they'd run across fences before
they didn't see my knees
crashing into cactus needles
that night one shoe slipped off

she says Coyote said
I'll carry him to your front door myself Pati

she didn't know 110 degrees
when like Colorado River toads
we slid under bushes

officers yelled
on your fucking knees

you couldn't have known this could happen
Mom
you couldn't have
no es su culpa
no lo es

i.

javier here you go
about same shit
when will your status change

when will you stop
not being that June 10
let it go man

you're not inside that Tucson fitting room
this is not Abuelita
who you couldn't call
those eight weeks she lit a candle every night
to light your path

Abuelita who you can't call
every two weeks
you can't even tell her la quiero
la quiero mucho
only here in a language
she don't speak

i.

I left Grandpa in Guatemala
for eight weeks no one heard my voice
for eight weeks
no one slept

twice parents packed the car said
I'm going to the border

then at 1 a.m.
someone called said
you the parent of javier nine years old
from El Salvador
yes

órale
it's gone be fifteen hundred
cash
can you get to Tucson
tomorrow
yes

órale
near Phoenix
call this number

i.

to write I look for words in books
little ants Abuelita calls words

right now it's *bonsai*
that makes me think *father*

he made the one in a black pot in the first living-room I saw
in this country

correction first *furnished* living-room in this country
my first dawn here I spent it dreaming
about what furniture should be where
on that living-room carpet used as coyote warehouse
in some Tucson suburb

the smell of all fifty of us who waited for family
to pay so we could take different vans
to different states

in that ceiling's white bumpy surface
I imagined a movie I wanted to see
Mi Vida Gringa

I was ready to be gringo
speak English
own a pool
Jeep convertible

i.

Abuelita won't leave the house
hasn't left in years
hasn't will not
leave
no bullshit
no metaphor

she won't shower
won't walk to the market
pero they'll talk
what will they say
she says

who is they
and who cares
we say through the phone
on the table
by her door
we've all walked out of

her hair knots a dread
in the back of her short hair

like a microphone head
cousin says

my little microphone head
won't shower
won't sit on a chair
watching people walk by
like she did
when we were there

i.

I wasn't born here
I've always known this country wanted me dead

do you believe me when I say more than once
a white man wanted me dead

a white man passed a bill that wants me deported
wants my family deported

a white man a white man a white man
not the song I wanted to hear

driving to the airport today
the road the trees the signs the sky the cars the walls the lights

told me we want you
out out out

i.

a few hours ago I boarded a plane
tried to cut ahead with Group A
usually I'm not caught I was stopped
the flight attendant told me wait
it's not your turn I started sweating
I wore white the worst
color for sweat my back drenched
until she let me through I was
in the gate in the plane 18F

when I got to SFO
I took Marin Airporter to San Rafael
same bus I took when I first saw
the Golden Gate
I'd never dreamed of it then
waiting in that line at the US embassy
when I tried and tried for a visa
like Mom like Dad like aunts
and we all got denied

i.

in public again writing at the corner
so people can't see line breaks
so they think I'm essayist

maybe I'm ashamed
maybe I don't want them reading this
that was not part of *Mi Vida Gringa*

Mi Vida Gringa not the movie I paid to see then
on that ceiling
but I still haven't exited in protest
haven't been kicked out
for not having a valid ticket
I sneaked in bought the popcorn drank the Coke
bonsai the word stuck in my brain
Dad a landscaper Mom a babysitter

I was supposed to be lawyer
businessman soccer player
Mom and Dad said
someone of value

i.

javier can you think of that date
without almost pissing yourself in La Migra's backseat
and in front of you people running
fast as we could

now I walk toward dawn
only when I'm fucked up
and if I'm blacked out
I want to shut the fuck up
those brown strangers
who didn't listen and ran
from Migra guns

but now in San Francisco
I'm half-drunk at 8 a.m.
stuffing shirts pants socks
into my carry-on

as if I had a flight today

I've carried this since that day
I'm talking about the flor de izote in our fence
the one Abuelita plucked
mixed with eggs that dawn she was crying
I didn't know why
come out come out of the house Abuelita
please

I'm soft I'm soft Grandpa says
who to this day goes out with his bad knee
to the fields and scrapes the grass
hunching down raking to blast the leaves on fire

and what do I do
I sit her type it's Monday
it's Tuesday it's Friday
type *first day inside a plane I sat by the window*

everyone's working
Mom Dad Tía Lupe Tía Mali
working under different names
I sit here writing our names

The TV is on
coffee is on
the couch is soft
my throat is dry
and sick and still
nothing has changed

NOTE

1. Javier Zamora, "June 10, 1999" from *Unaccompanied*. Copyright © 2017 by Javier Zamora. Reprinted with the permission of The Permissions Company, Inc., on behalf of Copper Canyon Press, www.coppercanyonpress.org. All rights reserved.

Chapter 2

Childhood, Violence, and Displacement

Experiences of Unaccompanied Immigrant Children from the Perspective of Human and Legal Service Providers in North and Central America

Maria Vidal de Haymes, Adam Avrushin, and Celeste Sánchez

UNACCOMPANIED IMMIGRANT CHILDREN IN THE UNITED STATES

The migration of unaccompanied children in the United States is not a new phenomenon, although the circumstances in which they migrated have varied over time. During the seventeenth and eighteenth century, children from Africa and Europe were kidnapped and brought to North America as enslaved persons and indentured servants, respectively.[1] During and after World War II, thousands of unaccompanied children were admitted to the United States through various refugee resettlement programs, including 5,000 British children evacuated during the German Air attacks under Operation Pied Piper;[2] 14,000 Cuban children evacuated under Operation Peter Pan following the 1959 revolution;[3] and 2,500 Vietnamese children evacuated under Operation Babylift during the Vietnam War.[4]

In more recent years, unaccompanied children have continued to come to the United States, although in an irregular fashion, entering the United States through the Southern border. These children come primarily from Mexico, El Salvador, Honduras, and Guatemala, making the difficult journey to the United States for multifaceted and complex reasons. Among the most common reasons given are these: to escape the high rates of violent crime in their home countries, family reunification, and limited economic opportunity.[5] The peak of this flow occurred in 2014, with a record number of 68,500 unaccompanied minors apprehended by US Border Patrol on the Southwest border of the United States.[6]

While most unaccompanied immigrant children (UIC) are apprehended at the Southern border or are identified at US ports of entry, a smaller number are apprehended in the interior and deemed to be unaccompanied minors.[7] The number of apprehensions have decreased since the 2014 peak, yet significant numbers of UIC continue to arrive, with 39,970 apprehended in 2015 and 59,697 in 2016.[8]

FACTORS CONTRIBUTING TO CONTEMPORARY UNACCOMPANIED CHILD MIGRATION TO THE UNITED STATES

A report authored by Elizabeth Kennedy (2014) of the US Immigration Council during the peak of unaccompanied minor arrival at the US southern border, and another by the United Nations High Commissioner for Refugees, UNHCR (2014) focused on why Mexican and Central American unaccompanied minors were migrating in such high numbers. She comes to the conclusion that "crime, gang threats, or violence appear to be the strongest determinants for children's decision to emigrate."[9] Similarly, the UNHCR report found that 58 percent of the children interviewed "suffered, [had] been threatened or feared serious harm of a nature that raises international protection concerns."[10] The conclusions drawn in these reports based on nonscientific samples of unaccompanied migrant children are supported by the well-documented high rates of violent crime, homicide, and organized crime and transnational gang presence in the region.[11] Unfortunately for many youth, violence is also present in the home and is reflected in the reported incidence of child abuse, neglect, and abandonment, also a motivating factor for some to migrate.[12]

General insecurity and direct violence in Mexico and the Northern Triangle region have become the predominant factor pushing youth to look for safety in the United States. Yet, situations of structural violence that contribute to this direct and widespread violence, such as poverty and state failure to provide needed protections and support, continue to be significant factors in motivating youth emigration. Furthermore, social problems associated with structural violence, such as abandonment and family separation are also significant factors propelling migration.

For children in Mexico and Central America, the separation from one or both parents due to migration for significant time periods is a common phenomenon with unfavorable psychosocial implications.[13] For example, irrespective of the rising rates of nonmarital births and divorce, the rising migration rates since the mid-1970s have moved migration from the least common to the most common cause for father household absence.[14] So significant is this trend that by the age of fifteen more than one in five Mexican children experience the absence of their father due to migration.[15] This trend toward transnational families and associated separations has been expanded and elaborated with growing rates of female migration (feminization of migration) and the migration of mothers that leave their children with caregivers in communities of origin (transnational motherhood) in recent decades, movements resulting in a "care deficit" in the global south.[16] Not surprisingly, Kennedy found that more than 90 percent of the 322 unaccompanied immigrant children she interviewed had a family member in the United States and a little over 50 percent had one or both parents in the United States, yet only one in three of the children interviewed identified family reunification as their primary reason for leaving.[17] Nevertheless, Donato and Sisk found that parental migration increases the likelihood of youth migrations.[18]

For many youth, particularly those from rural areas, extreme poverty and a desire to work contributed to their decision to migrate.[19] Limited opportunities for employment, high rates of poverty, and minimal state support and services leave many with few options outside of migration to provide for the material needs of their family.[20]

CHILDHOOD AS ANALYTICAL FRAMEWORKS

Childhood

Childhood is socially constructed and is understood according to various intertwined contextual factors including race, gender, culture, ethnicity, class and at different periods throughout history.[21] The traditional view of children is that they are incomplete adults with presumed deficits of maturity, competence, and significance. The more current and contrasting view is that children are social "beings" in their own right with their own status, agency, capacities, set of needs, and rights that evolve over time.[22]

Mayall argues that childhood is a politically determined category that is often derived from adult perspectives that view children as inherently, inferior to adults because they lack competence, maturity and the necessary capacity to make decisions in their own best interest. Views that purport that only adults know what is best for children place them in a subordinate position and impede any consideration of taking children's views seriously.[23]

A progressive view of childhood promotes children's status within society as equal to adults. Unlike the traditional view, children are viewed as contributing members of society, with agency and the ability to change their environment. The views of adults are not exclusive in determining children's needs and wishes. Children's own expressed views and beliefs are also relevant, if not critical, to the construction and implementation of social policies and practices.

John Tobin distinguishes the historical development of childhood through a legal lens and identifies three primary models of childhood: proprietary, welfare, and rights-based models. Through this approach, he demonstrates the interrelationship between the evolving notion of childhood, children's rights, and the obligation of families and the State.[24]

Proprietary Model of Childhood

Prior to the late nineteenth century, a proprietary model of childhood considered children the property of their parent and the family preeminent in all matters involving the child. Parents had the right of possession over their child until they reached adulthood, which for boys was, approximately, the age of fourteen and girls, the age of sixteen. The right of possession provided parents with full control over all aspects of a child's life without government or other nonfamilial interference. Government interference risked disrupting the family structure and, hence, society. In the English Common Law case, Re Egar Ellis (1883), Lord Justice Bowen declared that the court must not "interfere with the natural order and course of family life, the very basis of which is the authority of the father, except it be in those very special cases. . . . To neglect the natural jurisdiction of the father over the child would be to "set aside the whole course and order of nature, and . . . would disturb the very foundation of family life." Parents, or if absent, the child's family, ultimately decided what was best for the child.

Welfare Notion of Childhood

Beginning in the late nineteenth and into the mid-twentieth century, increased knowledge about children and their development resulted in the alternative welfare model of childhood. They are not property/chattel but, rather, vulnerable, incompetent, and immature human beings in need of protection and support from competent adults. The previous proprietary model failed to ensure the protection and welfare of children who risked being left in the care of potentially harmful adult family members. Adults and institutions created by the State (including courts) had an obligation to protect children against harm and to intervene to secure the child's best interest.

Although the notion of children as human beings resulted in increased protections, the general period view maintained that children lacked the maturity, capacity, and agency to protect themselves against harm or make decisions in their own best interest. This, consequently, not only impacted their private lives, but also their participation in political and civil society where they have little if any voice.

Rights-based Model of Childhood

Beginning in the middle of the twentieth century, a rights-based model promoted a more developed understanding about children and their development. It supported the view that children are particularly vulnerable to exploitation and maltreatment but, because they continue to grow and evolve, they have a right to determination in their own well-being, subject to their individual capacity and maturity. Children are human beings but, because of their vulnerable and evolving development, need special protections and rights that place added responsibilities on primary caregivers and the state to support their healthy development.

Internationally, this rights-based model is apparent in the U.N. Convention on the Rights of the Child (1989), which is ratified by every nation in the world except for the United States. This human rights treaty defines the civil, political, economic, social, and cultural rights of children and, notably, promotes the best interest of the child in all State actions concerning children (Article 3). It recognizes a child's right to express their views in all matters affecting them (Articles 12, 13, 14, and 15) thus, theoretically, guaranteeing a child's participation in political and civil society.

Children both affect and are affected by social structures and by the constructions of childhood.[25] Notable examples include the laws and related child-serving systems that address child labor and child welfare.[26] In their examination of applied notions of childhood, Somers, Herrera, and Rodriguez argue that child-serving laws and systems may disagree and result in alternative approaches to engaging and supporting young people.[27] In their historical analysis of legal systems for unaccompanied immigrant children, the authors highlight five constructions of childhood that are embedded in their structures and impact these children's experiences and perceptions: developmental, dependency, privacy, autonomous, and threatening.

- *Developmental Construction*—Children are in constant progression cognitively and social emotionally;
- *Dependency Construction*—Children need other adults, and adult-led organizations, to make necessary decisions to survive (food, shelter, healthcare, education). Children are the target for intervention but intervention goes through adults.

- *Privacy Construction*—Children do not have voice/agency within their environment. Children do not have input/voice into their needs and/or the interventions designed to support them.
- *Autonomous Construction*—Children are independent actors with voice and autonomy. Children have their own knowledge, experience, belief, and understanding about the world that is different, not inferior to adults. Children's views and ideas are valued and can inform and improve adult's understanding about the world. Children are viewed as active political, social, and economic partners in the world.
- *Threatening Construction*—Children are menacing, problematic, and a drain on society. Children are not valued contributors but rather negative influences on their environment.

In their historical examination of the US immigration system, immigration courts, and the US Office of Refugee and Resettlement social service organizations, Somers, Herrera, and Rodriguez conclude that child-serving laws and systems have over time presented all of these constructions of childhood, resulting in varied, and at times contradictory, approaches to unaccompanied immigrant children.[28] While all constructions of childhood are expressed throughout the custodial and legal immigration systems, the dependency and developmental constructions are more relevant for the custodial system because of the "historical marginalization of children in the immigration system."[29]

CURRENT STUDY

The current study is guided by an interest in understanding the varied perspectives regarding childhood and violence in the processes of social exclusion or integration of vulnerable Central American youth and UICs in the United States from the standpoint of a diverse sample of professionals working in systems that these youth encounter. The systems of interest broadly include family, economy, education, health, and security institutions, as well as immigration. The guiding questions for the secondary analysis were

1. What forms of violence did the study participants indicate the youth experienced in communities of origin, and destination? What impact do these forms of violence have on the integration or exclusion of these youth?
2. What were the perspectives regarding childhood reflected by the study participants?
3. How did the participants' views regarding childhood and violence inform their vision regarding desired social responses to address the situation of these youth?

Design and Procedures

The current study consists of a secondary analysis of two primary qualitative data sets that entailed transcripts from forty-six interviews conducted by the authors for two separate projects: one based in Chicago, Illinois, with a focus on the unaccompanied immigrant children in Chicago; and the second based in Guatemala City, Guatemala, and Tegucigalpa, Honduras, with a focus on marginalized youth in situations of high vulnerability and violence.

Such a design is appropriate given the fit between the primary data sets and the secondary research questions which apply a new conceptual focus to the original research issues presented in the primary studies.[30] The decision to conduct a secondary analysis is supported by several factors: 1) the research questions for the secondary analysis are sufficiently close to those of the primary research; 2) the data collection techniques and time frame for both primary studies were the same; and 3) the thematic analytic techniques in the primary study are similar to those applied in the secondary analysis; and furthermore, the ideas explored in this secondary analysis were identified during the analytic interpretation associated with the primary studies.[31]

Data Sources and Sample

As previously stated, this chapter draws on interviews from two separate primary studies. The Chicago study focused on the experiences and outcomes of unaccompanied immigrant children released to family/sponsors in the Chicago metropolitan area from an Office of Refugee Resettlement (ORR) facility and those who entered the United States undetected and did not engage with ORR. For this study, "Unaccompanied Immigrant Child" refers to children/youth, under the age of eighteen, who entered the United States without a legal primary caregiver and without lawful immigration status in the United States. In-depth semi-structured interviews were conducted with local human service, education, health, and legal advocacy professionals attending to unaccompanied immigrant children and the families reunited in Illinois with the purpose of gathering their perspective on: 1) the unique experiences and service needs of these UIC, 2) what formal services and supports were available to them, and 3) how state and local public policies and agency practices facilitate access to services and support that enhance the well-being and integration of this population?

The focus of the Tegucigalpa/Guatemala City primary study was to better understand: 1) the experience and context of youth in situations of violence in Honduras and Guatemala who have been displaced or are at risk for displacement; 2) the nature of the violence and displacement they experience and how it influences critical dimensions of their life, including family/household structure and relationships, education, employment, housing, health and mental health, migration, and the formation of their own families; and 3) what has been the humanitarian response to the precarious situation of these youth? In-depth semi-structured interviews were conducted with local human service, education, health, and legal advocacy organizations attending to this youth population.

A semi-structured interview guide was developed for each study. The interviews were conducted by the authors in the office/facility of the research participant. The Chicago interviews were conducted in English and the Tegucigalpa and Guatemala City interviews were all conducted in Spanish. Prior to initiating the interview, the participants were provided a verbal overview and written consent form detailing the purpose of the study, any risk or benefits and issues of confidentiality. Each interview lasted approximately one hour in length. All interviews were audiotaped and later transcribed for analysis. The Chicago interviews were conducted July through November of 2017, and the Guatemala City and Tegucigalpa interviews were conducted in July of 2017.

Chicago was selected as a project site for the UIC study because it is home to a large and diverse immigrant community, with a long tradition of immigrant reception, sanctuary, and integration, as well as vibrant immigrant organizations and residential enclaves.[32] Chicago is located in the state of Illinois, which ranks among the top six receiving states for new immigrants and sixth among states with undocumented residents.[33] More than 60 percent of the state's foreign-born live in the Chicago metropolitan area, a figure which includes 1,818 UIC who have been released by the Office of Refugee Resettlement to live with sponsors in Illinois since October 2013,[34] with the vast majority of whom (866) were placed in Cook County, the county housing the city of Chicago.[35] These youth join thousands more UIC who entered without detection and also live in the area.

Tegucigalpa and Guatemala City were selected because of their high rate of violence, gang-controlled neighborhoods, and forced displacement due to organized crime and transnational gangs, factors that impel the migration of youth from these countries. The informal communities on the periphery of these cities, as well as marginalized sectors in the interior are particularly targeted, as are the youth. Because of the indiscriminate, targeted violence and gang control of communities, the UNHCR estimates that over 215,000 people fled Honduras, Guatemala, and El Salvador primarily to the United States and Canada in the first half of 2017.[36] While both of these cities suffer tremendous violence, they were also selected because of the remarkable organizations and agencies that have emerged in response.

Sample

The sample included forty-six professionals drawn from diverse education, legal, and human service professions and roles in the public and private sector: twenty based in Chicago, nine from Guatemala City, and seventeen from Tegucigalpa. The participants were recruited for the primary studies because of their personal knowledge, experience, and insights regarding the unique service needs of vulnerable youth in Guatemala City and Tegucigalpa, and the UIC population settling in Chicago, Illinois, US metropolitan regions. Table 2.1 provides a summary of the Chicago study sample and Table 2.2 of the Guatemala City and Tegucigalpa study sample.

Table 2.1 Chicago Study Sample

Professional Role	*Frequency*
Former teacher in ORR facility	1
Case manager in ORR facility	1
Post release services administrator in ORR facility	1
Administrator of shelter for UIC that have aged out of ORR facility and have a pending asylum case	1
Case manager at shelter for UIC that have aged out of ORR facility and have a pending asylum case	1
Religious that provides pastoral accompaniment to UIC in ORR facilities	1
Administrator/program director in community-based human service organization that provides services to UIC	1
Former state human service director for immigrant services/current administrator in community-based service organization that provides services to UIC	1
Director of immigrant advocacy and resource organization	1
Attorney in Office of the Public Guardian	1
Attorney in clinic that provides pro bono representation of UIC	1
Social worker in legal clinic that provides pro bono counsel to UIC	1
Public school system administrator for Language and Cultural Services	1
Public school system administrator for college and career planning	1
Public school system administrator for Community Relations and Refugee Services	1
City colleges advisor and transitional language services program administrator	1
Former charter school network administrator/current director of education policy and parent advocacy organization	1
Social worker in public high school with immigrant welcoming center	1
Social worker in grade school with large immigrant population/ Former social worker in public high school with large immigrant population	1
Attorney with Guardian Ad Litem Office for minors	1

Table 2.2 Guatemala City and Tegucigalpa Study Sample

Professional Role	*Frequency*
Principal and religious sister of elementary school and community center in Guatemala City	1
Program coordinator in community organization focused on educational and occupational opportunities for marginalized youth in Guatemala City	1
Academic coordinator and teacher in community organization focused on educational and occupational opportunities for marginalized youth in Guatemala City	1
Director of nonprofit that provides legal and psychological services for youth and women survivors of violence in Guatemala	1
Executive coordinator of association of private and state organizations working toward migrant rights in Guatemala	1
Education director of nonprofit focused on education and life skills training for children and adults of communities surrounding Guatemala City garbage dump	1
Volunteer/tour guide of nonprofit focused on education and life skills training for children and adults of communities surrounding Guatemala City garbage dump	1
Youth advocate of Human Rights Headquarters in Guatemala City	1
Lawyer in nonprofit focused on youth survivors of sexual violence, exploitation and human trafficking in Guatemala	1
Missionary in youth outreach center in community of Tegucigalpa, Honduras	1
Coordinator of youth outreach center in community of Tegucigalpa, Honduras	1
Youth group coordinator of community church in Tegucigalpa, Honduras	1
Priest of community church in Tegucigalpa, Honduras	1
Researcher in Tegucigalpa, Honduras	1
Researcher and youth shelter worker in Tegucigalpa, Honduras	1
Communications director of organization comprised of volunteer youth focused on reducing violence in Honduras	1
Volunteer and member of organization comprised of volunteer youth focused on reducing violence in Honduras	2
Missionary of a Christian order focused on accompanying youth and families in community of Tegucigalpa, Honduras	2
Program director of shelter for youth experiencing homelessness and trafficked youth in Tegucigalpa, Honduras	1
National director of shelter for youth experiencing homelessness and trafficked youth in Tegucigalpa, Honduras	1
Social worker and former youth of residential care home for at-risk children in Honduras	1
Doctor and former youth of residential care home for at-risk children in Honduras	1
Human rights worker in UNHCR office in Honduras	1
NGO human rights advocate that works with youth experiencing homelessness in Honduras	1

Analysis

The authors conducted an inductive transcript-based analysis using open and axial coding with the interview transcripts to identify themes related to violence, notions of childhood and their interrelationships.[37] Dedoose, a web-based application for the coding and analysis of qualitative data, aided this process. Several strategies were employed to enhance rigor and quality, including an iterative transcript review process, independent coding of each transcript by two of the researchers and discussion until agreement was reached, documentation of coding development through memoing, rechecking coding against the data, and identification of direct quotes to support themes for transparency.

FINDINGS AND DISCUSSION

Perspectives on Child Vulnerability and Migration

In the Central and North American region, the number of youth that have experienced displacement due to structural and direct violence resulting from profound inequality, a legacy of war, devastating natural disasters, and transnational gangs and organized crime has escalated dramatically in the last decade. The displacement that youth experience can be internal or transnational, or have dimensions of both. This study gathered the perspectives of individuals who work(ed) in organizations that attend to youth who have been displaced or are at risk of displacement due to the structural and direct violence they experience. In Guatemala City and Tegucigalpa, the individuals interviewed worked with youth from highly marginalized communities who were at high risk of displacement, or had already been displaced, or had emigrated but had been deported. In Chicago, the individuals interviewed worked with unaccompanied immigrant children post release from an ORR detention facility or who had entered the United States undetected.

In both the US and Central American contexts, these youth were recognized as a particularly vulnerable population. The individuals interviewed saw these young people as vulnerable for numerous reasons related to their predicament. They understood that many migrated out of necessity to escape high rates of violence and extreme poverty, only to experience additional insecurity and harm along their journey. An increase in violence, extortions, kidnappings, and physical injuries, mutilations, and even deaths due to assaults and accidents add to the already physically and emotionally exhausting experience of traveling in a clandestine manner. Moreover, they understand these young people to be particularly vulnerable because they do not have a parent or primary caregiver to help make critical life decisions and someone who is able to protect them from the harms and mistreatment of other adults in their country of origin. The statement made by a post-release services administrator in ORR facility reflects this view of childhood as a social category that merits protection by adults:

> I think that, at the end of the day these are just kids. They really are. When you give them an opportunity to be just kids, you realize that they are no different than yours or mine, or your nephews, or your nieces. They are just kids, you know. Not some sort of political thing, not something that is here to drain the economy. . . . They are just kids that deserve protection. That deserve basic rights as children and first and foremost that is to be alive and not feel threatened, to have that sense of security. . . . We protect children. That is what we do. You wouldn't see a poor child walking down the street and cold and not say—Oh my God where is this kid's parents? These are kids, you know. I don't know how [to] describe that feeling; that need to really change the way we look at unaccompanied children. . . . They are children who come from horrific things that none of us could possibly understand.

Many of the participants in Guatemala City and Tegucigalpa believed that their organizations addressed governmental and institutional failures that left these youth unprotected and socially excluded, a condition that often was seen as leading to displacement from their communities of origin and for many the necessity to emigrate. After noting that Honduras, unlike other Central American countries plagued by violence, had invited the United Nations High Commission on Refugees (UNHCR-ACNUR in Latin America) to have a presence in Honduras due to the alarming level of internal displacement, a UNHCR human rights advocate described the multifaceted nature of violence experienced by youth in Honduras:

> I am going to give you an example of a child from any complicated neighborhood in Honduras. He has left the country and you ask him in the first interview why did you abandon your country? "I left because I needed money and I needed a job." Then one would think that it was for economic reasons. Later you ask why the United States and not another place? Because my parents live in the United States. So now the motives are familial and not violence. Finally in the third interview, you ask why did you leave, what did work have to do with it? "Well they told my mother that she had to pay her debts and then the extortion occurred." And that is the path that the violence continues. I conclude that the violence is multicausal.

Similarly, the individuals interviewed in Chicago, believed that the US government failed to protect these youth from additional harms after they arrived and integrated them into the local communities where they now live.

They believed that their organization, in some cases, needed to protect these young people from governmental abuses and harms that include not providing an attorney or guardian *ad litem* to advocate for them and/or represent their best interests in asylum interviews and/or removal proceedings, detaining the unaccompanied youth in inappropriate conditions, and repatriating them to their home nation without proper vetting. An attorney in the Office of the Cook County Public Guardian in Chicago summarized this concern regarding the vulnerability of children, the failure of the state to protect them, and the need for adults or adult-led institutions to intervene on their behalf to advance their best interest.

> It's horrible. It's absolutely horrible. How can you ship a kid back on a plane to nobody? How is that in the child's best interest? How you can put a kid in immigration court without a lawyer? The fact that we don't give them counsel is appalling; it's just down right appalling. I can understand you not wanting to use the best interest standard for anyone 18 or older, but anyone who is a child? You have to use the best interest equation even if that does open the floodgates. Even if the answer is well it's always in their best interest to get status. Ok so be it. Give them all status. I mean, where are you sending them back to? Like when did we turn into monsters? You know, and I understand we don't have enough resources for our own, you know, kids born here, but we gotta do better.

Unlike the US Department of Homeland Security and other law enforcement government agencies, the study interviews reflected that these human, educational, and legal service professionals did not consider these young people, generally, to be a threat to the community or a drain on society. Rather, they viewed these young people as not only particularly vulnerable and in need of their care and protection, but also having capacity to be either involved with or making decisions in their own best interest. They viewed them as possessing their own beliefs, ideas, and values that should guide and/or inform any decision made on their behalf.

Their view of these youth, and the manner in which the state and social institutions that youth encounter should offer them safety, stability, and an environment that promotes the development of their capabilities and well-being, included many elements of the constructions youth found in the Somers, Herrera and Rodriguez typology. More specifically, their understanding of the youth, while varied, presented elements of *developmental*, *dependency*, and *autonomous* constructions of youth. These constructions emphasize the importance of supporting adults and social institutions in promoting and guiding the progression of social and emotional development of children and youth, while recognizing the importance of the child/youth's perspective, desires, and autonomy.

In contrast, the interview transcripts indicated a view that the state and key social institutions in the lives of youth reflected indifference, at best, to sources of direct and structural violence in their lives. One study participant, an attorney who primarily attends to youth in the child welfare system but also to unaccompanied minors offered a hypothetical case of an unaccompanied minor released to a relative to contrast the dissimilar treatment of children in child welfare and immigration systems:

> The kids [unaccompanied minors] released, who are undocumented who are released from the [ORR] shelter to relative—Jenny in Alabama. There is no social worker for Jenny to call to get a list of service providers who can help, you know, little Abe who needs help. And there is no social worker who is going to follow up with Jenny and Abe to make sure that Abe is getting his services. So they are just released into the ether. And do they come to the next court date, that by the way is in Chicago? They have to get everything transferred to Alabama. Do they get a legal service provider? Well there is nobody in Alabama. Do they know who to call? . . . How can we better serve this population once they are spider webbed out around the country to their sponsors.

From their standpoint, their governments and key social institutions reflected elements of *privacy* and *threatening* constructions of youth, perspectives that disregard the voice, agency, and contributions of youth and rather view them as a threat and drain on society. In the context of Guatemala and Honduras, youth advocates and service providers often commented on governments that lacked a vision of youth as engaged citizens active in public life. As one youth advocate of a human right center in Guatemala City commented,

> There is no space for expression, there is no space for participation, there are no courts, there are no youth groups, they do not have health centers, etc. What we have is a non-growing state so the state has left us adrift, And, finally, the response that it gives is a repressive one. It isn't until there is an extreme act of violence, that there is an invasive situation,[that] authorities come into these places. But there is no preventative action, it is completely reactive in general terms.

We explore these constructions of youth through the perspectives of the study participants as reflected in the transcripts analyzed. In particular, we focus on several key institutions that children and youth encounter: family, school, economy, health/mental health and security institutions.

Family

The interviews revealed a number of troubling family dynamics that emerged from situations of extreme poverty and direct, generalized and structural violence. Study participants noted the common inability of parents in this context to provide for the material needs and safety of their children, despite their noble efforts. Sometimes these efforts included familial separation as adults went north to secure better paying jobs. Others noted the violence that was present in the home, as well as the street, with no reprieve for the children. In general, they described a home situation in which many children and youth commonly experience instability, fear, and abuse. These children and youth must accept these circumstances or look for other circumstances, which can also lead to additional risk exposure and danger, as they search for the support and attention that is absent in their home. Others noted what they viewed as early initiation into caretaking roles for these young individuals that received little care and protection themselves, thwarting their childhood and their long-term efforts to develop their capabilities, which adds to the cycle. The following quotes reflect some of these insights offered by the study participants.

> The topic of inclusion of the youth, boys, adolescents and girls, in gangs. . . . They see a support, they see them as family. For them, it is what has been missing on the other side. We have a lot to work on with family to create those affective bonds between children and parents.
>
> —Lawyer in nonprofit focused on youth survivors of sexual violence, exploitation, and human trafficking in Guatemala

> Violence starts in the home through abuse, physical abuse, psychological, emotional. That is how the expulsion of boys and girls to the street begins. And in that context, we fall into the phenomenon of children experiencing homelessness.
>
> —Human rights worker in Honduras

> Children of 13, 14 years of age that are taking care of children that are 2 years old or they are on their second pregnancy. It is difficult that a person be able to teach values that are needed to keep a society stable when the person is an adolescent [parent].
>
> —Physician and former resident of care facility for at-risk children in Honduras

Others noted the tremendous efforts that parents and youth made to reunify following long separations. In some cases they observed the great difficulty and fragility of these bonds. The director of a human service organization in Chicago that serves unaccompanied immigrant children and their family sponsors illustrates this difficulty and frustration experienced by the youth and parents in different ways.

> But you know we paid so much money [to bring him to the United States] and he wants to go back. And I say, "Why do you want to go back? You have nothing there. You are not going to be able to come back here." And they say, "Yes, I rather die there, better than being lonely [here]." . . . So we are talking about the teenagers to age 18, right, that moment that you haven't been with your parents and your mother here, or your father here, because they are separated; Nobody will wait for that many years. . . . Ok, that's my husband I will come back to him after 15 years of not having seen you, that doesn't work. So a lot of the parents here already have a new family, already built new relationships. . . . So when you bring your teenage son who has been separated when they go to school or start to go to college, or the university they are still with that loneliness, they miss their friends, they miss the culture, but also they don't fit in this new family. They see themselves as an outsider, but the parents don't see it that way. You are my child, equal like everybody else, you have the same, this is your room, this is your house but they feel emptiness internally. How can they build that relationship back? And of course rebellions are happening, to the new husband or the new wife . . . but parents don't understand that, after you bring [the youth] here and this person [new partner] helped me to pay for you to come here, and you are not appreciative and you want to go to college and but you still don't want to do it, you are in a rebellious situation.

An ORR-funded post-release services administrator for unaccompanied children offered a similar observation regarding the difficulty of reunification. He highlighted some of the underlying feelings of abandonment and resentment that may surface upon reunification, while the youth is simultaneously trying to adjust to a wholly new context.

> There is always an adjustment period for almost everyone. I think that if you think about any child placed in out of home care, when they return to home there is always like this period of like, this is weird, we haven't lived together for a while and now we have to get used to each other again. I think it's slightly a little more intensified for unaccompanied children because we are not just talking about out of home placement, we are talking out of life placement. We are talking about children who have not been with potentially a mother or a father for an extended period of time and we are not just re-introducing them to their parents, we are also introducing them to a new neighborhood, a new community a new world, a new political climate, a new . . . there is all these things that happening at the same time. So there is an adjustment period. It starts out easy, like "this is the greatest thing ever. I love this place. I missed you." And then

> there is the period of "You left me. I hate you. Why did you leave me. I don't like it here I want to go back." There is a whole lot of emotions that come with experiencing the trauma, just the trauma of separation. Needless to discuss the trauma that comes with traveling to get here, having to take these huge risks to be able to be with your mother again. So it's complicated. . . . A parent took a huge risk to be able to provide for their family, now that they are together maybe the child kind of needs to process the information to understand. Sometimes, its successful sometimes it's not.

School

All of the study participants emphasized the importance of education in the development of children and youth along cognitive, social, and civic dimensions, as well as providing practical knowledge and skills that could help advance them in further studies or employment. They saw schools as institutions with tremendous formative possibilities and responsibilities in the development of the youth's capacities, yet study participants in Tegucigalpa, Guatemala City, and Chicago invariably commented on the difficulty many of the youth experienced in accessing appropriate education in their communities of origin and in destination communities for migrating youth.

They highlighted the early departure from schooling for many of the youth, a common occurrence in the primary years of formal study. The need to work to help support themselves or assist with household chores and caretaking were common reason for this early departure. Similarly, several school-based service providers in Chicago noted how familial responsibilities continued in the US context for unaccompanied minors who were reunited with family or other sponsors.

> A lot of them do have jobs, if they are the oldest male in the house the expectation is for them to work and help support the family. And I know that in those cases it's very, very difficult for them to be involved in school activities.
>
> —Chicago School social worker who attends to unaccompanied minors and refugee children

> The parents, you know. The parents may prefer them to come home and cook or help with . . . which is also about education, you know, family support. But some of the parents don't see the critical age when the child needs to be in most engaged, especially if they are missing . . . if they are not at grade level. . . . Some swim or sink.
>
> —Public school system administrator for Community Relations and Refugee Services

Others spoke of lengthy disruptions to education to avoid school, which has become a site for gang recruitment, or due to internal displacement related to violence or to emigration. Yet others noted the disinvestment of government in education, the barriers that schools place on enrollment, and the irrelevance of education in a context that does not allow youth to realize their full potential or provide them with meaningful opportunities.

> There is nothing extra. They paint the school but there aren't any books, there is no other teaching system. It's the same orthodox system where the students sit at a desk and listen to the teacher. So I do not necessarily consider it a crime in its definition, but a sickness. It seems like there is no cure for poverty and there is very little interest on behalf of the people that govern to be able to give a better opportunity to this new population.
>
> —Physician attending to at-risk youth in residential facility in Honduras

> An example would be a 14–15-year-old minor who if you grew up in the U.S. you are required to go school. You know, there are truancy officers, people that force . . . make sure parents, make sure they enroll the kids in school. If you are talking a young man or woman in Guatemala where you have to have money to take them to school, they might have stopped going to school in second or third grade. So you take that 7–8-year-old, fast forward 10 years, they are 17 and they have to go to school. Enroll in school but they haven't had any formal education for that huge 10 year gap. Schools have difficulty with that, they don't understand. . . . What do you mean you weren't going to school? . . . The challenge there is for some of the older kids, it's hard to get some schools to accept those children and we have to remind them that, you know, the law says they are eligible and they can be enrolled there. Immigration status is irrelevant.
>
> —Post ORR release services administrator

However, several noted that when given the opportunity to study, paired with some sense of safety and support, kids became engaged and active learners eager to continue. A former teacher in an ORR facility shared one such example.

> We also started getting kids from Mexico who worked as polleros or coyotes [smugglers] and so those kids it was very hard for them to see how education was relevant to their lives. I had one kid, I think he was from Mexico who had a 4th grade education and he had been working as a pollero and he could hardly read and write and he just said "I am not good at this." He would say "Yo no soy hecho para esto [I'm not made for this]." It's not part of their world. He didn't feel he could be successful or he could see how this was relevant to his life, I guess. . . . But I saw over time with him that he started gaining confidence

and then started seeing that it was interesting and he could connect and engage with school. And so he started studying and working really hard and ended up deciding that he didn't want to go back to Mexico.

Health/Mental Health

An examination of data from both US and Central American study sites finds that despite great need among the youth populations, communities and organizations often lacked the resources necessary to provide needed mental health services. In the Tegucigalpa and Guatemala City contexts such services were practically nonexistent. In the US context, culturally sensitive, trauma-informed, mental health services in the young person's primary language were not uniformly available. According to participants in the Chicago study, although a great desire exists within the community and among service providers to offer these necessary services, they often struggle to find the resources to provide them. Many lack funding to offer these services to all who need them and they often are challenged to find individuals who possess the skills and training to provide the necessary care.

In Chicago, public schools and private community organizations provide much of the mental healthcare for school-aged children. In schools, the availability and quality of mental health services varies greatly between schools, as does the student population. Some schools are demographically diverse and have students from different racial, ethnic, cultural, and linguistic backgrounds, while student populations at other schools are relatively homogenous. Schools make considerable efforts to address the diverse social-emotional needs of these and other vulnerable students, but the quality and availability of services depends on the school. Generally, however, mental health services are lacking for these and other vulnerable immigrant children. As a Chicago Public Schools (CPS) administrator states, with the exception of a few schools with substantial need, mental health services across the district are "widely inadequate." As a CPS Support Staff explains, "each school has a trained counselor. . . . It is better than nothing . . . but, if you figure that some schools serve 100 children and there is one counselor and if they do other stuff too, . . . it is a challenge."

For young people with greater mental health needs and/or whom cannot/will not be served at their public school, community-based organizations are often tasked with providing necessary services. Unfortunately, community-based mental health services for many UIC and other vulnerable migrant children are not a viable option. Few community-based mental health providers offer free care or accept a medical card to cover the costs of services and, those providers who do, often have waiting lists that extend weeks or months and may not have staff that can provide care in a child's primary language.

An administrator of an ORR-funded post-release service program summarized the situation in the following manner:

> The need for mental health services is the number one need. Basic human rights: so access to healthcare, education, ensuring that they have access to any kinds of benefits. So even if it's nutrition, pregnant teens might need access to prenatal care as well OBGYN for delivery. But top priority would be mental health services. There is a lot of these children who are coming with a significant history of trauma.

The lack of mental health services can impact the youth's ability to focus on their studies and engage in school. For others it can impact their asylum case. The following quotes from social workers that work with unaccompanied minors in Chicago in school and legal service settings, respectively, describe the impact of unaddressed mental health needs in the lives of these youth.

> A lot of those students that do have work because they have to support the family they end up acting out in school. But that is where I come in, and I work with them and I talk to them, you know, about their challenges and why they work. A lot of them they tell me, yeah I work for my family, but also work because I don't want to think about the things that happened in my country. Because when I work I don't have to think about those things.
>
> —School social worker

> So one thing I would say is that some kids very quickly, very easily can tell their story to an attorney and it's easy for that attorney to clearly say yes you are qualified for a form of relief. Some kids cannot, and I think trauma plays a huge role in that, so we sometimes need time to really go through that with a child and help them understand that coming to this country means they can have some form of protection and sometimes things happen in their home country that allows them to be protected. But I think since in some of these communities the violence is so normalized they do not realize that their story that can open this window [of protection] for them. So for kids who usually tell their story and can express themselves very clearly, it's not a barrier but if we think about highly traumatized children or very young children or pre-verbal children or children who have developmental delays or any type of special needs—that attorney needs a chronological story and to get that child to that point can be a long road. So what we have done in some cases is we will reach out to find a pro bono mental health evaluator to do an evaluation. Either a trauma-informed, intellectual capacity or competence issue, developmental needs [assessment], to help contextualize some of this, to help look at what are the impacts of trauma on memory. For that attorney to understand that there is in fact a credible story. Cause I mean the attorneys are faced with meeting all the legal arguments and

> immigration law and we have to find, create a way to help that child, help that attorney.
>
> —Social worker in legal clinic

A director of a community-based agency that serves unaccompanied immigrant minors in Chicago lamented that the critical need for mental health services for these children and youth is because "they have seen so much more than what they should. They should know less than what they know in real life." A coordinator of a youth outreach program in Tegucigalpa, Honduras described the heightened state of arousal and fear experienced by the youth as a result of the violence they have witnessed or experienced directly. She states, "the instability, feeling fear, being in a state of alert . . . so many kids that are growing up so close to violence, not only because of what they see or what they feel or what they are suffering personally but because many families . . . they have many close family members who were murdered." Unfortunately, youth have few options for mental health or health services in their communities of origin.

> For many it is difficult in a country where, for example, 17% of the population does not have access to healthcare even though there is a public system. That is big and we have a population of 8.5 million people. So not having access to healthcare [means] not only that there isn't a [hospital] building close to you, it's also that the building does not have anything inside. It doesn't have medicine. It's that people do not have money to even take the bus to go there or that people have to walk two or three hours to be able to get a bus.
>
> —Physician working in medical clinic serving at-risk youth in Honduras

Economy

The study participants described how children and youth, despite their tender age, have had to make tough choices in order to help support themselves and their family's basic economic needs. One human rights advocate in Honduras expressed the motives for such tough choices as, "wanting to see your family be in a different situation or because at 15 years he is a dad and he does not have anything to feed his children." Often their options and support systems were so limited that they sometimes turn to informal and at times illegal, options that offer them financial solutions to their immediate needs. Unfortunately, many times youth have to take one of the very few available employment options that also come with many limitations and end up trapping the youth in vulnerable circumstances with very little opportunities and support for mobility. A director of a nonprofit agency that provides legal and psychological services for youth and women survivors of violence in Guatemala summarized the situation of youth in marginalized communities as one in which:

> There is no state—drug trafficking is the authority. No one enters [these communities] and so the most vulnerable groups will always be women, children, and adolescents. Young adults have no choice and, because of a lack of expectations, because they see that they will take 30 years to possibly have their own house [working a formal job], when drug trafficking offers them all of that in five years.

Security

All noted the level of violence present in the Northern Triangle countries of Central America. Some blamed the state for a lack of will or inability to protect the safety of youth. In the words of one Honduran human rights advocate, "The violence is so generalized, so generalized that we have a failed state. A completely failed state because there is not a governmental response." A missionary at a youth outreach center in the community of Tegucigalpa offers another criticism of the government, stating that "there should be a presence of the security authority instead of the violence [that is present]. There should at least be laws that do not favor violence. I feel that the laws do favor it and that there is a lot of corruption in favor of violence. Corruption fuels violence the most."

The view of youth, particularly male youth, as a threat was commonly heard in the interviews conducted in Guatemala City and Tegucigalpa. Study participants frequently noted the mistreatment and misrepresentation of youth by the media and police, and society in general. Many felt that these institutions, rather than considering them as children or youth who should be protected and supported in their development as valuable members of society, positioned them as a social problem to be controlled. Interviewee participants frequently reported that the government approach to generalized crime and violence has been to criminalize youth, labeling them as delinquents and parasites, rather than social assets and contributing actors. A missionary in a Tegucigalpa youth outreach center described this social perception of youth in the following manner, "The stigma is that a young man that is here and not doing anything productive, or in other words, is moving from one street to another, is a young threat. He has a tattoo, so the notion is that he is a threat. I think the government sees that in the youth. And it's seen more in communities on the outskirts. They are a threat."

A human rights advocate in Honduras went further to suggest that the police are often involved with organized crime, stating that, "we enter a very difficult state of organized crime with gangs that, because of territory, begin to kill each other, but in collusion with the auxiliary system of justice of the country—the police." A Fulbright researcher studying the experiences of unaccompanied youth in the Northern Triangle drew parallels between the marking of youth as a delinquent by the police and the false labeling of peasants as guerrillas in the Salvadoran civil war as a pretext to repression and the use of force against youth:

> The number of homicides among children has increased, both boys and girls and when you read the news articles on the report that they get, it's almost always attached to they were alleged gang members or collaborator of gangs. So there is this same marking that was done during civil war [in El Salvador] quite frankly, because every young person that was killed then they said oh it's a collaborator of the guerrillas and now they are doing the same thing with adolescent kids from the wrong neighborhoods. Dark skin, like . . . but according to them that is not happening.

This researcher posited another view that was supported by the human service professionals. She indicated that rather than being gang members, they were actually migrating to avoid forced gang recruitment. A similar observation was made by the director of a Guatemalan NGO that provides legal and psychological services for youth and women survivors of violence. As she indicated, "These same groups harm other youth that do not want to integrate [into gangs]. So what happens? There enters the theme of migration. Many are living in surroundings where there is a lot of conflict. What they do is flee that conflict. They go to USA looking for . . . better security conditions and also a way to help their family." For some there is no other option, as many observed that the violence and reach of the gangs has grown exponentially, as has their recruitment of younger and younger children.

> This whole thing of the presence of gangs and it's all because they have also had an evolution because there has always been gangs but they weren't as violent as they are now. They also recruit children now. You wouldn't see that before in the communities and now you do. So we also see a lot of deaths of children because some of the children maybe do not want to be part of the gang so for them it is easy to kill them. So the negative social aspects have had an evolution and with that everything that the government or the state cannot provide the citizens.
>
> —Member of a voluntary organization comprised of youth focused on reducing violence in Honduras

A director of a community-based human service agency that provides services and support to unaccompanied youth and their sponsors discussed how the US government continued the criminalization of these youth. She tried to place herself in the experience of the youth when facing immigration officials and how a child might interpret and internalize the experience.

> I mean it's a traumatic situation for a child to be handcuffed. I [have] never been handcuffed in my life, but I think I would just be afraid. I would be vulnerable, and that impacts your life. You are a bad person because that is what it means for children. That's why you have handcuffs, because you are a bad person and [they] didn't know that until they told us.

A former ORR facility teacher commented on the limited autonomy of the youth while in ORR custody. She indicated that while the facility staff tried to make the situation more welcoming for the children and youth, in the end it was still detention, leaving the youth without a voice or say in decisions that impacted them.

> It was very hard because it is so structured and it's a detention center. They don't have very much autonomy and like staff are pretty tied . . . like your hands are tied in a lot of ways. Like you have to enforce certain rules and policies and stuff like that. You kind of had to meet them where they are at and tell them, like "hey I know you are not used to being in this type of a situation and I get that." You know, kind of recognize and affirming their life experience too. And that they have a lot of things that they can bring to a classroom that other people couldn't because of their life experience.

CONCLUSION

In our exploration of the perceptions of human and legal service professionals that work with marginalized youth in Guatemala and Honduras, primary sending countries for unaccompanied immigrant children, and UICs in the United States through the analytical lens of childhood, we found that the lives of children are deeply impacted by the systems that they encounter. These systems are multiple and diverse, ranging from the family, economy, education, health, and security institutions, and for a growing number of children, the immigration system as well.

We also found that the political, cultural, social, and economic forces and constraints shape these systems encountered by youth in which the professionals interviewed work are simultaneously informed by images of childhood. The analytical framework of childhood provided insight into how these various systems advance inclusion or exclusion of these youth in the context of countries of origin and destination. In both sending and destination contexts we found that the human service professionals and legal and human rights advocates who were interviewed presented their governments and key social institutions as reflecting constructions of youth that diminished their agency and viewed them as social problems to be controlled, often in contrast to the official rhetoric of the state which positioned itself as the guardian of youth.

They gave numerous examples of how the state policies and officials disregard the voice, agency, and contributions of youth, and ignore their safety and well-being. Rather, they indicated that the state responded to them as a menace to society and a drain on its resources. Many of the individual interview transcripts suggested a belief that nongovernmental organizations such as theirs addressed governmental and institutional failures that left these youth unprotected and socially excluded, a circumstance that frequently lead to internal displacement, and for many the necessity to emigrate. In many ways they presented a view of civil society as the protectors of childhood, a critical moment in life that should be marked by supportive adults and institutions that promote security, well-being, development, and a flourishing of youth as active political, social, and economic partners in the world.

NOTES

1. Lauren Heidbrink, *Migrant Youth, Transnational Families, and the State: Care and Contested Interests* (Philadelphia: University of Pennsylvania Press, 2014).
2. Angus Calder, *The People's War: Britain 1939-45* (London: Jonathan Cape Ltd., 1969).
3. Maria Vidal de Haymes, "Operation Peter Pan: One Family's Journey to the U.S.," *Journal of Poverty* 2, no. 8.4 (2004): 119–123.
4. Everett Ressler, Neil Boothby, and Daniel Steinbock, *Unaccompanied Children: Care and Protection in Wars, National Disasters and Refugee Movements* (New York: Oxford University Press, 1988).
5. Katharine M. Donato and Samantha L. Perez, "Crossing the Mexico-U.S. Border: Illegality and Children's Migration to the United States," *The Russell Sage Foundation Journal of the Social Sciences* 3, no. 4 (2017): 116–135; William Kandel, Andorra Bruno, Peter Meyer, Clare Ribando Seelke, Maureen Taft-Morales and R. E. Wasem, "Unaccompanied Alien Children: Potential Factors Contributing to Recent Immigration," Congressional Research Service (Washington, DC, 2014).
6. William Kandel, "Unaccompanied Alien Children: An Overview," Congressional Research Service (Washington, DC, 2017), https://fas.org/sgp/crs/homesec/R43599.pdf.
7. Ibid.
8. Ibid.

9. Elizabeth Kennedy, "No Childhood Here: Why Central American Children are Fleeing their Homes," American Immigration Council, 2014, http://www.immigrationpolicy.org/sites/default/files/docs/no_childhood_here_why_central_american_children_are_fleeing_their_homes_final.pdf.

10. United Nations High Commissioner for Refugees (UNHCR), "Children on the Run: Unaccompanied Children Leaving Central America and Mexico and the Need for International Protection" (Washington, DC, 2014), http://www.unhcr.org/56fc266f4.html.

11. Ibid.; United Nations Office on Drugs and Crime (UNODC), *Global Study on Homicide 2013* (Vienna, 2014), https://www.unodc.org/documents/gsh/pdfs/2014_GLOBAL_HOMICIDE_BOOK_web.pdf.

12. UNHCR, "Children on the Run," 2014.

13. Carola Suárez-Orozco and Maria G. Hernández, "Immigrant Family Separations: The Experience of Separated, Unaccompanied, and Reunited Youth and Families," in *The Impact of Immigration on Children's Development: Contributions to Human Development,* ed. Cynthia Garcia Coll, 24 (2012): 122–148, doi:10.1159/000331032.

14. Jenna Nobels, "Migration and Father Absence: Shifting Family Structure in Mexico," *Demography* 50, no. 4 (August 2013): 1303–1314, doi:10.1007/s13524-012-0187-8.

15. Ibid.

16. Pierette Hondagneu-Sotelo and Ernestine Avila, "I'm Here, but I'm There: The Meanings of Latina Transnational Motherhood," *Gender & Society* 11, no. 5 (1997): 548–560.

17. Kennedy, "No Childhood Here," 2014.

18. Katharine M. Donato and Blake Sisk, "Children's Migration to the United States from Mexico and Central America: Evidence from Mexican and Latino American Migration Projects," *Journal of Migration and Human Security* 3, no. 1 (2015): 58–79, doi:10.14240/jmhs.v3i1.43.

19. Kennedy, "No Childhood Here," 2014.

20. Dennis Stinchcomb and Eric Hershberg, "Unaccompanied Migrant Children from Central America: Context, Causes, and Responses," Working Paper Series No. 7., American University Center for Latin American & Latino Studies (Washington, DC, 2014), http://ssrn.com/abstract=2524001.

21. See Sultana Ali Norozi and Torill Moen, "Childhood as a Social Construction," *Journal of Educational and Social Research* 6, no. 2 (2016): 37–38, http://doi.org/10.5901/jesr.2016.v6n2p75; Michael Freeman, "The Sociology of Childhood in Relation to Children's Rights," *International Journal of Children's Rights* 6, no. 4 (1998): 433–444; Chris Jenks, "Constructing Childhood Sociologically," in *An Introduction to Childhood Studies*, ed. M. J. Kehily (Berkshire, UK: Open University Press, 2004), 77–95; and Alan Prout and Allison James, "A New Paradigm for the Sociology of Childhood? Provenance, Promise and Problems," in *Constructing and Reconstructing Childhood*, eds. Alan Prout and Allison James (New York: The Falmer Press, 1990), 7–34.

22. See Jenks, "Constructing childhood sociologically."

23. Berry Mayall, "The Sociology of Childhood in Relation to Children's Rights," *International Journal of Children's Rights* 8, vol. 3 (2000): 243–259.

24. John Tobin, "Courts and the Construction of Childhood: A New Way of Thinking," in *Law and Childhood Studies: Current Legal Issues*, ed. M. Freeman (Oxford: Oxford University Press, 2012), 55–74.

25. David Oswell, *The Agency of Children: From Family to Global Human Rights* (New York: Cambridge University Press, 2013).

26. See Ali Norozi, et al., "Childhood as a social construction"; and William A. Corsaro, "Children's Peer Cultures and Interpretive Reproduction," in *Sociology of Childhood* (California: Pine Forge Press, 1997).

27. M. Aryah Somers, Pedro Herrera, and Lucia Rodriguez, "Construction of Childhood and Unaccompanied Children in the Immigration System in the United States," *UC Davis Journal of Juvenile Law and Policy* 14, no. 2 (2010): 311–382.

28. Ibid.

29. Jacqueline Bhabha and Susan Schmidt, "Seeking Asylum Alone: Unaccompanied and Separated Children and Refugee Protection in the U.S.," *Journal of the History of Childhood and Youth* 1, no. 1 (Winter, 2008): 126–138.

30. P. S. Hinds, R. J. Vogel, and L. Clarke-Steffen, "The Possibilities and Pitfalls of Doing a Secondary Analysis of a Qualitative Dataset," *Qualitative Health Research* 7, no. 3 (1997): 408–424.

31. Tracy Long-Sutehall, Magi Sque, and Julia Addington-Hall, "Secondary Analysis of Qualitative Data: a Valuable Method for Exploring Sensitive Issues with an Elusive Population?" *Journal of Research in Nursing* 16, no. 4 (2010): 335–344.

32. Jessica Martone, Danielle Zimmerman, Maria Vidal de Haymes, and Lois Lorentzen, "Immigrant Integration through Mediating Social Institutions: Issues and Strategies," *Journal of Community Practice* 22, no. 3 (2014): 299–323.

33. Pew Research Center, "U.S. Unauthorized Immigration Population Estimates," 2016, accessed October 20, 2017, http://www.pewhispanic.org/interactives/unauthorized-immigrants.

34. U.S. Office of Refugee Resettlement, "Unaccompanied Alien Children Released by State," accessed July 5, 2017 at https://www.acf.hhs.gov/orr/resource/unaccompanied-alien-children-released-to-sponsors-by-state.

35. U.S. Office of Refugee Resettlement, "Unaccompanied Alien Children Released to Sponsors by County," accessed October 20, 2017 at https://www.acf.hhs.gov/orr/resource/unaccompanied-alien-children-released-to-sponsors-by-county.

36. United Nations High Commissioner for Refugees, "Honduras: UNHCR Report Urges Reforms to Defend Displaced People's Lands," September 29, 2017, https://reliefweb.int/report/honduras/honduras-unhcr-report-urges-reforms-defend-displaced-people-s-land.

37. See Yvonne Lincoln and Egon Guba, *Naturalistic Inquiry* (Beverly Hills, CA: Sage Publishing, Inc., 1985); Long-Sutehall, et al., "Secondary analysis"; Anselm Strauss and Juliet Corbin, *Basics of Qualitative Research Techniques and Procedures for Developing Grounded Theory*, 3rd ed. (Thousand Oaks, CA: Sage Publications, 2008).

BIBLIOGRAPHY

Ali Norozi, Sultana, and Torill Moen. "Childhood as a Social Construction." *Journal of Educational and Social Research* 6, no. 2 (2016): 37–38. http://doi.org/10.5901/jesr.2016.v6n2p75.

Bhabha, Jacqueline, and Susan Schmidt. "Seeking Asylum Alone: Unaccompanied and Separated Children and Refugee Protection in the U.S." *Journal of the History of Childhood and Youth* 1, no. 1 (Winter, 2008): 126–138.

Calder, Angus. *The People's War: Britain 1939–45*. London: Jonathan Cape Ltd., 1969.

Corsaro, William A. "Children's Peer Cultures and Interpretive Reproduction." In *Sociology of Childhood*. California: Pine Forge Press, 1997.

Donato, Katharine M., and Blake Sisk, "Children's Migration to the United States from Mexico and Central America: Evidence from Mexican and Latino American Migration Projects." *Journal of Migration and Human Security* 3, no. 1 (2015): 58–79, doi:10.14240/jmhs.v3i1.43.

Freeman, Michael. "The Sociology of Childhood in Relation to Children's Rights." *International Journal of Children's Rights* 6, no. 4 (1998): 433–444.

Heidbrink, Lauren. *Migrant Youth, Transnational Families, and the State: Care and Contested Interests*. Philadelphia: University of Pennsylvania Press, 2014.

Hinds, P. S., R. J. Vogel, and L. Clarke-Steffen. "The Possibilities and Pitfalls of Doing a Secondary Analysis of a Qualitative Dataset." *Qualitative Health Research* 7, no. 3 (1997): 408–424.

Hondagneu-Sotelo, Pierette, and Ernestine Avila. "I'm Here, but I'm There: The Meanings of Latina Transnational Motherhood." *Gender & Society* 11, no. 5 (1997): 548–560.

Jenks, Chris. "Constructing Childhood Sociologically." In *An Introduction to Childhood Studies*, edited by M. J. Kehily, 77–95. Berkshire, UK: Open University Press, 2004.

Kandel, William. "Unaccompanied Alien Children: An Overview." Washington, DC: Congressional Research Service, 2017, https://fas.org/sgp/crs/homesec/R43599.pdf.

Kandel, William, Andorra Bruno, Peter Meyer, Clare Ribando Seelke, Maureen Taft-Morales, and R. E. Wasem. *Unaccompanied Alien Children: Potential Factors Contributing to Recent Immigration*. Washington, DC: Congressional Research Service, 2014.

Katharine M. Donato, and Samantha L. Perez, "Crossing the Mexico-U.S. Border: Illegality and Children's Migration to the United States." *The Russell Sage Foundation Journal of the Social Sciences* 3, no. 4 (2017): 116–135.

Kennedy, Elizabeth. "No Childhood Here: Why Central American Children are Fleeing their Homes." American Immigration Council, 2014, http://www.immigrationpolicy.org/sites/default/files/docs/no_childhood_here_why_central_american_children_are_fleeing_their_homes_final.pdf.

Lincoln, Yvonne, and Egon Guba. *Naturalistic Inquiry*. Beverly Hills, CA: Sage Publishing, Inc., 1985.

Martone, Jessica, Danielle Zimmerman, Maria Vidal de Haymes, and Lois Lorentzen. "Immigrant Integration through Mediating Social Institutions: Issues and Strategies." *Journal of Community Practice* 22, no. 3 (2014): 299–323.

Mayall, Berry. "The Sociology of Childhood in Relation to Children's Rights." *International Journal of Children's Rights* 8, no. 3 (2000): 243–259.

Nobels, Jenna. "Migration and Father Absence: Shifting Family Structure in Mexico." *Demography* 50, no. 4 (August 2013): 1303–1314, doi:10.1007/s13524-012-0187-8.

Oliviera, Gabrielle. "The Impact of Mexican Maternal Migration of Children's Future Ambitions." Migration Policy Institute, November 2016, https://www.migrationpolicy.org/print/15770#.WunNJNMvwUE.

Oswell, David. *The Agency of Children: From Family to Global Human Rights*. New York: Cambridge University Press, 2013.

Pew Research Center. "U.S. Unauthorized Immigration Population Estimates." 2016. Accessed October 20, 2017. http://www.pewhispanic.org/interactives/unauthorized-immigrants/.

Prout, Alan, and Allison James. "A New Paradigm for the Sociology of Childhood? Provenance, Promise and Problems." In *Constructing and Reconstructing Childhood*, edited by Alan Prout and Allison James, 7–34. New York: The Falmer Press, 1990.

Ressler, Everett, Neil Boothby, and Daniel Steinbock. *Unaccompanied Children: Care and Protection in Wars, National Disasters and Refugee Movements*. New York: Oxford University Press, 1988.

Somers, M. Aryah, Pedro Herrera, and Lucia Rodriguez. "Construction of Childhood and Unaccompanied Children in the Immigration System in the United States." *UC Davis Journal of Juvenile Law and Policy* 14, no. 2 (2010): 311–382.

Stinchcomb, Dennis, and Eric Hershberg. "Unaccompanied Migrant Children from Central America: Context, Causes, and Responses." Working Paper Series No. 7. American University Center for Latin American & Latino Studies. Washington, DC, 2014. http://ssrn.com/abstract=2524001.

Strauss, Anselm, and Juliet Corbin. *Basics of Qualitative Research Techniques and Procedures for Developing Grounded Theory*. 3rd ed. Thousand Oaks, CA: Sage Publications, 2008.

Suárez-Orozco, Carola, and Maria G. Hernández. "Immigrant Family Separations: The Experience of Separated, Unaccompanied, and Reunited Youth and Families." In *The Impact of Immigration on Children's Development: Contributions to Human Development*, edited by Cynthia Garcia Coll, 122–148. 24: (2012). doi:10.1159/000331032.

Tobin, John. "Courts and the Construction of Childhood: A New Way of Thinking." In *Law and Childhood Studies: Current Legal Issues*, edited by M. Freeman, 55–74. Oxford: Oxford University Press, 2012.

Tracy Long-Sutehall, Magi Sque, and Julia Addington-Hall. "Secondary Analysis of Qualitative Data: a Valuable Method for Exploring Sensitive Issues with an Elusive Population?" *Journal of Research in Nursing* 16, no. 4 (2010): 335–344.

United Nations High Commissioner for Refugees (UNHCR). "Children on the Run: Unaccompanied Children Leaving Central America and Mexico and the Need for International Protection." Washington, DC, 2014. http://www.unhcr.org/56fc266f4.html.

———. "Honduras: UNHCR Report Urges Reforms to Defend Displaced People's Lands." September 29, 2017. https://reliefweb.int/report/honduras/honduras-unhcr-report-urges-reforms-defend-displaced-people-s-land.

United Nations Office on Drugs and Crime (UNODC). "Global Study on Homicide 2013," Vienna, 2014. Accessed May 1, 2018. https://www.unodc.org/documents/gsh/pdfs/2014_GLOBAL_HOMICIDE_BOOK_web.pdf.

U.S. Office of Refugee Resettlement. "Unaccompanied Alien Children Released by State." Accessed July 5, 2017. https://www.acf.hhs.gov/orr/resource/unaccompanied-alien-children-released-to-sponsors-by-state.

———. "Unaccompanied Alien Children Released to Sponsors by County." Accessed October 20, 2017. https://www.acf.hhs.gov/orr/resource/unaccompanied-alien-children-released-to-sponsors-by-county.

Vidal de Haymes, Maria. "Operation Peter Pan: One Family's Journey to the U.S." *Journal of Poverty* 2, no. 8.4 (2004): 119–123.

Chapter 3

Trauma, Detachment, and Non-Belonging

The Plight of Migrant and Refugee Children

Stephanie N. Arel

According to the United Nations Department of Economic and Social Affairs, in 2017, 258 million people were migrants.[1] This number equates to 3.4 percent of the world's population. Half of the world's refugees are children,[2] who in greater numbers, and with greater frequency, are travelling alone. In an effort to escape violence, war, torture, forced marriages, and recruitment as child soldiers, to name but a few root causes, children flee. Defined by the United Nations High Commissioner for Refugees (UNHCR) as unaccompanied persons under the age of eighteen, separated from both parents and not cared for by "an adult who by law or custom has responsibility to do so,"[3] the millions of unescorted children on the run suffer compounded trauma and grief, before, during, and after their flight. Traumatically uprooted and detached from culture, family, and what they knew of home, vulnerable, unaccompanied minors confront further trauma and detachment as they face innumerable dangers in order to seek a better life, often doing so to reunite with family and caregivers who have also escaped violent environments at home. Simone Weil's pronouncement that "to be rooted is perhaps the most important and least recognized need of the human soul"[4] presses both the admission of the grave mental, physical, and spiritual risks that minors travelling alone encounter and a societal response.

In his memoir, *The Lightless Sky*, Afghani refugee Gulwalāy Passarlay recounts his experience being smuggled at the age of twelve to England. Passarlay recounts being present when a gunfight with American soldiers killed his father and grandfather—believed to be Taliban sympathizers during the war in Afghanistan who harbored weapons that killed other Americans. His torturous, migratory route included seven countries, imprisonment, a near drowning, and being trapped in a chicken coop for days. Despite the dangers and the endured trauma, Passarlay made it to England. Although he was eventually granted asylum, members of the Kent Social Services in England assessed his age as sixteen and a half, instead of thirteen (age assessment is a problem for children seeking asylum as governments can more easily deport adults and so benefit from determining that children are older than they are).[5] Although by all accounts Passarlay was lucky, he found himself depressed and desperately lonely in England, craving his old life and familial connections. He experienced a sense of estrangement and non-belonging, and he endured this alone. In deep isolation in England, Passarlay attempted to kill himself from a pill overdose. His experiences echo Rosemarie Perez Foster's findings that "the sense of isolation and absence of familial support serves as yet another strike against the already stressed newcomer,"[6] emphasizing the desperate conditions of a child migrating and seeking asylum alone.[7]

Passarlay's experience reflects the types of trauma minors encounter before and after they flee home countries. Perez Foster classifies the traumas sustained by migrant children into four categories organized by stages: traumatogenic experiences that occur prior to migration, traumatic events during transit, continuing trauma in efforts of asylum seeking, and conditions in the host country that lead to inadequate care.[8] The fact that so many children are in transit alone without parents or other family members compounds such traumas. Minors that have lost caregivers through death or separation after leaving home countries, or who have experienced their caregivers' own psychological impairment, must survive without interpersonal attachments which offer safety and security. The absence of caregivers and supportive adults is a severe blow to minors on the run.

Children at every stage of development need to have secure relationships to navigate the world. Others, especially those who serve as secure attachment figures, help children build basic trust, establish a sense of safety (internally and environmentally), secure a sense of self and self-worth, and sustain emotional relationships into adulthood. Furthermore, secure and reliable attachment figures provide a crucial defense against stress and trauma. A child who travels alone, with no access to a primary caregiver at all, whether temporarily or permanently, faces the greatest challenges. With the lack of supportive loved ones who mitigate the negative effects of traumatogenic experiences endured before, during, and after migration, minors suffer impairment to healthy development, which perpetuates problems with intimacy, attenuates the feeling of security in relationships, and disrupts their general sense of well-being in the world.[9] Travelling alone, minors must survive with little to no assistance, navigating external threats and managing internal states. What may be most debilitating is that the disruption of attachment constitutes what

Marco Mazzetti calls a "vulnerability factor" which inhibits the development of resilience in migrants and, subsequently, impedes their ability to confront the challenges of adaptation in a host country.[10]

Without social or familial support, minors often struggle against isolation that engenders a deep sense of alienation, bereft of the sense of belonging afforded to them in home countries and within their own families. Without this fundamental base, the need to be rooted, as Simone Weil asserts, goes unmet. For Weil, having roots consists of having an "active and natural participation in the life of a community" which evolves automatically in stable environments.[11] In the case of the unaccompanied minor, rootedness, along with its automatic evolution, is unattainable on the move and at best difficult after arrival in a host country. Acclimating to host countries' cultures, languages, and social mores poses an additional set of challenges to the active and natural involvement in social life, challenges that are magnified in the face of traumatization and detachment.

In order to probe the effects of the traumatogenic experiences of migration magnified by the loss endured in the absence of a primary attachment figure, and the impact that this loss has in the long term, I will focus on psychological studies. The purpose is to illuminate why unaccompanied children need targeted support systems to cope with the multiple traumas that they have suffered—independent of how necessary or reasonable it is for them to leave their countries and families. In the following sections, an exploration of emotional attachment alongside trauma theory will ground a consideration of how attachment forms in infancy and early childhood. Early attachment is critical to human well-being and secures connections with others who are foundational to personality development.[12] Understanding that minors travelling alone are distanced from such connections and often sustain severe trauma leads, in the second section, to the examination of the lasting effects of being deprived of positive and nurturing bonds with parents and/or other consistent caregivers when minors are most in need.

Elucidating the impact of losing parents or close family ties at particular stages of development reinforces an appreciation of the residual effects of detachment from family members, communities, and home, pressing on communities of care to address this gap. The loss of the primary attachment figure establishes a state of disconnection and non-belonging that persists into adulthood. The risks of detachment in adulthood include impairment of basic interactional skills, lowered ability to regulate emotionally, and weakened resilience. The deprivation of core relationships that provide love and nurturing also perpetuates an internal, and often external, state of isolation and makes children especially vulnerable to groups or individuals who exploit their need to belong. The importance of providing unaccompanied migrant children with attachment figures is crucial because what is at stake is not only their future mental and physical health, but the overall health of the community in which they reside.

OVERVIEW OF ATTACHMENT THEORY

Attachment theory, established through research on primates by John Bowlby, and the "Strange Situation Protocol" developed by Mary Ainsworth, offers a lens through which to view early trauma and the magnified effects of trauma on minors who travel alone. Formed through the early child-caregiver relationship, attachment defines the nature of the exchange between a child and a primary caregiver or attachment figure, considered critical by attachment theorists.[13] When the caregiver is physically and mentally attentive to the child, secure, attuned attachment develops. Secure attachment enables the child to feel safe, to trust in the primary attachment figure, to regulate affect, and to have the support to develop autonomy and a sense of self-worth. In contrast, when the caregiver is mentally or physically absent, unable for whatever reason to attune to the child, the secure base that typically forms from that relationship falters. In this case, the attachment becomes insecure. Insecure attachment relationships fall into three categories: avoidant, ambivalent, or disorganized.[14] The negative effects of a deficit or disturbance in primary attachment reflected in these styles and subsequent relationships are shown to persist trans-culturally.[15]

Psychologist Jean Mercer emphasizes that attachment theory speaks to a specific set of developmental stages itself based on infant attachment. Her work highlights cognitive and emotional development and attachment addressing significant age periods which theorists have correlated with predictable attachment events for minors: (1) birth to six to eight months; (2) eight months to two and a half years of age; (3) the preschool period—two and a half to five years; (4) the elementary school years; and (5) adolescence.[16] Migrant children of all age ranges travel alone and so remain vulnerable at all stages of development. This is the case even for infants, often born to mothers en route, but who lose parents to death or mothers to sexual violence; therefore, the infants rely on the care of strangers or services of aide in host countries.[17] A high percentage of these children travelling alone also undergo trauma. Trauma may occur at home; for instance, 77 percent of Palestine refugee children from Syria aged one to fourteen experience at least one source of violent discipline.[18] Children in the first five years of life are found to be the most vulnerable to violence during travel and the most underserved by social services in host countries.[19] Further, younger children are the most susceptible to early attachment trauma suffered when they are victims of violence in the home or isolated from a primary caregiver.

Relationships, especially with caregivers and family members, mitigate negative affects, such as fear and shame generated by trauma, serving as powerful forces in nature and constituting deep, genuine connections. From this place of resonance, persons are aware of and responsive to one another. Such connection provides the essential means for the mastery of negative emotional experiences, such as those faced by all, but in greater numbers and severity by refugees, and forms a child's capacity to adapt to external stresses or to recover from trauma. The ability to express positive emotion to others, develop and communicate compassion, tolerate vulnerability, and to both sustain and enjoy the intimacy of interpersonal relationships are foregrounded by having healthy relationships with caregivers and family; migrant children travelling alone are deprived from these nurturing bonds.[20] While some of these children are often reunified with caregivers, those who are not are even more vulnerable. In the absence of a caregiver, family members, or a community to call home, refugee and migrant children face not only uncertain futures but also the fear and apprehension of not having a support network.

Attachment relationships enable a general sense of trust that ensures that susceptibility to negative emotional experiences does not result in such damage to the self or others. In fact, the ability to tolerate negative affect leads to trust of the other and of the self. Stable, secure relationships foster confidence in the constructive responses of others and instill the assurance that negative affective states can be integrated into the self; therefore, these are not denied or repressed.[21] Without someone to whom children of any age can attach, children in general have more painful or frustrating experiences regarding the responses of others and are at an increased risk for repressed affect and defensiveness.[22]

Further, damage to or severing of emotional attachment bonds, as in the lives of minors travelling alone, magnifies the impact of trauma. Susan M. Johnson addresses this phenomenon in her work on strengthening attachment bonds when she discusses how trauma disturbs life, perpetuates suffering, and effects how interpersonal attachments offer relief from trauma's symptoms.[23] In addition, she categorizes isolation and the lack of secure attachments—categories of existence for migrant children—as undermining to resiliency.[24] In an essay surveying longitudinal studies on resilience, Emmy E. Werner surmises that the ability to adapt at forty reflects the nature of primary attachment and can be explained by earlier predictors of resilience primarily in the first decade of life.[25] She groups these predictors into four categories corresponding with greater adaptation, autonomy, less stress, and the ability to attract more sources of emotional support throughout development. It includes the mother's positive interactions with her child at one and two, various sources of emotional support from immediate and extended family between ages two and ten, academic competence at age ten, and the child's physical health, between birth and two years for girls and between birth and ten years for boys.[26]

The absence of attachment figures, thus, impedes the development of resistance, intensifying and perpetuating the consequences of trauma. Traumatic aftermath includes the victim's being flooded with fear, a vision of the world as dangerous, a state of overwhelming emotional chaos, threats to a cohesive sense of self, interference in the ability to have self-control, and the muddling of a person's ability to engage in the present.[27] Secure attachment relationships answer such trauma by providing comfort and safe space while providing affect regulation, opportunities for personal integration, self-confidence, new learning and risk taking.[28] Thus, without a safe and loving person to whom they can turn, minors of any age suffer serious deficits and live in a world where human contact represents a threat and not a comfort.

SEVERED ATTACHMENT AND TRAUMA

A child who experiences trauma needs attachment figures in order to adjust to loss and integrate trauma. This figure can be a parent or another adult, who Bowlby calls a "substitute mother."[29] The need for the attachment figure is more critical than who functions in this role (mother, father, aunt, etc.). Without someone in the primary caregiver role, sustained traumas arrest development and leave permanent wounds in the child's psyche that have both mental and physical repercussions. Confirmation of this phenomenon can be found in the method for treating traumatized children: "what works best," as Perry and Szalavitz assert, "is anything that increases the quality and number of relationships in a child's life."[30]

From a developmental perspective, the longer a child has a secure attachment with a parent, regardless of a loss of that parent, the better. Children who never have secure attachment, or who live with trauma from an early age and then lose parents, are especially at risk.[31] Migrants travelling alone belong to this category. A 2012 study on trauma history of sixty war-affected refugee children in the United States shows that minors generally experience traumatic loss, bereavement, and separation; forced displacement; and community and domestic violence concomitantly.[32] Traumatic loss co-occurred with exposure to war or political violence at a rate of 60.0 percent but was also linked with experiences of domestic violence (35.0 percent), physical abuse (31.7 percent), emotional abuse (30.0 percent), or impairment in the child's caregiver due to depression, other illness, drug or alcohol abuse, or extreme poverty, inhibiting the effective role of the caregiver.[33]

A later 2017 report summarizing research on the traumatogenic experiences of migrant children that present risk factors to growth and flourishing show similar trends and can be categorized according to Perez Foster's stages. Jennifer Teska and Megan Rabin detail the common traumatic events migrant minors travelling alone sustain prior to departing from home countries:

> exposure to conflict, war, and/or persecution, being confined to their homes or forced to flee because of chaos and violence, being separated from families, witnessing the death or disappearance of family and/or community members, and being threatened, physically and/or sexually abused, held captive, tortured, and/or forced to participate in violence.[34]

In addition, these children may have also endured trauma that their respective cultures sanctioned such as female genital mutilation or child marriage prior to departure. During transit, unaccompanied children face harsh circumstances such as "starvation, mistreatment by smugglers, exploitation, and trafficking."[35] Their plight is often not lessened by arrival in host countries where continuing trauma emerges in the efforts of asylum seeking, as a result of conditions in a host country that lead to inadequate care, and in being confronted with different laws, customs, and language barriers.[36] Facing such obstacles alone constitutes a challenge for children of any age.

Further, a report by the UNHCR on the susceptibility of migrant children and caregivers to trauma recognizes that unaccompanied and separated children are "highly vulnerable," and at higher risk for either serious immediate or future harm if children have endured physical, sexual, or emotional abuse at home, neglect, or exploitation (being forced to work).[37] The reality of not having an attachment figure in such cases is severe. The lack of provision of secure attachment ensures that a child's exposure to trauma such as war constitutes a more severe problem than the impact of war on parents or even the physical and sexual abuse inflicted on a child by a parent.[38] The greatest loss amounts to the loss of someone who provides attachment, comfort, and support.

Having experienced oppression, torture, and other forms of organized violence along with suffering the trauma of war, the absence of a migratory plan (likely the case for children), poverty, loss, and stresses related to learning a new culture (not understanding the language of the host country and going from rural to urban environments), children face serious impediments in their ability to recover from trauma. Further, the permanent or temporary severing of familial bonds undermines the ability to trust others. The struggle to trust obstructs adaptation to environments in host countries as it accounts for trepidation in approaching adult relationships, difficulty in expressing emotions, and obstacles to forming shared communities in the new foreign home. The failure to develop basic levels of trust manifests in children who have suffered war-related experiences and psychosocial stress (separation from a parent), as they are more likely to develop depression, anxiety, and aggression.[39] The result is fear and distance from others. These minors cannot with ease settle into a relationship and may, instead of adhering to rules and regulations, thwart authority figures that represent them. Alternatively, they may be easily persuaded by authority figures, as in the case of children recruited to be child soldiers. This persuasion, a current and increasing area of study, cajoles children who are isolated in refugee camps, and therefore economically exploited, to become part of a group that often both offers an adult leader and some promise of payment or moral reward.[40]

A failure to develop basic levels of trust also leads to the inability to feel secure and safe in the world, inhibiting self-regulation and the skills needed to modulate "physiological, emotional, behavioral, and cognitive experience."[41] Marked by the ability to self-soothe and to control impulses, regulation includes the self's ability to make corrective adjustments in behavior that originates from within.[42] Attachment to primary caregivers provides the context for understanding how to make such adjustments and safely connect to others.[43] Damage to the caregiving relationship results in an undermining of the ability to regulate leading to a dysregulated internal state, impeded decision making, and the inability to respond with flexible emotional reactions to external stimuli. Furthermore, in a state of dysregulation or alarm, a child cannot process verbal information or engage in learning, a serious impediment for migrant children adapting to a host country.[44] Instead, dysregulation impairs the ability to focus on future planning and so therefore disenables a child from being able to assess the repercussions of their behavior. Dysregulation can also happen with very little incitement, triggered by seemingly innocuous stimuli including eye contact and friendly touch.[45] This is due to impediments in the "regulating capacities of the cortex: the brainstem acts reflexively, impulsively and often aggressively to any perceived threat."[46]

Perhaps one of the greatest and most insidious consequences of the inability to self-soothe and connect to others as a result of severed attachment is the inability to modulate shame. Shame, recognized as a primary affect underlying insecure attachment and symptoms related to post-traumatic stress disorder, interferes with a sense of self-worth. Shame also arrests the instinct to connect with other people. Physiologically, the affect literally motivates the body to withdraw—at the point of contact—with averted eyes or slumped shoulders—or after the point of contact—where any self-exposure becomes embarrassing, and the simple act of being vulnerable through eye contact is painful. Shame also motivates violence, a more obvious manifestation of the rejection of another person. Severed attachments therefore have the effect of disturbing a person's sense of wholeness. As a result, pathologies centered on acquiring safety replace empathetic modes of being, and shame inhabits the body, truncating the possibility for further empathic connection.

For migrant and refugee children, this could manifest in depression and hopelessness, affective barriers to making the necessary human connection needed to acquire and establish safety which then supports empathic development. Non-belonging to a social group and language barriers also serve as obstacles for the exchange of empathy with people from the host country, as does political rhetoric of stigmatization, to these marginalized and therefore shamed groups.

When situations of trauma accompany severed attachment, the stakes increase. The default mode of reaction to stress becomes the flight/fight/freeze response, which takes place in the sympathetic nervous system communicating to the body a need to escape, exert violence, or feign death. Affectively, these urges can be articulated as a shame response in the form of withdrawal, attack, or avoidance. According to Babette Rothschild, shame renders individuals speechless in the flight/fight/freeze response, but shame also disables the ability to either refute or respond to intimacy often manifested in physical touching. In the case of abusive or intrusive contact, the trauma survivor interprets the experience of freezing, or "going dead," as a failure to act; the experience of shame accompanies this perception of failure. This situation emerges in cases of rape, torture, and physical/sexual violence and abuse, where survivors fault themselves for somehow causing the attack and for being unable to respond to attackers in any form of defense.[47] Thus, in trauma, the proximity and sense of closeness that eases shame becomes inaccessible because that very closeness constitutes a threat. If safety is a prerequisite to human functioning, and safety is lacking, a pattern often experienced by unaccompanied migrant children who have endured compounded trauma, then the key to adjustment and acclimation—connection with others—cannot be fully accessed.

Shame also emerges when an individual feels stigmatized or perceives him/herself as existing outside of a group. For migrants and refugees, this status can nearly always be assumed. Stigmatization and ostracization evoke powerful feelings of non-belonging. This emotional state can be debilitating. In such cases, the stigmatized person might bear a posture of "false bravado," or conversely, assume a posture of "defensive cowering" and the impetus to hide manifested in shame.[48] Most often, the stigmatized vacillate rapidly between these two poles. Postures of "toughness" or "bravado" constitute attempts of the person in shame to experience an affect perceived as less painful than shame. Patterns of defense include withdrawal (escape), avoidance (repression), attacking the self, and attacking the other.[49] Within each category, an entire behavioral repertoire persists consisting of an aggregate system of affect management or ways that an individual has adapted to manage the shame affect. The function and aim of the strategy is to transmute shame, "to make it feel different."[50] Each defense serves as a means of burying shame beneath some other affective experience to greater or lesser degrees. Relationships suffer, and instead of turning toward others to seek attunement, the shamed self falls deeper into a sense of isolation and affective humiliation. Passarlay recounts this in his own narrative—acknowledging that without his foster parents, his situation would have turned grave and isolation would have overcome him.

NON-BELONGING AND THE DESIRE FOR THE GROUP

Simone Weil presents her concept of rootedness through the image of the tree, which needs roots in order to grow and bear fruit. Without roots, this tree will fall "at the first blow."[51] Every human, in her estimation, like the tree, "needs to have multiple roots,"[52] otherwise the person experiences a state of "uprootedness," which Weil likens to a disease provoked by at least two scenarios: money and war.[53] Her metaphors are apt. The toppled tree which can no longer grow replicates an illness that adversely affects a person's physical and mental health. Children travelling alone suffer from the "disease" of uprootedness. On the move alone, children suffer multiple wounds, from the loss of attachment figures to the stigmatization of being an outlier in a new host country, which alters their self-perception, coping styles, psychological well-being, and the ability to integrate traumatic experiences. These minors experience a dramatic shift in the psyche that produces, in Mazzetti's words, "an irreversible change in how they viewed themselves in the world"[54] which disrupts the ability to assimilate to a new culture or worse, to develop a sense of belonging in that society.

When minors reach a host country, the pain of migration might be ameliorated to some degree, but without familial or social ties sociocultural adjustment presents itself as an arduous, even seemingly insurmountable undertaking. These children are challenged to find a support network or develop a sense of belonging in their new environment. Without stable human connection and reciprocity, the status of "going alone" is amplified. "Human[s] have a deep psychological need to belong,"[55] and this need goes unmet. If, as Farhad Dalal asserts, "one's psychological health depends enormously on the kinds of places one finds oneself belonging to,"[56] the isolated minor severed from family connections is left with a severe deficit.

Despite the risks related to the group to which one attaches, the desire to attach indicates that the motivational system of attachment has not been completely ruptured. The longing to attach evidences the presence of resilience. The search to find a group to which to belong is combined with the need to establish safety, attain emotional regulation, intimacy with others, and the ability to share emotional experiences. Research has shown that group growth relies on interpersonal bonds.[57] Many different types of people, not solely family members, can fulfill attachment figures; for the refugee child, this can sometimes be a detriment. Refugee youth are often recruited to be child soldiers. Commanders sometimes become attachment figures for these children.[58] In many circumstances, children have been forced to commit atrocities against their families, with the purpose of breaking bonds and preventing them from returning to their communities. In addition to the suffering and abuse incurred by removal from the primary caregiver, children develop ambiguous loyalty as "insiders."[59] Stigmatization as "rebels," by both family and community, hinders children from developing normal social contacts and reintegrating into civilian society.[60]

Connections to any attachment figures are critical for recruitment and retention of minors. In the building of insurgent or deviant groups, attachment to group members is privileged over acceptance of ideology and also a prerequisite, so necessary for the initial formation of the group and for continued engagement.[61] Randy Blazak's ethnographic research on hate group consolidation shows that men who identify as Nazi skinheads understand when youth experience themselves as anomalous or unusual, therefore outside of "normal" social groups, including boys of nonwhite ethnicity, and solicit them for group allegiance.[62] "These populations [are] targeted," Blazak writes, "because of their desire for structure, a subcultural solution to their anomie, as well as their need for consistent models of authority and masculinity. They [are] easily manipulated and brought into the fray of right-wing hate groups."[63] Without a connection to a secure attachment figure who helps a child build both self-worth and a sense of purpose in the world, such manipulation is made easier. Addressing this need in refugee children would help thwart this kind of manipulation.

Group leaders understand their positions as attachment figures, articulating their roles as "big brothers" or "friends in need." In targeting boys who identify as abnormal, stigmatized, or isolated, they offer "a sympathetic ear, a critical explanation of the problem, and an action program that appears to (somewhat) resolve the problem."[64] Successful recruiting to any group is based on the need to have a personal, nurturing connection. These relationships form the cornerstone of group growth and illustrate that emotional reciprocity and trust are key to building the group.

Passarlay records in his memoir how he himself was at risk for solicitation from a deviant group, reflecting the precarious lives of children who find themselves separated from primary attachment figures and angry about their situations.

> Some of my friends got involved in extremist radical Islamist groups. These groups prey on the vulnerable and the lonely. They offer friendship and

> brotherhood and are masters at seizing on and manipulating a person's trauma or unsolved issues. I was still angry inside and struggling to find my way in a new culture, so it wouldn't have been hard to brainwash me. I was invited to attend talks and certain mosques that had more radical agendas, but luckily for me I was too busy to go because I had all my other activities going on. Without that I might have gone down the extremist path myself.[65]

At least two things enabled Passarlay to refute solicitation. First, his separation from his mother or primary caregiver happened when he was twelve, so that his more formative years were shaped by her care. Second, as he articulates, he was busy, but also at this point in the narrative he was living with a foster family "which helped his depression fade away."[66] His connection to this family was crucial. He expresses concern for his friends not as fortunate as he was and who were drawn to radical preachers because "they were lonely, and had nothing to do, no money, no support."[67] Passarlay's words emphasize the importance of human to human connection, and how with it, children are healthier, resilient, and capable of thriving. For migrant minors then, reunification and education about trauma-related stress and response is useful, but also minors benefit from developing friend networks among other children who have travelled alone in order to develop resilience and engage in shared problem solving.[68]

In a report for the United Nation Children's Fund, An Michels emphasizes the need for connection among children, vulnerable to subsequent abuse and exploitation, who are subjected to the loss of an attachment figure. Michels points out that migrant children travelling alone have "often limited access to basic necessities such as shelter, education, and health" which has "important implications for their physical and psychosocial development."[69] Furthermore, and perhaps most egregiously, the absence of an attachment figure and a subsequent "social support system can make it more difficult for children to participate safely in transitional justice systems," set up to protect their human rights.[70] Thus, support systems that work toward security for these minors serve both as a means of protection and as a defense against the multiple traumas inherent in migration. Such systems which offer emotional connection, as well as social and legal assistance, must be established as expeditiously as possible for minors seeking refuge in host countries.

The importance of bonding and attachment has not gone unrecognized by the Catholic Church. In fact, the United States Conference of Bishops calls for the rapid identification of unaccompanied and separated children as refugees and as children in need of protection. They urge the State Department to take action by establishing comprehensive systems for unaccompanied and separated refugee minors which connect early identification with assessments of vulnerability, provisions for care, timely solutions, and adjustments to care and long-term solutions for children "as circumstances change, or new opportunities or new risks emerge (durable solutions include resettlement, local integration, and voluntary repatriation)."[71] At the heart of the Bishops' argument rests Catholic Social Teaching, namely that the human person is both sacred and *social.* At the root of the social character lies the family, where the person "learns how to interact with and engage the wider community."[72] This assertion corresponds to a great degree with the psychological presupposition that relationality is the key to resilience, and that attachment to caregivers provides the framework from which to function in healthy human relationships. Accordingly, the bishops recognize the limitations of shelters, and the need for children to be reunited with family members or placed into community-based foster care as rapidly as possible. The initiatives pressed by the bishops correspond with research showing that migrant and refugee minors must be provided with a platform, whatever the method may be, of establishing safety and trust.[73]

CONCLUSION

In facing the crisis of migrant minors travelling alone, understanding the cumulative trauma that these children experience is imperative. The effects of trauma of any kind increases and is made worse by severed attachment. Those who are at most risk are minors travelling alone who have experienced trauma prior to migration. Regardless of trauma endured before, during, and after migration, detachment from a primary caretaker remains a serious deficit to children of any age in their adjustment to host countries. Lack of a primary caregiver that promotes secure attachment is a major inhibitor of wellness, adaptation, and assimilation/ integration. This leaves children vulnerable and at risk for a variety of maladaptive responses to migration. Issues of non-belonging and desires to belong are compounded in this climate.

The challenge to researchers, ethicists, and community members is how to provide secure attachment to children who, having travelled alone, arrive in host countries without parents. Agencies, institutions, organizations, and individuals would be best to understand that attachment is critical for these children so that they begin to embrace self-worth and a sense of purpose, so that they are able to make meaning of their suffering. These capabilities do not occur in isolation after extensive trauma. It is worth repeating Perry and Szalavitz's assertion that helping children who have endured trauma includes increasing the number of relationships they form. This sentiment is shared by other researchers and finds strong support in Catholic Social Teaching. In speaking about the plight of migrant minors, Jessica Stern responded to an audience member's question related to what we can do: the most vulnerable refugees, she asserted, are those who feel alienated.[74] "Any way that we address this alienation," she posited, "is a step in the right direction."[75]

NOTES

1. "New UN DESA report finds numbers of migrants continue to rise," United Nations Department of Economic and Social Affairs, Accessed January 3, 2018, https://www.un.org/development/desa/en/news/population/international-migration-report-2017.html.

2. "UNHCR Age, Gender, and Diversity Accountability Report 2016," The UN Refugee Agency, Accessed January 12, 2018, http://www.unhcr.org/en-us/protection/women/595cdf5c7/unhcr-age-gender-diversity-accountability-report-2016.html.

3. "Guidelines of Policies and Procedures in dealing with Unaccompanied Children Seeking Asylum February 1997," The United Nations High Commissioner for Refugees, Accessed March 2, 2018, http://www.unhcr.org/3d4f91cf4.pdf.

4. Simone Weil, *The Need for Roots: Prelude to a Declaration of Duties towards Mankind*, trans. Arthur Wills (1952; reprint, New York: Routledge, 2003), 43.

5. Gulwali Passarlay, *The Lightless Sky: A Twelve-Year-Old Refugee's Extraordinary Journey Across Half the World* (New York: Harper Collins: 2016).

6. RoseMarie Perez Foster, "When Immigration is Trauma: Guidelines for the Individual and Family Clinician," *American Journal of Orthopsychiatry* 71, no. 2 (2001): 158.

7. Passerlay's story is not an isolated one, and it raises issues of young people's perceptions of their own situations, their integration into society or not, and the governmental and policy impacts created by the number of minors travelling alone. These concerns and many more are outlined, discussed, and analyzed from various viewpoints through research conducted by Elain Chase, Nando Sigona, and their research team, funded by the Economic and Social Research Council in the United Kingdom. See especially the Becoming Adult Conference proceedings (2017) at "Becoming Adult: Researching Young Migrants' Uncertain Futures," Economic and Social Research Council, University of Oxford, and University of Birmingham, Accessed July 13, 2018, https://becomingadult.net.

8. Ibid., 153–170.

9. Corinne Rees, "Childhood Attachment," *British Journal of General Practice* 57, no. 544 (2007): 921.

10. Marco Mazzetti, "Trauma and Migration: A Transactional Analytic Approach Towards Refugees and Torture Victims," *Transactional Analysis Journal* 38, no. 4 (2008): 289–290.

11. Weil, *The Need for Roots*, 43.

12. Judith Herman, *Trauma and Recovery* (New York: Basic Books, 1992): 52.

13. See John Bowlby, *Attachment and Loss*, Vol. 1. (1969; reprint, London: Penguin Books, 1971), 300; and Mary D. Ainsworth, Mary C. Salter, Everett Waters Blehar, and Sally N. Wall, *Patterns of Attachment: A Psychological Study of the Strange Situation* (New York: Halsted Press, 1978).

14. See Mary Main and Judith Solomon, "Discovery of a New, Insecure-Disorganized/Disoriented Attachment Pattern," in *Affective Development in Infancy*, eds. T. B. Brazelton and M. Yogman (Norwood, NJ: Ablex, 1986), 95–124.

15. Mazzetti, "Trauma and Migration," 289.

16. Jean Mercer, *Understanding Attachment: Parenting, Child Care, and Emotional Development* (Westport, CT: Praeger, 2006), 55–56.

17. Aware Migrants, "The Odyssey of Infant Migrants: A Tragedy within a Tragedy," September 5, 2016, accessed March 15, 2018, https://www.awaremigrants.org/infants-in-the-migrants-odyssey-a-tragedy-in-the-tragedy.

18. "Lebanon Crisis Response Plan 2017–2020," The UN Refugee Agency, accessed March 13, 2018, https://data2.unhcr.org/en/documents/download/62236, 134.

19. Ibid.

20. See Mario Mikulincer, Phillip R. Shaver, Omri Gilath, and Rachel A. Nitzberg, "Attachment, Caregiving, and Altruism: Boosting Attachment Security Increases Compassion and Helping," *Journal of Personality and Social Psychology* 89, no. 1 (2005): 817–839.

21. Mario Mikulincer, and Phillip R. Shaver, *Attachment in Adulthood: Structure, Dynamics, and Change* (New York: Guilford Press, 2007), 191–192.

22. Ibid., 202.

23. Susan M. Johnson, *Emotionally Focused Couple Therapy with Trauma Survivors: Strengthening Attachment Bonds* (New York: The Guilford Press, 2005).

24. Ibid., 37.

25. Emmy E. Werner, "What Can We Learn about Resilience from Large-Scale Longitudinal Studies?" in *Handbook of Resilience in Children,* eds. Sam Goldstein and Robert B. Brooks (New York: Springer, 2013), 94.

26. Ibid., 94–95.

27. Johnson, "Emotionally Focused Couple Therapy," 37.

28. Ibid., 37–38.

29. John Bowlby, "The Nature of the Child's Tie to His Mother," *International Journal of Psycho-Analysis* 39 (1958): 350–373.

30. Perry and Szalavitz, "*The Boy who was Raised as a Dog,*" 80.

31. Marina A. Zelenko and Anne Benham, "Attachment Theory, Loss, and Trauma: A Case Study," *Clinical Child Psychology and Psychiatry* 7, no. 2 (2002): 201.

32. Theresa S. Betancourt, Elizabeth A. Newnham, Christopher M. Layne, Soeun Kim, Alan M. Steinberg, Heidi Ellis, and Dina Berman, "Trauma History and Psychopathology in War-Affected Refugee Children Referred for Trauma-Related Mental Health Services in the United States," *Journal of Traumatic Stress* no. 25 (2012): 684.

33. Ibid.

34. See Jennifer Teska, and Megan Rabin, *Immigrant Children, Unaccompanied: An Overview Evidence-Base Care Sheet* (Glandale, CA: Cinahl Information Systems), 2017.

35. Ibid.

36. Ibid.

37. United Nations High Commissioner for Refugees, "RRP6 Output 1: Vulnerabilities of children and caregivers reduced and their resilience strengthened," 2014, accessed March 12, 2018, https://data2.unhcr.org/en/documents/download/41572.

38. David J. Kinzie, "Immigrants and Refugees: The Psychiatric Perspective," *Transcultural Psychiatry* 43, no. 4 (2006): 587.

39. See James Garbarino, and Kathleen Kostelny, "What do We Need to Know to Understand Children in War and Community Violence?," 36 and Mona Macksoud, J. Lawrence Aber, and Ilene Cohn, "Assessing the Impact of War on Children," 220 in *Minefields in their Hearts: The Mental Health of Children in War and Communal Violence,* eds. Roberta J. Apfel and Bennett Simon (New Haven: Yale University Press, 1996).

40. Sarah Kenyon Lischer, *War, Displacement, and the Recruitment of Child Soldiers* (Pittsburg: Ford Institute for Human Security, 2006), 3–7.

41. Maragaret E. Blaustein, and Kristine M. Kinniburgh, *Treating Traumatic Stress in Children and Adolescents: How to Foster Resilience through Attachment, Self-Regulation, and Competency* (New York: Guilford Press, 2010), 38.

42. Charles S. Carver, and Michael F. Scheier, "Self-Regulation of Action and Affect," in *Handbook of Self-Regulation, Third Edition: Research, Theory and Applications,* ed. Kathleen D. Vohs and Roy F. Baumeister (New York: Guilford Press, 2017), 3.

43. Blaustein and Kinniburgh, *Treating Traumatic Stress,* 38.

44. Perry and Szalavitz, "*The Boy who was Raised as a Dog*," 249.

45. Ibid., 250.

46. Ibid.

47. Babette Rothschild, *The Body Remembers: The Psychophysiology of Trauma and Treatment* (New York: W. W. Norton & Company, 2000), 11.

48. Erving Goffman, *Asylums: Essays on the Social Situation of Mental Patients and Other Inmates* (New York: First Anchor Books Edition, 1961), 17.

49. Donald L. Nathanson, *Shame and Pride: Affect, Sex, and the Birth of the Self* (New York: W. W. Norton & Company, 1992), 250 and 318–319.

50. Ibid., 312.

51. Weil, *The Need for Roots*, 49.

52. Ibid., 43.

53. Ibid., 44 and 47–50.

54. Mazzetti, "Trauma and Migration," 286.

55. Farhad Dalal, "The Paradox of Belonging," *Psychoanalysis, Culture & Society* 14, no. 1 (2009): 77.

56. Ibid.

57. M. Sageman, *Understanding Terror Networks* (Philadelphia: University of Pennsylvania Press, 2004).

58. An Michels, "Psychosocial Support for Children: Protecting the Rights of Child Victims and Witnesses in Transitional Justice Practices," Innocenti Working Paper, UNICEF (2010), https://www.unicef-irc.org/publications/pdf/iwp_2010_14.pdf., 5.

59. Ibid.

60. Ibid.

61. Jessica Stern, "Terrorism," Webinar, January 24, 2018.

62. Randy Blazak, "White Boys to Terrorist Men: Target Recruitment of Nazi Skinheads," *The American Behavioral Scientist* 44, no. 6 (2001): 982–1000.

63. Ibid., 993 and 994.

64. Ibid.

65. Passarlay, *The Lightless Sky*, 343–344.

66. Ibid., 342.

67. Ibid., 344.

68. Kimberly A. Ehntholt, and William Yule, "Practitioner Review: Assessment and Treatment of Refugee Children and Adolescents who have Experienced War-Related Trauma," *Journal of Child Psychology and Psychiatry* 47, no. 2 (2006): 1205–1206.

69. Michels, "Psychosocial Support for Children," 4.

70. Ibid., 3–5.

71. United States Conference of Catholic Bishops, "Building Capacity to Protect Unaccompanied and Separated Refugee Children," July 2014, accessed March 12, 2018, http://www.usccb.org/about/migration-policy/upload/Durable-Solutions_URM.pdf.

72. United States Conference of Catholic Bishops, "Catholic Social Teaching and Unaccompanied Migrant Children," July 2014, accessed March 12, 2018, http://www.usccb.org/about/migration-policy/upload/Catholic-Social-Teaching-and-Unaccompanied-Migrant-Children.pdf.

73. Ehntholt and Yule, "Practitioner Review," 1202.

74. Jessica Stern, "Terrorism," Webinar 2018 at Boston University.

75. Ibid.

BIBLIOGRAPHY

Ainsworth, Mary D. Salter, Mary C. Blehar, Everett Waters, and Sally N. Wall. *Patterns of Attachment: A Psychological Study of the Strange Situation.* New York: Halsted Press, 1978.

Aware Migrants. "The Odyssey of Infant Migrants: A Tragedy within a Tragedy." September 5, 2016. Accessed March 15, 2018. https://www.awaremigrants.org/infants-in-the-migrants-odyssey-a-tragedy-in-the-tragedy/.

Betancourt, Theresa S., Elizabeth A. Newnham, Christopher M. Layne, Soeun Kim, Alan M. Steinberg, Heidi Ellis, and Dina Berman. "Trauma History and Psychopathology in War-Affected Refugee Children Referred for Trauma-Related Mental Health Services in the United States." *Journal of Traumatic Stress* no. 25 (2012): 682–690.

Blaustein, Maragaret E., and Kristine M. Kinniburgh. *Treating Traumatic Stress in Children and Adolescents: How to Foster Resilience through Attachment, Self-Regulation, and Competency.* New York: Guilford Press, 2010.

Blazak, Randy. "White Boys to Terrorist Men: Target Recruitment of Nazi Skinheads." *The American Behavioral Scientist* 44, no. 6 (2001): 982–1000.

Bowlby, John. 1969. *Attachment and Loss*, Vol. 1. Reprint, London: Penguin Books, 1971.
———. "The Nature of the Child's Tie to His Mother." *International Journal of Psycho-Analysis* 39 (1958): 350–373.
Carver, Charles S., and Michael F. Scheier. "Self-Regulation of Action and Affect." In *Handbook of Self-Regulation, Third Edition: Research, Theory and Applications* edited by Kathleen D. Vohs and Roy F. Baumeister, 3–23. New York: Guilford Press, 2017.
Dalal, Farhad. "The Paradox of Belonging." *Psychoanalysis, Culture & Society* 14, no. 1 (2009): 74–81.
Economic and Social Research Council, University of Oxford, and University of Birmingham. "Becoming Adult: Researching Young Migrants' Uncertain Futures." Accessed July 13, 2018. https://becomingadult.net.
Ehntholt, Kimberly A., and William Yule. "Practitioner Review: Assessment and Treatment of Refugee Children and Adolescents who have Experienced War-Related Trauma." *Journal of Child Psychology and Psychiatry* 47, no. 2 (2006): 1197–1210.
Garbarino, James, and Kathleen Kostelny. "What do We Need to Know to Understand Children in War and Community Violence?" in *Minefields in their Hearts: The Mental Health of Children in War and Communal Violenc*e, edited by Roberta J. Apfel and Bennett Simon, 33–51. New Haven: Yale University Press, 1996.
George, C., N. Kaplan, and Mary Main. *The Adult Attachment Interview*. Unpublished, 1985.
Goffman, Erving. *Asylums: Essays on the Social Situation of Mental Patients and Other Inmates*. New York: First Anchor Books Edition, 1961.
Herman, Judith. "Shattered Shame States and their Repair." Presentation, The John Bowlby Memorial Lecture from Harvard Medical School, Cambridge, Saturday March 10, 2007.
———. *Trauma and Recovery*. New York: Basic Books, 1992.
Johnson, Susan M. *Emotionally Focused Couple Therapy with Trauma Survivors: Strengthening Attachment Bonds*. New York: The Guilford Press, 2005.
Kinzie, J. David. "Immigrants and Refugees: The Psychiatric Perspective." *Transcultural Psychiatry* 43, no. 4 (2006): 577–591.
Lischer, Sarah Kenyon. "War, Displacement, and the Recruitment of Child Soldiers." Pittsburg: Ford Institute for Human Security, 2006: 1–27.
Lisseth Rojas-Flores, Mari L. Clements, J. Hwang Koo, and Judy London. "Trauma and Psychological Distress in Latino Citizen Children following Parental Detention and Deportation." *Psychological Trauma: Theory, Research, Practice and Policy* 9, no. 3 (2017): 352–361.
Macksoud, Mona, J. Lawrence Aber, and Ilene Cohn. "Assessing the Impact of War on Children." In *Minefields in their Hearts: The Mental Health of Children in War and Communal Violence,* edited by Roberta Apfel J. and Simon Bennett, 218–230. New Haven: Yale University Press, 1996.
Main, Mary. "Introduction to the Special Section on Attachment and Psychopathology: 2. Overview of the Field of Attachment." *Journal of Consulting and Clinical Psychology* 64, no. 2 (1996): 237–243.

Main, Mary, and Judith Solomon. "Discovery of a New, Insecure-Disorganized/Disoriented Attachment Pattern." In *Affective Development in Infancy*, edited by T. B. Brazelton and M. Yogman, 95–124. Norwood, NJ: Ablex (1986).

Masten, Ann S., Karin M. Best, and Norman Garmezy. "Resilience and Development: Contributions from the Study of Children Who Overcome Adversity." *Development and Psychopathology* 2, no. 4 (1990): 425–444.

Mazzetti, Marco. "Trauma and Migration: A Transactional Analytic Approach Towards Refugees and Torture Victims." *Transactional Analysis Journal* 38, no. 4 (2008): 285–302.

Mercer, Jean. *Understanding Attachment: Parenting, Child Care, and Emotional Development.* Westport, CT: Praeger, 2006.

Michels, An. "Psychosocial Support for Children: Protecting the Rights of Child Victims and Witnesses in Transitional Justice Practices." Innocenti Working Paper, UNICEF, 2010. Accessed December 10, 2017. https://www.unicefirc.org/publications/pdf/iwp_2010_14.pdf.

Mikulincer, Mario, and Phillip R. Shaver. *Attachment in Adulthood: Structure, Dynamics, and Change.* New York: Guilford Press, 2007.

Mikulincer, Mario, Phillip R. Shaver, Omri Gilath, and Rachel A. Nitzberg. "Attachment, Caregiving, and Altruism: Boosting Attachment Security Increases Compassion and Helping." *Journal of Personality and Social Psychology* 89, no. 1 (2005): 817–839.

Moretti, Marlene M., and Maya Peled. "Adolescent-Parent Attachment: Bonds the Support Healthy Development." *Paediatrics Child Health* 9, no. 8 (2004): 551–555.

Passerlay, Gulwali. *The Lightless Sky: A Twelve-Year-Old Refugee's Extraordinary Journey Across Half the World.* New York: Harper Collins, 2016.

Perez Foster, RoseMarie. "When Immigration is Trauma: Guidelines for the Individual and Family Clinician." *American Journal of Orthopsychiatry* 71, no. 2 (2001): 153–170.

Perry, Bruce D., and Maia Szalavitz. *The Boy who was Raised as a Dog.* New York: Basic Books, 2006.

Rees, Corinne. "Childhood Attachment." *British Journal of General Practice* 57, no. 544 (2007): 920–922.

Rothschild, Babette. *The Body Remembers: The Psychophysiology of Trauma and Treatment.* New York: W. W. Norton & Company, 2000.

Sageman, M. *Understanding Terror Networks.* Philadelphia: University of Pennsylvania Press, 2004.

Schore, Allan. *Affect Regulation and the Origin of the Self.* Hillsdale, NJ: Lawrence Erlbaum Associates, Publishers, 1994.

Stern, Jessica. "Terrorism," Webinar 2018 at Boston University.

Teska, Jennifer, and Megan Rabin. *Immigrant Children, Unaccompanied: An Overview, Evidence-Base Care Sheet.* Glandale, CA: Cinahl Information Systems, 2017.

The UN Refugee Agency. "Lebanon Crisis Response Plan 2017–2020." Accessed March 13, 2018. https://data2.unhcr.org/en/documents/download/62236, 127–147.

———. "UNHCR Age, Gender, and Diversity Accountability Report 2016." Accessed January 12, 2018. http://www.unhcr.org/en-us/protection/women/595cdf5c7/unhcr-age-gender-diversity-accountability-report-2016.html.

United Nations Department of Economic and Social Affairs. "News." Accessed January 3, 2018. https://www.un.org/development/desa/en/news/population/international-migration-report 2017.html.

United Nations High Commissioner for Refugees. "Guidelines of Policies and Procedures in dealing with Unaccompanied Children Seeking Asylum February 1997." Accessed March 2, 2018. http://www.unhcr.org/3d4f91cf4.pdf.

———. "RRP6 Output 1: Vulnerabilities of Children and Caregivers Reduced and their Resilience Strengthened." 2014. Accessed March 12, 2018. https://data2.unhcr.org/en/documents/download/41572.

United States Conference of Catholic Bishops. "Building Capacity to Protect Unaccompanied and Separated Refugee Children." July 2014. Accessed March 12, 2018. http://www.usccb.org/about/migration-policy/upload/Durable-Solutions_URM.pdf

———. "Catholic Social Teaching and Unaccompanied Migrant Children," July 2014. Accessed March 12, 2018. http://www.usccb.org/about/migration-policy/upload/Catholic-Social-Teaching-and-Unaccompanied-Migrant-Children.pdf.

Weil, Simone. 1952. *The Need for Roots: Prelude to a Declaration of Duties Towards Mankind.* Translated by Arthur Wills. Reprint, New York: Routledge, 2003.

Werner, Emmy E. "What Can We Learn about Resilience from Large-Scale Longitudinal Studies?" in *Handbook of Resilience in Children*, edited by Sam Goldstein and Robert B. Brooks, 87–102. New York: Springer, 2013.

Zelenko, Marina A., and Anne Benham. "Attachment Theory, Loss, and Trauma: A Case Study." *Clinical Child Psychology and Psychiatry* 7, no. 2 (2002): 1359–1045.

Chapter 4

Unaccompanied Refugee Children and Adolescents and Access to Vocational Training in Germany—with a Focus on Bavaria

Philip M. Anderson

This chapter deals with the situation of young unaccompanied minors in Germany with specific reference to their access to vocational training. It is based on findings from a four-year research project the author completed in 2016 which was commissioned by the Schools Department of the City of Munich municipality. The chapter focuses on the situation in Bavaria, which was a main receptor of the hugely increased flow of refugees[1] in 2014–2016.

This chapter will not treat the mass immigration of refugees into Germany between 2014 and 2016, but it is the "game changing" background that puts the pedagogic-political strategies that this chapter examines into stark focus.

After a brief consideration of the role of intercultural skills, the broad educational situation of unaccompanied minors (henceforth UMs, the expression employed in German debate) is discussed, detailing the Vocational Integration Courses (VIC) which have been phased in and greatly expanded in the 2011–2017 period in Bavaria.

These classes have attained a role-model character across Germany as preparation and orientation of refugees on the path to vocational training. These are two-year courses for 16 to 21-year-olds (with exceptions up to 25 years) that convey language skills and a grounding in the German school system as well as a phase of vocational training orientation through internships. They culminate in a school certificate, which—ideally—result in an apprenticeship in a recognized trade.

With the huge rise in asylum seekers entering Germany in the period of 2014–2016 these classes have expanded enormously, from a few hundred students in the principal cities of Munich and Nuremberg in 2011–2012 to a total of 1,150 classes with places for 22,000 pupils in the 2016–2017 school year.[2]

The article features the UMs' own view of their educational, job, and social situation. This was a central aspect of the author's findings, and discussions with practitioners showed these results to be of particular interest. The article concludes with an assessment of ongoing intercultural pedagogic and job-training challenges and some suggestions on how to address these at local level.

CULTURALLY SENSITIVE WORK APPROACHES

In pedagogic or social work contexts it is always important to be aware of a tendency toward a Eurocentric view, or a more subtle potpourri of assumptions which are culturally determined. In the German context training courses on developing intercultural skills have increased enormously, corresponding in the last few years to a drastic increase in demand from a whole range of professions in the social, health, and educational sectors–from social pedagogues via child and adolescent psychiatrists to teachers in schools/classes of every type and grade.

Professionals working in particular with asylum seeker families or unaccompanied refugee children have to be aware of the dangers of "culturally tinted spectacles" as the German expression has it. Thus the ability to change one's culturally determined perspective (*What is the other person's take on this situation?*) is an essential element in developing culturally sensitive skills and minimizing potential sources of conflict.[3]

On the one hand, it is important not to ignore one's own values and concepts; on the other to display a readiness for culturally sensitive dialogue and exchange. This is all the more true when dealing with refugees who have entered Germany in recent years who—in contrast to the generation of those with a migration background who have grown up in Germany—have experienced social conditioning outside the European context. The great majority of those entering the country as asylum seekers experience a "steep learning curve" in the course of a process of forced migration. They encounter, and must come to grips with, people with differing cultural, religious, and ethnic backgrounds on a daily basis and in varied contexts.

Discussions on the need for a "guiding culture" (*Leitkultur*), which have been a staple of German intercultural and migration debate for over a decade, are of little help in professional, social, health, and educational practice. Taking on board a "dynamic" notion of culture is more appropriate, that is, one which does not pin down refugees to a specific ethnic-cultural-religious context, but rather views them as actors in a framework of the multilayered process of mixed and forced migrations.[4]

Set against this background the statement of an Anglican pastor in a parish in East London (United Kingdom) in the course of a discussion with the author some years ago may be deemed appropriate. At that time, an African family facing deportation had been living for nearly three years in "sanctuary" on the grounds of the church.

His view regarding processes of long-term intercultural understanding was that "*Sex is a great leveler!*" What he meant was that in conditions of ever-increasing global mobility manifold encounters and relationships—including those of an erotic nature—lead to transnational connections of an increasingly varied and complex character. Rigid immigration regimes are per se inflexible and anachronistic in the face of this unprecedented dynamism in human reach and global mobility. It is the task of receiving societies in times such as these to meet this challenge as constructively as possible.

UNACCOMPANIED MINORS ARRIVING IN GERMANY: THE SOCIAL AND EDUCATIONAL SITUATION

Unaccompanied minors under eighteen years of age are absorbed into the youth service system and after an initial *clearing phase* are allotted a place in a residential group for unaccompanied minors—assuming there are no adult relatives in the European Union with whom family reunion can be initiated.[5] The first goal of the newly arrived is to get their bearings, in the comprehensive sense to actually "arrive" in the here and now. In this context, the broad range of supportive networks for refugees which sprouted everywhere in Germany in the period 2014–2015 is very important. Voluntary helper groups in larger and medium-sized towns as well as in rural villages often provide sustained longer-term support both for refugee families and unaccompanied young people. This mobilization of local policy-makers, administration and professionals, especially in the educational, health, and social sectors—together with civil society engagement—has enabled absorption and day-to-day integration of refugees. It has also turned their reception into a "mainstream" topic in German public discourse and policy-making.

If we examine the lives of the newly arrived unaccompanied minors we get an idea of the range of challenges they face. The top priority is learning the language, but they have to cope with the challenges of strange cultural surroundings, homesickness, grief, and loss of their loved ones. Then there is the issue of trauma. Studies proceed from the assumption that at least 50 percent of unaccompanied minors suffer from some degree of traumatization.[6] One of the important tasks facing care and social workers, teachers and other professionals is recognizing the symptoms: sudden outbreaks of fright, blackouts, aggressive outbursts—but also apathy, pronounced sensitivity to light or loud noises, insomnia, or acute withdrawal behavior. In the Bavarian context the special training courses and professional counseling offered by the *Refugio* organization, based in Munich, are of great value. This psychotherapeutic institute has specialized in the treatment of traumatized refugees and the victims of torture for over twenty years and has developed considerable expertise in therapeutic sessions conducted through specially trained interpreters.[7]

Practitioners emphasize the importance of getting access to language courses off the ground as soon as possible. The legal terrain is complex here, as access to courses is dependent on the intermeshing constellation of the individual asylum application, residential status, and availability of courses on the ground. In practice, local voluntary networks often work in tandem with residential unit care workers to enable participation in a language course as soon as possible. Over time—and especially with the drastic reduction of new entries from 2017—provision of language tuition has been made possible on a comprehensive basis.

THE UNACCOMPANIED MINORS' VIEW

The author's interviews and research form the basis of the following observations on the situation of the unaccompanied minors in Germany.[8] Apart from young asylum seekers themselves, expert interviewees/interlocutors included teachers, social workers, therapists, administrative workers, local politicians, and others.

The group of refugees that has entered Germany in the last few years is extremely heterogeneous. This fact was emphasized repeatedly by expert interviewees, and herein reside the educational and vocational training challenges. Their social and educational backgrounds vary enormously and these factors intermesh with intellectual and experiential elements to determine levels of performance and achievement. Some unaccompanied minors will begin by wrestling with the basics of literacy in order to begin to learn the (German and native) language. At the other end of the spectrum there will be pupils who have had nine or ten years of schooling, speak good English, have a grounding for an academic course in the foreseeable future—and may well have thought ahead to save their certificates in their cell phones before taking flight.

Soft skills are an essential part of the picture in terms of social acceptance, especially by their central European peer group: the young Syrian from Aleppo who speaks good English, has varied contacts on Facebook and Instagram, followed the latest Hollywood films and is conversant with hip-hop culture will establish contact much more easily than, say, the young Afghan from a mountainous region with very little schooling, possibly a long and stressful period of forced migration because of lack of funds—as well as little experience of young women of his age who do not wear the veil. The latter will feel much more inhibited by the notion of *do's and don'ts in the German disco* than will his Syrian counterpart.

In interviews emphasis was put upon how important it is for young people to feel free and autonomous. After a time of insecurity and the tribulations of the migration process these young people need a time to get acclimatized, to *just be*, in order to recover something of their lost childhood (as one therapist put it). The need for support and for role models is an essential element in this, and the social workers in residential units or teachers and social workers at school are often key figures who can assume this role.

From a (social) pedagogic point of view it should be borne in mind that these young men (more than 80 percent are men) have an "assignment" to fulfill: they have been chosen to have the chance to get a good qualification and find a job in order to earn a good income. This is why the family of origin "invested" a considerable sum in the form of payment to the human smuggler. In an age of virtual communication these familial expectations are much more ever-present (in the classroom, wherever the adolescent is living, in their contacts with other young people from their home area) than, say, twenty years ago. The social media, the tweets, or the mobile phone messages mean that family members are consistently in the picture–sometimes, so teachers report, almost to the extent of being invisible presences in the classroom.

The accommodation situation plays a vital role in success or failure at school or during an apprenticeship. In residential groups for unaccompanied minors the young people have as a rule a) the peace and quiet to do their school and homework, b) the resources to get extra tutorship if required, and c) most important, the professional guidance and support to enable them to navigate their way among the 550-odd trades and vocations available in the German system. Thus they can be in a position to make informed choices about a potential apprenticeship or other venues of qualification.

The situation is very different for those over eighteen years who are likely to be in a much more difficult position, because they may well be living in a hostel, maybe sharing a room with three to four other people, mostly adults and often with considerable burdens and stresses of their own. There will be little space and scarcely the requisite peace and quiet to do their homework, after-school tutoring may well not be available, advice on vocational training and apprenticeships will be at a premium. Moreover, there is the "social space" aspect: the young refugees will be acutely aware that they are in a social no-man's land. The hostel (mostly located in less desirable parts of town) is not the kind of place you invite your class friends to for a party or to impress your new European girlfriend. Young refugees have to learn to deal with feelings of embarrassment or shame in this context.

Searching for security and a sense of belonging, these young people are constantly undermined by a lack of secure residential status or recognition as a refugee in the narrower legal sense. Professionals pointed out in the interviews that even the fear of an impending deportation order can undermine their charges and render them incapable of concentration on their studies and everyday lives for weeks at a time.

As regards taking on an apprenticeship, the UMs are faced with different types of pressure. There is the economic burden of having to pay back the debt to the human smuggler—who may well be tightening the screw on the home family to receive his money. The relatives will in any event be expecting some kind of "payback" from their sponsored relatives soon, and they may find it hard to grasp why training over three or more years should even be necessary ("What do you mean sales training? You've been a salesman in our shop for years!").

In addition to this certain types of professions may be regarded as less prestigious, for instance in some cultures, working in the building trade is looked down upon as "dirty work." The issue of working with one's hands in any context may well be problematic for a young man who has been told by relatives that he *must* attain a university qualification. This is in turn a challenge for the social workers or teachers who have established a trusting relationship with their charges: keeping them on course for an apprenticeship. For, as the latter come to realize how long and stony the path to well-paid work in a qualifications-oriented society like Germany can be, there is the danger they may simply give up in frustration or turn to apparently "easier" but more fraught, and possibly illegal, ways of making quick money.

It is important for the receiving society in general to realize that these processes take time. UMs are (or should be viewed as) candidates for life-long learning. Resources should be made available so that they can have a second (or third) attempt at learning a trade. Once they have learned how things function in Germany, have mastered the language to the extent of comprehending the nuances of specialist terms and have a broader awareness of the range of vocations that they might choose from, the playing field begins to become level. Under these circumstances stable and trusting relationships with experienced and caring professionals (as role models) will be the essential bricks and mortar to motivate the UMs to stay for the long haul into the world of work and not to succumb to a sense of resignation.[9]

Once students have completed their two-year course in the VIC, they hope to find a place for an apprenticeship. Experience has shown that, if possible, some form of *mentoring* is advisable during the initial phase of vocational training. The linguistic and specialist challenges both at the workplace and at vocational school are considerable. Moreover, whereas the UMs have enjoyed intensive tuition in the (smaller) VIC classes to date, at "conventional" vocational school they are faced with the challenge of specialist language terms relating to their field as well as front-on classroom teaching with limited or no resources for support teaching in smaller groups. In rural areas the pupils may also have to wrestle with the additional difficulty of the strong regional (Bavarian) dialect the teachers may speak. Linguistically and socially, it may well be hard for them to meet the challenges of the different "life worlds" of small-scale business and vocational school.[10]

Nonetheless, there has been over the last few years a coordinated development of supportive labor market integration instruments at the local level for this specific target group. For example, the local labor offices provide resources for measures like the assisted training program, whereby a young asylum seeker is given language and vocational guidance by a social worker on a one-to-one basis. Problems arising at the workplace can also be dealt with, the social worker acting as intermediary, if required. Training supervisors at work, particularly in small and medium-sized enterprises (SME) are often grateful for culturally sensitive advice regarding their charges, such as information on aspects of Arab custom, culture, and Islam or advice on how to detect signs of trauma. Professional bodies such as the Chambers of Trade and of Industry and Commerce have supported integration at the workplace over the last few years by appointing refugee ombudsmen who advise and organize courses for the SMEs.[11]

ONGOING CHALLENGES AND POTENTIAL REMEDIES

One of the greatest challenges facing the adolescents is the lack of secure residential status and the uncertain perspective of remaining in Germany. This is particularly true if students come from "countries of safe origin," such as Balkan states like Kosovo and Montenegro, but most controversially from Afghanistan. Policy has become much stricter regarding this group since 2016. The number of Afghani UMs has consistently been among the highest among all UMs. Many young people facing potential deportation have been in Germany for a number of years and are either in training or already have jobs. They dread the "yellow letter" from the Aliens' Office, stating that they must leave the country voluntarily, failing which they face deportation.

Practitioners complain of a constant sense of underlying uncertainty, which undermines the students' ability to concentrate on school, become adjusted to life in their new surroundings, and plan for the future. This is why employers have consistently called for a guarantee that asylum seekers who have not attained recognition as a refugee or another form of secure residential status will be able to remain at least for three years' training plus an additional two years as qualified workers, the so-called *3+2 arrangement*. In practice, this principle has—after much criticism of restrictive policy on the part of the Bavarian Ministry of the Interior (responsible for issuing permits enabling UMs to begin apprenticeships via the Aliens Offices at local level)—been conceded.[12]

There is an ongoing need for access to good-quality language teaching from as early as possible after arrival in the country. Professionals argue that *learning German is the key to integration* and essential even for those asylum seekers whose prospects of remaining are uncertain. They need to lead their everyday lives in Germany; language skills are essential for this and even in the case of removal, knowledge of German may well be regarded as a recognized skill in the home region.

Social participation is a valuable dimension in developing a sense of belonging. Here the voluntary sector is of great importance. One of the striking facts about the influx of refugees from 2014 onward has been the degree of civil society engagement. Rural areas in particular, with the long-established tradition in Germany of people being involved in clubs (*Vereine*) of all kinds, have provided a basis for community involvement. Whether it is the local choir, music and sports clubs, or the local (voluntary) fire service, these spaces allow people to get to know each other and share activities and interests in this broader interactive context where good language skills are not necessarily a prerequisite. Particularly for young asylum seekers soccer is an ideal way to get to know one another and promote uncomplicated inclusive processes with one's peers.[13]

Good intermeshing cooperation on the part of local actors at the municipal level is of particular importance. Some cities have much more experience of development of intercultural policies to prevent conflict between communities and enhance the quality of life for minorities than others, for example, Munich or Nuremberg. Professionals in the social, educational, and health sectors in cities like Munich working in government offices, local government, grassroots initiatives, or campaigning groups have developed networks over the years and meet regularly in workshops and seminars. This has helped bridge ideological gaps, overcome conflicts, and promote a sense of a shared search for practicable, professional solutions to problems. Good, regular communication and mutual respect for differing institutional roles and interests are essential elements in this.

Structures of the youth service need to be flexible and needs-oriented. This means it is important to implement *transitional structures* for those eighteen-year-olds who have lived in residential units and have to move out into hostels or their own accommodation. They still require counseling on vocational training and jobs as well as support in dealing with the demands of everyday life. The German youth service has good models for promoting independent living for young people who have lived in care. These can be amended for the needs of this target group.

Then there is the need for broad-based *psychotherapeutic support* (for traumatized clients) and training courses and supervision for professionals working with them. These courses should be made available for volunteers as well as the professionally trained. Beyond this there has been a steep rise in the need for supplementary training for child and adolescent psychiatrists as well as for outpatients departments of psychiatric clinics. The issue here for example is how do psychiatric professionals deal with asylum seekers who go into psychosis as a result of their experiences during forced migration? Equally important is the need to provide for qualified interpreters who can meet the challenge of therapeutic translation in a crisis-induced context.[14]

In summary, linguistic, social, and educational integration processes take time. Helping young people with a refugee background adapt to the needs of the vocational training and job market requires a targeted and well thought-out use of resources, and these should be employed on a sustainable basis. Quite apart from the humanitarian-moral dimension of this commitment, it is a long-term "investment" in societal and economic development that will prove to be well worth it.

NOTES

1. Unless otherwise stated, the term "refugee" will be used in the colloquial sense to describe people with a flight background, irrespective of their status in the asylum system. It will be used interchangeably with "asylum seeker" for easier readability.

2. "Kultusministerium/Bavarian Ministry of Education," https://www.km.bayern.de/lehrer/meldung/3755/junge-asylbewerber-und-fluechtlinge-koennen-in-ganz-bayern-berufsintegrationsklassen-besuchen.html.

3. See Astrid Erll, and Marion Gymnich, *Interkulturelle Kompetenz—erfolgreich kommunizieren zwischen den Kulturen* (Stuttgart: Klett, 2013).

4. See Georg Auernheimer, ed., *Interkulturelle Kompetenz und pädagogische Professionalität* (Wiesbaden: VS Verlag, 2013).

5. "Bundesarbeitsgemeinschaft BAG Landesjugendämter: Handlungsempfehlungen zum Umgang mit unbegleiteten minderjährigen Flüchtlingen. Inobhutnahme, Clearingverfahren und Einleitung von Anschlussmaßnahmen," http://www.bagljae.de/downloads/118_handlungsempfehlungen-umf_2014.pdf.

6. On the social and therapeutic dimensions of traumatization through forced migration, see Sonja Bergler, *Unbegleite minderjährige Flüchtlinge. Vom Aufbruch im Herkunftsland bis zur Ankunft in Deutschland* (Norderstedt: GRIN Verlag, 2015), and Brigitte Hargasser, *Unbegleitete minderjährige Flüchtlinge. Sequentielle*

Traumatisierungsprozesse und die Aufgabe der Jugendhilfe (Frankfurt am Main: Brandes & Apsel, 2014).

7. http://www.refugio-muenchen.de.

8. See Philip Anderson, *"Lass mich endlich machen!" Eine Strategie zur Förderung in der beruflichen Bildung für junge berufsschulpflichtige Asylbewerber und Flüchtlinge (BAF).* Study for the City of Munich: Landeshauptstadt München, Referat für Bildung und Sport (RBS) 2016.

9. For a culturally sensitive view of the challenges faced by migrants in small and medium-sized enterprises, see Katharina Scharrer, Sybille Schneider, and Margit Stein, eds., *Übergänge von Schule in Ausbildung und Beruf bei Jugendlichen Migrantinnen und Migranten. Herausforderungen und Chancen* (Bad Heilbronn: Klinkhardt, 2012).

10. See documentation with practical tips on preparing young refugees for the challenges of an apprenticeship: ISB (Staatsinstitut für Schulqualität und Bildungsforschung) Handreichung: *Berufsschulpflichtige Asylbewerber und Flüchtlinge*, München 2014, https://www.isb.bayern.de/download/15501/handreichung_baf_beschulung.pdf.

11. See "Chamber of Trade and support for vocational training for refugees," Zentralverband des deutschen Handwerks, https://www.zdh.de/fachbereiche/arbeitsmarkt-tarifpolitik/integration-von-fluechtlingen.

12. See "Flyer on 3+2 issued by the local Chamber of Trades/ Bayerische Industrie und Handelskammer," https://www.ihk-muenchen.de/ihk/documents/Fl%C3%BCchtlinge/BIHK-Flyer-3-2-Regelung.pdf.

13. See "Street football league in Munich set up in the 1990s, specifically for asylum seekers who—at that time—were unable to access the local youth football clubs," http://buntkicktgut.de.

14. See "Interpreters service in Bavaria specializing in translation in therapeutic and legal contexts for refugees," http://www.bayzent.de/dolmetscher-service/informationen.

BIBLIOGRAPHY

Anderson, Philip. *"Lass mich endlich machen!" Eine Strategie zur Förderung in der beruflichen Bildung für junge berufsschulpflichtige Asylbewerber und Flüchtlinge (BAF).* Landeshauptstadt München, Referat für Bildung und Sport (RBS), 2016.

Auernheimer, Georg, ed. *Interkulturelle Kompetenz und pädagogische Professionalität.* Wiesbaden: VS Verlag, 2013.

Bayerische Industrie und Handelskammer: *3+2* https://www.ihk-muenchen.de/ihk/documents/Fl%C3%BCchtlinge/BIHK-Flyer-3–2-Regelung.pdf.

Bergler, Sonja. *Unbegleite minderjährige Flüchtlinge. Vom Aufbruch im Herkunftsland bis zur Ankunft in Deutschland.* Norderstedt: GRIN Verlag, 2015.

Bundesarbeitsgemeinschaft BAG Landesjugendämter. *Handlungsempfehlungen zum Umgang mit unbegleiteten minderjährigen Flüchtlingen. Inobhutnahme,*

Clearingverfahren und Einleitung von Anschlussmaßnahmen. http://www.bagljae.de/downloads/118_handlungsempfehlungen-umf_2014.pdf.

Buntkicktgut. http://buntkicktgut.de.

Erll, Astrid, and Marion Gymnich. *Interkulturelle Kompetenz – erfolgreich kommunizieren zwischen den Kulturen.* Stuttgart: Klett, 2013.

Hargasser, Brigitte. *Unbegleitete minderjährige Flüchtlinge. Sequentielle Traumatisierungsprozesse und die Aufgabe der Jugendhilfe.* Frankfurt am Main: Brandes & Apsel, 2014.

Institut für Schulqualität und Bildungsforschung: Handreichung, *Berufsschulpflichtige Asylbewerber und Flüchtlinge*, München, 2014. https://www.isb.bayern.de/download/15501/handreichung_baf_beschulung.pdf.

ISB (Staatsinstitut für Schulqualität und Bildungsforschung) Handreichung. *Berufsschulpflichtige Asylbewerber und Flüchtlinge*, München, 2014, https://www.isb.bayern.de/download/15501/handreichung_baf_beschulung.pdf.

Korntheuer, Annette,and Anderson, Philip: *Zwischen Inklusion und Exklusion. Die Rolle der Sozialen Arbeit in Bildungsprozessen junger Flüchtlinge* in: Migration und Soziale Arbeit (ISA). Frankfurt am Main, Oktober 2014, Heft 4, 2014: 320–327.

Kultusministerium/Bavarian Ministry of Education. "junge-asylbewerber-und-fluechtlinge-koennen-in-ganz-bayern-berufsintegrationsklassen-besuchen." https://www.km.bayern.de/lehrer/meldung/3755/junge-asylbewerber-und-fluechtlinge-koennen-in-ganz-bayern-berufsintegrationsklassen-besuchen.html.

Scharrer, Katharina, Sybille Schneider, and Margit Stein (Hrsg.): *Übergänge von Schule in Ausbildung und Beruf bei Jugendlichen Migrantinnen und Migranten. Herausforderungen und Chancen.* Bad Heilbronn: Klinkhardt, 2012.

Zentralverband des deutschen Handwerks. "Chamber of Trade and support for vocational training for refugees," https://www.zdh.de/fachbereiche/arbeitsmarkt-tarifpolitik/integration-von-fluechtlingen.

Part II

CHILDREN'S RIGHTS?

Chapter 5

Betraying Children's Rights

Unaccompanied Immigrant Children in the United States

Katherine Kaufka Walts

The world is experiencing the greatest migration crisis since World War II. It is estimated that of the 65.6 million people displaced today, including refugees, children represent more than half of global refugees.[1] Many factors account for the increased migration, including conflict, poverty, violence, corruption, climate change, and extractive development policies. Opportunities for family unification and increased economic and physical security also continue to be compelling pull factors that contribute to global migration. All these elements affect migration to the United States, one of the top destination countries in the world. The United States has more international migrants than any other country in the world, and the Mexican migration corridor is one of the most heavily traveled.[2]

People, particularly children and youth, who move out of necessity rather than free choice, are more at risk of human rights violations during their migration and at their country of destination. Among the millions of children[3] on the move worldwide, hundreds of thousands of children and adolescents undertake dangerous journeys without an adult or guardian accompanying them. Child migrants are particularly vulnerable, and this vulnerability is recognized under both international and domestic laws. Laws on paper versus laws in practice, however, are two different matters. Since October 2013, the US government has apprehended more than 250,000 unaccompanied immigrant children[4] at its southern border, the largest number of youth recorded. Most of the children are arriving from Central America (El Salvador, Guatemala, Honduras) and Mexico. Over 135,000 of these children have been placed with adult sponsors who care for the children in communities throughout the United States.[5] Countless other youth have entered the United States without inspection.

This chapter provides an overview of the practice by which the US government processes unaccompanied immigrant minors and critically examines the systemic gaps that currently exist to protect their rights under both domestic and international laws and norms, applying the "best interests standard" articulated under Article 3 of the United Nations Convention on the Rights of the Child (CRC). Part 1 briefly introduces the children's rights movement and the CRC. It describes the "best interests of the child" principle defined by CRC, and provides a brief summary of US laws related to unaccompanied immigrant children seeking entry into the United States. Part 2 profiles the unaccompanied children and youth who are entering the United States and the experiences they face pre- and post-migration. Part 3 analyzes the systemic ways children's rights are violated under immigration policies and practices, emphasizing the absence of a child-centered approach under US immigration laws, and the importance of applying a "best interests standard" under the UN CRC.

CHILDREN'S RIGHTS IN THE UNITED STATES

The notion of children as rights holders may seem obvious but, in fact, this is still a relatively new concept in both international and domestic laws and norms. Although human rights applied to adults became a norm after World War II with the Universal Declaration of Human Rights proclamation of 1948, the notion of children as rights holders did not occur until much later. For example, in nineteenth-century America, many children were viewed as the property of their parents or employers, and child labor and indentured servitude for arriving youth migrants was rampant. In 1989, the international community adopted the CRC, the first human rights instrument to establish the human rights of children and the standards that all governments must aspire to achieve for realizing these rights, which include political, civil, economic, and social rights. The drafting of the CRC was the culmination of eight preceding decades of nation-states around the globe, including the United States, setting standards and policies addressing the rights of the child. The CRC was also the first human rights instrument to consider the child to be a "subject" of rights versus the "object" of concern for the state or private philanthropy.[6] To put it another way, the CRC recognized that children were not adults in miniature, the property of their parents or objects of charity, and that given their developing minds and bodies, children required additional protections as human beings. It recognized that how children experience situations and how their social and physical environment affects their developing minds and bodies is quite different from that of adults. States, civil society, and parents are all tasked with protecting and implementing these rights under the CRC.

The CRC embodies four (interconnected) principles:

1. The best interests of the child shall be a primary consideration in all actions affecting children (Article 3).
2. There shall be no discrimination on the grounds of race; color; sex; language; religion; political or other opinions; national, ethnic or social origin; property, disability, birth, or other status (Article 2).
3. States Parties recognize that every child has the inherent right to life and shall ensure to the maximum extent possible the survival and development of the child (Article 6).
4. Children shall be assured the right to express their views freely in all matters affecting them, their views being given due weight in accordance with the child's age and level of maturity (Article 12).

Article 3 of the CRC outlines the standard by which "the best interests of the child must be the primary concern in making decisions that may affect them."

1. In all actions concerning children, whether undertaken by public or private social welfare institutions, courts of law, administrative authorities or legislative bodies, the best interests of the child shall be a primary consideration.
2. States Parties undertake to ensure the child such protection and care as is necessary for his or her well-being, taking into account the rights and duties of his or her parents, legal guardians, or other individuals legally responsible for him or her, and, to this end, shall take all appropriate legislative and administrative measures.
3. States Parties shall ensure that the institutions, services and facilities responsible for the care or protection of children shall conform with the standards established by competent authorities, particularly in the areas of safety, health, in the number and suitability of their staff, as well as competent supervision.

The "best interests of the child" standard is a feature of both US child protection laws and international guidelines such as the CRC governing the treatment of children. In the United States, all fifty states require consideration of a child's best interests in any decision "about a child's custody or other critical life issues."[7] "Best interests" encompasses both a substantive right—the child's right to have his or her best interests considered in any decision about him or her—and procedural protections to ensure that there is "an evaluation of the possible impact" of decisions upon a child or group of children.[8] These procedural protections in the context of US domestic child welfare law factors entering into the determination of best interests vary case by case and are not universally defined. Nevertheless, three factors—safety, well-being, and permanency—appear consistently in statutes, case law, regulations, and policies defining best interests across all states. In 2013, the Committee on the Rights of the Child, the appointed governing body of experts overseeing the implementation of the CRC, articulated seven specific elements for assessing a child's best interests:

1. The child's views
2. The child's identity
3. Preservation of the family environment and maintaining relations
4. The care, protection, and safety of the child
5. A situation of vulnerability
6. The child's right to health
7. The child's right to education

Under US child protection law, the "best interests of the child" standard is perhaps most visible in placement and custody determinations, safety and permanency planning, and proceedings for termination of parental rights. Every state in the United States has child welfare laws requiring courts to consider the "best interests" of children who are separated from their parents or legal guardians. "Best interests" determinations are made by considering several factors related to the child's circumstances and the parents' or caregiver's circumstances and capacity to parent, the child's age, and other vulnerabilities, with the child's ultimate safety and well-being as the main priority. Often, these considerations take into account the recommendation of several individuals, including an advocate or guardian ad litem, a state's attorney, a juvenile court judge, family members, other experts, and the expressed wishes of the child.

Today, the CRC is the most universally recognized human rights instrument, with every nation-state in the world ratifying the instrument with the notable exception of one: the United States. Although there is still much debate about the effectiveness and impact of the CRC, it has undoubtedly elevated the notion that children require special protections to ensure their safety, health, and well-being, particularly in legal proceedings. It has created an international reporting and monitoring mechanism to report on nation-state compliance with the CRC. And while the United States has not ratified the CRC, its principles are embodied in its child welfare systems, particularly around the policies and practices that incorporate the "best interests of the child" standard in every state.

One of the most notable areas where the absence of a commitment to children's rights and welfare has the most profound effects on children is under US immigration law. Unlike all other legal arenas in which children are subjects of a legal proceeding, there is little recognition of children's rights or the statutory "best interests of the child" standard codified in US immigration law. While both the Homeland Security Act of 2002[9] and the TVPRA (2008) introduce "best interests of the child" language, this fundamental principal of children's rights is largely absent from the practice of immigration law. In fact, children are processed in immigration legal proceedings systems the same way adults are, with little to no recognition of the unique developmental needs and differences of children's minds, bodies, and well-being. This deficiency is most evident in how unaccompanied immigrant children are apprehended in the United States, how their immigration cases are adjudicated, and how they are released into US communities or repatriated back to their home countries.

ARRIVING UNACCOMPANIED: IMMIGRANT MINORS IN THE UNITED STATES

Unaccompanied immigrant minors, referred to as "unaccompanied alien minors," under US federal law, are defined by statute as children who lack lawful immigration status in the United States, who are under the age of eighteen, and who are either without a parent or guardian in the United States, or without a parent or legal guardian in the United States who is not available to provide care and physical custody.[10] It is important to note that this definition applies at the point of apprehension. Many unaccompanied children and youth have parents, family members, or guardians, but may not be traveling with them when they are apprehended by officials. For example, many youth travel to the United States to reunify with parents or family members who migrated earlier to the United States. Due to their vulnerability, unaccompanied minors receive additional protections under US immigration laws. Under the William Wilberforce Trafficking Victims Protection Reauthorization Act of 2008, or TVPRA 2008, unaccompanied minors from noncontiguous countries are provided additional protections, most notably the opportunity for a hearing before an immigration judge. The policy behind this provision is a recognition that Central American unaccompanied immigrant children are uniquely vulnerable to human trafficking, and therefore more rigorous policies and practices need to be implemented to protect them. There is little empirical evidence that Mexican nationals do not suffer similarly, but that is beyond the scope of this chapter.

For many years, the number of unaccompanied immigrant minors and women and their children entering the United States has been increasing steadily. During the Obama administration, the United States saw an increase in the detention of women and children and unaccompanied minors. The year 2014 became a "tipping point" for the US government's as well as media attention to the issue, with more than 68,000 unaccompanied immigrant children arriving at the southern border, most from Central America and Mexico (but also India, China, and other countries).[11] The exponential increase in unaccompanied immigrant minors at the border was referred to as a "humanitarian crisis." That same year, the United Nations High Commissioner for Refugees (UNHCR) reported a 712 percent increase in asylum applications by children in the neighboring countries to Honduras, Guatemala, and El Salvador.[12]

While there is much political debate about why so many children have been arriving, available research tells us that most child migrants are seeking safety and family reunification, fleeing violence, conflict, poverty, and abuse. A UNHCR report, titled *Children on the Run*, found that more than 58 percent of arriving children are eligible for international protection, documenting extreme levels of violence in home communities that children are victims of and witnesses to, among other crimes. Unstable political environments resulting in systemic violence and crime, declining economic stability, and other forms of crime are driving the large wave of undocumented migration of children, adults, and families from Central America. For example, the United Nations has declared San Pedro Sula, Honduras, the "murder capital of the world," with young men having an incredibly high—1 in 300—chance of being murdered. In addition, 75 percent of Guatemalans live in poverty, with 29 percent living in extreme poverty.

It is also important to note that there is much diversity within these "sending countries" in Central America, and the push factors for migration may differ among communities within each country. Research in Guatemalan highland communities, for example, shows that many youth who are migrating are doing so to fulfill social and familial expectations rooted in economic necessity and a long history of migration.[13] These highland communities view migration as a collective investment in the family and community.

Although current US governmental data suggests that unaccompanied child migration has declined since January 2018, presumably because of the Trump administration's hardline stance against immigrants, evidence shows that children are continuing to migrate and that their numbers continue to rise.[14] This includes data showing that migration to and application for asylum in neighboring countries, not just to the United States, is on the rise. This is predictable given that the root causes and push factors for child migration have not changed, even in the face of greater enforcement measures in the United States.

APPREHENSION, ADJUDICATION, AND REPATRIATION OF UNACCOMPANIED MINORS AND THE ABSENCE OF THE BEST INTERESTS STANDARD

When children are apprehended at a border or port of entry, the "nation-state" becomes involved, and international and domestic protocols around receiving migrant children can be invoked. Most unaccompanied immigrant children are apprehended at the US southern border with Mexico, with many presenting themselves to border officials and requesting assistance and protection after suffering traumas before or during migration.[15] Under the TVPRA 2008,[16] a child from a noncontiguous country who arrives at the US border without a parent or guardian is designated as an "unaccompanied child" under US federal law. The unaccompanied child is afforded additional protections under this designation, including a right to a hearing before an immigration judge to determine if the child is eligible for forms of immigration relief.[17] However, several systemic barriers exist, adverse to a child's "best interests," to access such protections. These systemic barriers and practices begin with the first entry point into the United States and continue through the child's processing within the interior of the United States and possible removal back to the child's country of origin.

To begin, after an unaccompanied child seeking "admission" to the United States is apprehended at the US border or a port of entry, the child meets with a US customs and border patrol (CBP) officer. The officer is in uniform and often armed, with little to no training on interviewing children and is tasked with three main screening determinations:[18] (1) if the child is a victim of human trafficking, (2) if the child fears returning to their country of origin owing to a credible fear of persecution, and (3) if the child is able to make an independent decision to withdraw their application for admission to the United States.[19] This screening takes very little time, in the course of one interview. These are often held in a public room, with little privacy. As noted, the officers are often armed, and it can be incredibly intimidating, especially for smaller children, to have a weapon in such close proximity to their line of sight and body.

The notion that a child, particularly one who has been traveling alone and has either witnessed or experienced traumatic experiences, will be able to respond to such inquiry in a satisfactory way is contrary to research, norms, and common sense regarding eliciting information from children. Attorneys working with both children and adults often argue that it takes at least several interviews, often over the course of a year or more, to build rapport and trust to elicit information necessary to determine if a client is eligible for immigration relief. Moreover, many children may not speak Spanish or English, making the CBP officer's task even more challenging. Non-governmental organizations and immigrant advocates working at the border have reported that officials routinely fail to notify detained children of their right to meet with and notify a consular official before the repatriation decision is made, that they have a child in their custody.

Child development and mental health research shows that children and adolescents do not have full maturity in areas of cognition, language, emotional development, and judgment.[20] Exposure to trauma also shapes the development and behavior of children and youth,[21] and has serious implications for both assessment of and intervention with unaccompanied minors at the border. The majority of children fleeing Central America have experienced trauma because of the extremely violent communities they fled and adverse experiences en route to the United States. El Salvador, Mexico, and Honduras experience the highest homicide rates in the world.[22] Children who have experienced chronic trauma—multiple and pervasive violent events, including those that may make them eligible for asylum or protections as trafficking victims—have been shown to be even more difficult to interview, as the effects of this level of trauma can hinder communication between children and adults.[23]

The process by which children are apprehended and screened for possible immigration relief and protection at the border does not demonstrate any appreciation for the child's development, experience, situation of vulnerability, nor practices maintained in the United States. For example, every state in the United States has interdisciplinary Child Advocacy Centers (CACs), comprised of child development, medical, mental health, and law enforcement personnel. CACs provide a multidisciplinary and developmentally trained approach to interviewing and responding to children who are victims of crime. Similarly, these practices are reflected in the TVPA and TVPRA, which recognize that law enforcement agencies are not appropriate bodies to make initial determinations of humanitarian aid for minors. The TVPRA, for example, explicitly assigns the Department of Health and Human Services the responsibility to "make determinations for interim relief for potential trafficked children."[24]

The current screening process at the border does not incorporate any "best interests of the child" standards of inquiry used and applied in domestic child screening or interviewing contexts. In fact, the process does not reflect *any* child-centered practices or attention to the developmental, mental, and physical distinctions between children and adults.[25] In response, some advocates have suggested that CBP officers be trained in child development and culturally informed interviewing practices and techniques, with some advocates taking this a step further and recommending that the CBP be completely replaced by child welfare professionals. At this time, not one of these suggestions has been implemented, and there is even greater pressure under the Trump administration to deter all immigrants, including children, from entering the United States.

Yet another violation against children's rights and the child's best interests is demonstrated by the administration's proposal and practices to separate parents from their children at the border. This involves detaining parents and sending children to Office of Refugee Resettlement (ORR) facilities in other parts of the country—often with no notification to the parent regarding the child's location or status. In December 2017, the Department of Homeland Security introduced a new policy[26] to begin separating parents and children arriving at the border by detaining or deporting parents and sending their children to governmental facilities across the country. Although some cases of family separation[27] were reported under the Obama administration, the new policy, combined with increased reporting of family separation at the border by advocates and attorneys, demonstrates that incidents of separating children from their parents at the border are both on the rise and intentional.[28] This practice violates both international and domestic laws and norms related to preservation of family unity, including the best interests standard under the CRC. Family separation has long-term implications on the mental, emotional, and physical well-being of children and is clearly adverse to their best interests.

Since Donald Trump's election, there has been an increase in family separation at the border, with little transparency about criteria the CBP uses in making such determinations.[29] In March 2018, the American Civil Liberties Union filed a class action lawsuit, charging the Trump administration with separating hundreds of immigrant parents from their children as they await asylum claims.[30] The suit accuses the government of "forcible separation of parents from their young children for no legitimate reason." As of April 2018, over seven hundred children were reported separated from their families.[31] The administration has excused this policy by describing family separation as serving the "best interests" of the children, while also framing this as a deterrence tactic to prevent more immigrants from arriving at the border.

If separation of a child from their parent or guardian is not cruel and traumatic enough, in May 2018, Attorney General Jeff Sessions announced a new policy to criminally prosecute parents caught crossing the border without permission, in addition to separating them from their children. In his speech, Attorney General Sessions referred to parents traveling with children to the border as "smugglers of children."[32] This is a dramatic shift from the fact that most immigration violations, including unlawful entry, have fallen under civil administrative law, not criminal law. This new policy criminalizing parents traveling to the United States with their children ignore the bonds between children and their parents and caretakers, and is a clear violation of the human rights of both parents and the children, as well as the best interests of the child principal. Furthermore, the policy creates larger numbers of children separated from their children and placed in the care and custody of the US government.

US law requires that when an unaccompanied immigrant child is taken into US custody, CPB must transfer custody of the child to the US Department of Health & Human Services, ORR within seventy-two hours.[33] The child is also issued a "Notice to Appear" and placed in removal proceedings. At this point in the process, there is a formal recognition of the best interests standard, with policies stating that children should be placed within the "least restrictive setting" according to the best interest of the child.[34] The placements can vary from secure facilities that operate much like jails, to foster care, group homes, or residential treatment centers.[35] While in these settings, the clock begins ticking with the adjudication and disposition of the child's immigration case still pending. The average period of time a child is within ORR custody is approximately sixty–ninety days. During this time, ORR begins to explore the identification of an appropriate "sponsor," often a family member, to whom the youth is released. This release procedure is called reunification (even if the youth did not previously live with the sponsor).

This then leads to another systemic failure in applying a child's best interest standard in immigration proceedings—the lack of due process via limited access to an attorney or an advocate. Immigration law is complex and fast changing, and is often compared to tax law in its complexity and level of expertise needed to navigate. Despite this, children are treated similarly to adults and, like immigrant adults, have no statutory right to an appointed lawyer.[36] Although the Department of Health & Human Services makes arrangements for legal representation and provides referrals to an attorney, there is no obligation under US law for the government to provide paid counsel to undocumented immigrants, including children.[37] In fact, a qualified attorney only represents about one-third of unaccompanied immigrant children.[38] These children are engaging in adversarial proceedings, often in courtrooms together with adults, without an advocate or attorney to represent their voice or interests. With no guarantee or right to counsel, unaccompanied children must meet the same procedural, evidentiary, and legal requirements as adults. This would be challenging for any adult US citizen under civil or criminal justice proceedings, much less a foreign national child with limited to no language skills and little knowledge of our legal systems or immigration laws. The practice of children appearing in court alone and unrepresented is a practice the United States abolished in domestic child welfare proceedings, recognizing that children require more developmentally informed systems and advocacy. Moreover, the outcomes of these civil proceedings have tremendous consequences for a child. It can mean life or death to the child.

Since a 2016 class action lawsuit on behalf of eight named plaintiffs aged ten to seventeen, *J.E.F.M v. Lynch*, civil rights groups have challenged the federal government's practice of deporting unrepresented children.[39] Children as young as two are appearing in court alone, with one immigration judge in

Virginia bragging that he "taught immigration law literally to 3-year-olds and 4-year-olds."[40] Unfortunately, whether or not these children are afforded an attorney has a strong impact on the case outcome. Of unrepresented children, 90 percent are ordered deported versus only 18 percent of represented children, demonstrating the importance of representation in the outcome of the minor's court cases.[41]

Moreover, even if an immigration attorney represents a child, that attorney may not advocate the child's best interest. The role of the immigration attorney is to advocate for their client's (here, the child's) expressed wishes. For example, if a child has been placed in an ORR shelter or facility for any extended period of time, that experience will likely have psychological effects on that child; depression and anxiety are not uncommon. It is therefore not unusual for that child to express that they would do anything to leave the confinement of the shelter or facility as soon as possible, even if they may have a potential claim to a form of immigration relief to remain in the United States or returning to their home country is unsafe. This places the immigration attorney in an awkward position, but their ethical and professional duty is to represent the asserted wishes of their client, regardless if the return to the home country may or may not be safe or in the best interest of the child.

An exploration of a similar scenario in a domestic child welfare proceeding can provide perspective on the different outcomes if a "best interest of the child" standard is applied. For example, if a child is sexually abused by their parent, the child will likely be removed from the home by a public child protection agency. The child may then assert their wishes to be reunited with the parent, regardless of the sexual abuse. The subsequent adjudication and determination of the placement of the child, in contrast to immigration proceedings, would include a "best interest of the child" assessment, which varies by state, but would likely include whether or not it was safe for the child to return to their parent, regardless of the child's expressed interest. The process would also include input from a variety of stakeholders, including judges, advocates, family members, experts, and the child. This does not mean that the child's expressed interest is not part of a best interest determination—it is just one factor.

Unfortunately, when immigrant children enter the care and custody of the United States, this practice, or "best interest determination," does not formally exist under US immigration law. While the immigration system is responsible for making critical placement and service decisions similar to state child welfare systems, the US immigration system has limited consideration of a child's age and related vulnerabilities in making important determinations about their care, custody, release or repatriation, and even immigration status. Currently, only one organization, namely the Young Center for Immigrant Children's Rights, provides advocates to the most vulnerable children identified by the

US government. It convenes "best interest determination" panels related to care, custody, and release of some unaccompanied immigrant children, but this is not a nationally applied program and only serves a small number of unaccompanied migrant children in the United States.[42] This has tremendous implications on the safety and well-being of children, particularly as many unaccompanied immigrant children have experienced some form of trauma and have little knowledge of their rights. Most stakeholders interacting with unaccompanied immigrant children have no specialized training on developmentally informed practices, including interviewing skills.

Even if a child is represented by a qualified attorney, a "release" from a shelter or other facility does not mean that the child's future is certain or that their safety and well-being are secure. Most unaccompanied immigrant children in federal (ORR) custody are released to an eligible adult "sponsor." The sponsor can be a family member (more than 50 percent of sponsors are parents already residing in the United States, another 20 percent are other family members) or another caregiver deemed eligible to be a sponsor for the child.[43] While ORR generally applies a best interest standard for service and placement decisions, it can also be a highly stressful time for children, particularly for those whose families have been separated for years or who have been released to adults with whom they have little to no previous relationship. Once a child is released to a sponsor, ORR and the federal government relinquish custody of the child and provide little to no additional services, follow-up, or oversight, with the exception of children who qualify for "post release services," addressed below. Even in these situations, the services provided are very limited.

For children who have had little prior contact with their sponsor, their risk factors are even higher. In one of the most extreme examples, in 2014, eight unaccompanied immigrant boys who had traveled to the United States from Central America were released from custody to child labor traffickers posing as "sponsors." The boys were made to debeak chickens at an egg farm for twelve hours a day, six days a week, for as little as two dollars a day in pay. They were forced to live in unheated, cockroach-infested trailers in Ohio in the dead of winter, and they were told that if they tried to escape, they would be killed. In December 2014, federal agents and local officers raided the egg farm and rescued the boys, charging their employers with labor trafficking.[44] For other children, they may be forced to pay off existing smuggling debts or placed in abusive situations. However, absent situations where a child has a qualified attorney, there is no oversight or case management by government officials of post-release placements to ensure the health and safety of the child.

For children who are released from ORR facilities, the disposition of their legal cases is still pending, rendering the children ineligible for many forms of public assistance, including Temporary Assistance for Needy Families,

Medicaid, Children's Health Insurance Program, and Supplemental Nutrition Assistance Program. Children and their sponsors/families are further discouraged from seeking public assistance under the Trump administration's new executive order from 2017, titled "Enhancing Public Safety in the Interior of the United States," which seeks to curtail applications for any public benefits by unauthorized immigrants.[45] This provides tremendous limitations on ensuring the child's well-being during a period of immense transition into US communities.

In comparison, under US domestic child welfare practices, a child would not be released into the custody of a parent or family member with whom the child had not lived with prior without some sort of follow-up to ensure the health, safety, and well-being of the child. Some unaccompanied immigrant children may be eligible for "post release services," which include the assignment of a case manager and referral to services.[46] Eligibility for these services, however, is extremely limited to those children who have been trafficked, had a disability, or had been a victim of physical or sexual abuse. Additionally, the process for discerning these eligibility requirements is still arbitrary and not always developmentally or trauma-informed. The screening process for post-release services is legally required by the TVPRA 2008, but the act does not mandate that all children receive these services. Considering that most unaccompanied children entering the United States have experienced some sort of trauma, including trauma induced by migration, apprehension, and detention at the border and placement within the care and custody of ORR, all unaccompanied children should be eligible for post-release services to ensure their safety and well-being. Additionally, while most of the children are released to family members, the sponsors are often adults who the child has not had contact with for a long period of time. This is highly stressful and may put some children at risk. Again, releasing a child to the custody and care of an adult they have had limited contact with and not giving follow-up services or case management is contrary to standards and best practices under domestic child welfare proceedings.

In addition to considerations regarding a child's best interest in adjudicating cases, applying a child's best interest standard is equally as important in cases involving the safe repatriation of children back to their home country. For families who incur debt to send youth to migrate to other countries, including the United States, deportation is not a determent to migration because their debt continues to exist. Children often will make multiple attempts to reenter the United States. For example, 60 percent of youth deported back to Guatemala will attempt at least one, sometimes two additional crossings into the United States.[47] Their exposure to dangers en route to the United States, as well as their treatment by officials when they attempt reentering, however, will not improve.

Although the TVPRA 2008 creates a clear expectation that vulnerable children not be returned to unsafe or inhumane situations in their countries of origin, in practice, little resources are devoted to this issue, both within the United States and within countries of origin, to effectively implement this provision. In 2014, several Honduran children deported by the US government were killed after being repatriated to Honduras.[48] These cases show that a lack of systemic practices and procedures to ensure that a child's best interest is being considered in repatriation and deportation cases can have the gravest of consequences.

Some advances have, however, been made regarding the United States taking steps to incorporate the best interest standard into policy and practice. The TVPRA 2008 includes the first reference to the "best interest of the child" applying to arriving immigrant children, providing for child advocates, similar to "guardian ad litems" in domestic child welfare proceedings, to be appointed to vulnerable unaccompanied immigrant children to represent their "best interests." Child advocates have more flexibility than immigration attorneys do in advocating for a child's best interest and can convene "best interest determination" panels to assert a child's best interest in immigration proceedings and provide recommendations to judges and other administrative decision makers. These panels often include experts across disciplines from both the United States and the child's home country who make decisions about a child's placement, adjudication, or repatriation. Although advocates are not appointed for all unaccompanied children, it is a modest step in acknowledging the importance of applying best interest of the child standards in immigration proceedings.

In 2016, the Inter-agency Working Group on Unaccompanied and Separated Children, comprising representatives from the Department of Homeland Security, Department of Justice, Department of State, and Department of Health & Human Services, in collaboration with the Young Center for Immigrant Children's Rights, released the *Framework for Considering the Best Interests of Unaccompanied Children ("Framework").* The framework establishes that decisions involving unaccompanied immigrant children should take into account the child's best interest, including the child's safety, well-being, expressed interests, health and family integrity, and liberty.[49] The framework provides guidance to stakeholders and agencies involved in adjudicating unaccompanied immigrant minor cases on how to uphold the child's best interest, which closely parallels the CRC's factors for consideration, including[50]

- safety and well-being
- the child's expressed interests, in accordance with the child's age and maturity

- health
- family integrity
- liberty
- development (including education)
- identity

While the framework is a critical step in protecting children's rights, it is a guiding document and not binding. Unfortunately, the Trump administration's efforts to increase enforcement (deportation) measures, including family separation and expedited removal, and to deter immigrants from migrating to the United States have already demonstrated that there is little regard for children's best interests in immigration proceedings. Current proposals include expediting the screening of all unaccompanied children (including Central Americans), subjecting children to more restrictive detention, and forcing the government to adjudicate cases before the children have an opportunity to find their bearings and trust an adult with their traumatic stories.[51] If enacted, these proposals would likely return thousands of children to harm, or even death, in their home countries.

CONCLUSION

The number of children around the world, including the Western Hemisphere, who can no longer live safely in their country and therefore decide to immigrate is at an all-time high. How these children are treated and protected by receiving governmental systems is a reflection of their commitment to children's rights. Treating vulnerable children differently than adults is the hallmark of every democratic and advanced governmental system that makes decisions about children. While there have been modest improvements in US immigration law to apply the universally adopted "best interest of the child" standard, the immigration system largely does not recognize children as unique from adults and requiring special protections or developmentally appropriate procedures. This occurs in poor screenings for immigration relief at the border, family separation at the border, the absence of due process and court-appointed attorneys for all children in immigration proceedings, and decision-making and services related to the care and custody of children repatriated home or released to US communities. This has profound implications on the child's well-being, safety, development, and access to protections guaranteed to them under both domestic and federal law. It also violates principles outlined under the CRC, and practices maintained in domestic child-serving systems. More research and advocacy needs to be done to demonstrate the significant human rights abuses that happen to children in the absence of a "best interest of the child" standard applied in immigration law.

The notion that different standards apply to children in our own child protection systems and arriving immigrant children seeking safety, sanctuary, or family reunification at our border should be a concern for all of us. While immigrant attorneys and advocates have long been engaged in advocacy to elevate the issues that unaccompanied children face, there are opportunities for other disciplines and stakeholders, including (but not limited to) faith-based organizations, sociology, theology, child development, pediatrics, social work, psychology, child welfare, education, and public health—to weigh in and amplify these efforts through their own lens and expertise. For example, the writings and work of activist and social worker Jane Addams had significant impact on the development of separate courts and systems for children versus adults. The research of child development and psychology experts about the different ways children's brains work from adults, as well as principles of the CRC, have all had profound influence on the development of our current child welfare and juvenile justice systems in the United States, which recognize that children's brains and bodies work differently than fully matured adults. Together, we are more powerful and effective advocates of the rights of those most vulnerable among us—children.

NOTES

1. "Figures at a Glance," graph, The UN Refugee Agency, *UNHCR*, June 19, 2017, http://www.unhcr.org/en-us/figures-at-a-glance.html.

2. Philip Conner, *International Migration: Key Findings from the U.S., Europe and the World* (Pew Research Center, December 2016), http://www.pewresearch.org/fact-tank/2016/12/15/international-migration-key-findings-from-the-u-s-europe-and-the-world/.

3. The terms *child* and *children and youth* may be used intermittently throughout the chapter. *Child* refers to anyone less than eighteen years of age, under both US federal and international law.

4. The author will use the preferred term *unaccompanied immigrant child* (UIC) in place of the legal term codified under the US Immigration and Nationality Act (INA) of *unaccompanied alien child*, commonly referred to as "UAC" by both attorneys and government officials. UAC is defined by statute as children who lack lawful immigration status in the United States, who are under the age of eighteen, and who are either without a parent or legal guardian in the United States or without a parent or legal guardian in the United States who is available to provide care and physical custody. Two statutes and a legal settlement directly affect US policy for the treatment and administrative processing of UAC: the Trafficking Victims Protection

Reauthorization Act of 2008 (P.L. 110-457), the Homeland Security Act of 2002 (P.L. 107-296), and the Flores Settlement Agreement of 1997.

5. "Unaccompanied Alien Children Released to Sponsors by State," Office of Refugee Resettlement, June 2017, https://www.acf.hhs.gov/orr/resource/unaccompanied-alien-children-released-to-sponsors-by-state.

6. Mark Ensalaco, and Linda C. Majka, *Children's Human Rights, Progress and Challenges for Children Worldwide* (Lanham, MD: Rowman & Littlefield Publishers, 2005), 14.

7. Child Welfare Information Gateway, "Determining the Best Interests of the Child," Children's Bureau, US Department of Health & Human Services, 2013, https://www.childwelfare.gov/systemwide/laws_policies/statutes/best_interest.pdf; see also B. A. Carr, "Incorporating a 'Best Interests of the Child' Approach into Immigration Law and Procedure," *Yale Human Rights & Development Law Journal* 12 (2008): 120, 124 (identifying the "best interests of the child" as a "common legal standard for cases that involve children").

8. United Nations Committee on the Rights of the Children, General Comment No. 14 (2013) on the right of the child to have his or her best interests taken as a primary consideration (art. 3, para.1), ¶6, U.N. Doc. CRC/C/GC/14 (May 2013), http://www2.ohchr.org/English/bodies/crc/docs/GC/CRC_C_GC_14_ENG.pdf ("the child's best interests is a threefold concept . . . (a) A substantive right . . . (b) A fundamental, interpretative legal principle . . . (c) A rule of procedure").

9. Homeland Security Act of 2002, Pub. L. No. 107-296,116 Stat. 2135.

10. 6 U.S. Code § 279.

11. Lutheran Immigrant Relief Services, "Annual Report," 2015, https://www.speakcdn.com/assets/2474/lirs-2015-annual-report.pdf.

12. Tom K. Wong, "Statistical Analysis Shows that Violence, Not Deferred Action, Is Behind the Surge of Unaccompanied Children Crossing the Border," *Center for American Progress*, July 8, 2014, https://www.americanprogress.org/issues/immigration/news/2014/07/08/93370/statistical-analysis-shows-that-violence-not-deferred-action-is-behind-the-surge-of-unaccompanied-children-crossing-the-border/.

13. Lauren Heidbrink and Michele Statz, "Parents of Global Youth: Contesting Debt and Belonging," *Children's Geographies* 15, no. 5 (2017): 545–557, https://doi.org/10.1080/14733285.2017.1284645.

14. US Customs and Border Patrol, "Southwest Border Migration," April 4, 2018, https://www.cbp.gov/newsroom/stats/sw-border-migration.

15. Karen Musalo, Lisa Frydman, and Pablo Ceriani Cernadas, *Childhood and Migration in Central and North America: Causes, Policies, Practices and Challenges* (San Francisco: Center for Gender & Refugee Studies & National University of Lanus, 2015).

16. William Wilberforce Trafficking Victims Protection Reauthorization Act § 235(b)(3), 8 U.S.C. 1232 (2008).

17. The TVPRA 2008 was intended to "strengthen US efforts to stop the abhorrent practice of human trafficking both in the United States and around the world." The TVPRA 2008 also recognized the extreme circumstances that many Central American

children were fleeing from. Recognizing that "unaccompanied alien children are the most vulnerable immigrants," deserving of both humane and fair treatment while in custody, the TVPRA 2008 requires that children from noncontiguous countries be placed in removal proceedings before an immigration judge, have the right to apply for legal relief and receive counsel "to the greatest extent practicable."

18. Immigration and Nationality Act § 235(b).

19. William Wilberforce Trafficking Victims Protection Reauthorization Act § 235(b)(3), 8 U.S.C. 1232 (2008).

20. Sroufe, L. A., Egelund, B., Carlson, E.A., and Colins, W.A. *The Development of the Person: The Minnesota Study of Risk and Adaptation from Birth to Adulthood* (New York: Guilford, 2005); Daniel Siegel, *The Developing Mind: How Relationships and the Brain Interact to Shape Who We Are,* 2nd ed. (New York: Guilford Press, 2012); Daniel Siegel, "Toward an Interpersonal Neurobiology of the Developing Mind: Relationships, 'Mindsight,' and Neural Integration," *Infant Mental Health Journal* 22 no. 1–2. (2001): 67–94; Bruce D. Perry, "Childhood Experience and the Expression of Genetic Potential: What Childhood Neglect Tells Us about Nature and Nurture," *Brain & Mind* 3, no. 1 (2002): 79–100; Laurence Steinberg, and Elizabeth S. Scott, "Less Guilty by Reasons of Adolescence: Developmental Immaturity, Diminished Responsibility and the Juvenile Death Penalty," *American Psychologist* 58, no. 12 (2003): 1009–1018.

21. For more on trauma, unaccompanied minors, and attachment theory, see Stephanie Arel, Chapter 2 in this volume.

22. "The World's Most Dangerous Cities," graph, Igarape Institute, The Data Team, *The Economist*, March 31, 2017, https://www.economist.com/blogs/graphicdetail/2017/03/daily-chart-23.

23. United Nations High Commissioner for Refugees (UNHCR), "Children on the Run: Unaccompanied Children Leaving Central America and Mexico and the Need for International Protection" (Washington, DC, 2014), http://www.unhcr.org/56fc266f4.html; *See also* Lisa Frydman, Elizabeth Dallam, and Blaine Bookey, *A Treacherous Journey: Child Migrants Navigating the U.S. Immigration System* (San Francisco and Washington, DC: Center for Gender & Refugee Studies and Kids in Need of Defense, 2014), http://www.uchastings.edu/centers/cgrs-docs/treacherous_journey_cgrs_kind_report.pdf.; Judith A. Cohen, "Practice Parameter for the Assessment and Treatment of Children and Adolescents with Posttraumatic Stress Disorder," *Journal of the American Academy of Child & Adolescent Psychiatry* 49, no. 4 (2010): 414–430.

24. William Wilberforce Trafficking Victims Protection Reauthorization Act § 212(a)(2)(F)(i), 8 U.S.C. 1232 (2008).

25. Betsy Cavendish and Maru Cortazar, *Children at the Border: The Screening, Protection and Repatriation of Unaccompanied Mexican Minors* (Washington, DC: Appleseed, 2011), http://appleseednetwork.org/wp-content/uploads/2012/05/Children-At-The-Border1.pdf.

26. Caitlin Dickerson and Ron Nixon, "Trump Administration Considers Separating Families to Combat Illegal Immigration," *New York Times*, December 21, 2017, https://www.nytimes.com/2017/12/21/us/trump-immigrant-families-separate.html.

27. Parent-child border separations refer to the physical and prolonged separation of a parent from his or her child immediately following apprehension along the border or at a port of entry.

28. Women's Refugee Commission, *The Separation of Family Members Apprehended by or Found Inadmissible while in U.S. Customs and Border Protection (CBP) Custody at the U.S.-Mexico Border*https://www.womensrefugeecommission.org/images/zdocs/Family-Separation-Complaint-FINAL-PUBLIC-12-11-17.pdf, 6.

29. Customs and Border Patrol, "National Standards on Transport, Escort, Detention, and Search (TEDS)," available at: https://www.cbp.gov/sites/default/files/assets/documents/2017-Sep/CBP%20TEDS%20Policy%20Oct2015.pdf. For further discussion on the lack of clear mechanisms and policies to track and identify separated family members, see Betraying Family Values, 4.

30. *See* Ariane de Vogue and Tal Kopan, "ACLU Class Action Lawsuit Seeks to Block Immigrant Family Separations," *CNN*, March 9, 2018, https://www.cnn.com/2018/03/09/politics/aclu-lawsuit-separating-immigrant-families/index.html.

31. Caitlin Dickerson, "Hundreds of Immigrant Children Have Been Taken From Immigrant Parents at US Border," *New York Times*, April 20, 2018, https://mobile.nytimes.com/2018/04/20/us/immigrant-children-separation-ice.html?login=email&auth=login-email.

32. Benjamin Hart, "Trump Administration Will Separate Parents from Children At Border," *New York Magazine*, May 7, http://nymag.com/daily/intelligencer/2018/05/trump-administration-to-separate-parents-children-at-border.html; "US to Stiffen Border Rules and Separate Children from Parents," *Reuters*, May 7, 2018, https://www.theguardian.com/us-news/2018/may/07/us-border-rules-prosecutions-parents-families.

33. William Wilberforce Trafficking Victims Protection Reauthorization Act § 235(b)(3), 8 U.S.C. 1232 (2008).

34. The Flores Agreement, which still is in force, established the principle that minors are "particularly vulnerable" and are entitled to be treated "with dignity, respect and special concern"; it also mandated that children should be placed in the "least restrictive setting" appropriate for the child, provided the child's appearance in immigration proceedings can be assured. The Flores Agreement arose out of the 1997 settlement of Flores v. Meese, brought in 1985 on behalf of a class of minors in the custody of immigration authorities.

35. "Children Entering the United States Unaccompanied: Section 1," U.S. Department of Health and Human Services, Office of Refugee Resettlement, last modified January 30, 2015, https://www.acf.hhs.gov/orr/resource/children-entering-the-united-states-unaccompanied-section-1#1.1.

36. See 8 U.S.C. § 1229(b)(4) (2012).

37. "Services Provided," U.S. Department of Health and Human Services, Office of Refugee Resettlement, accessed March 26, 2018, https://www.acf.hhs.gov/orr/about/ucs/services-provided.

38. Transactional Records Access Clearinghouse, *TRAC Series on Juveniles and Families in Immigration Court: Representation for Unaccompanied Children in*

Immigration Court (Syracuse, NY: Transactional Records Access Clearinghouse, 2014), accessed March 26, 2018. http://trac.syr.edu/immigration/reports/371.

39. *See* J.E.F.M. v. Lynch, 837 F.3d 1026 (9th Cir. 2016).

40. Molly Hennessy-Fiske, "This Judge Says Toddlers Can Defend Themselves in Immigration Court," *Los Angeles Times*, March 6, 2016, http://www.latimes.com/nation/immigration/la-na-immigration-judge-20160306-story.html.

41. Sarah Pierce, *Unaccompanied Child Migrants in U.S. Communities, Immigration, Court, and Schools* (Washington, DC: Migration Policy Institute, 2015), https://www.migrationpolicy.org/research/unaccompanied-child-migrants-us-communities-immigration-court-and-schools.

42. See Young Center for Immigrant Children's Rights and TVPRA 2008, which provides that vulnerable UIC be provided "child advocates," https://www.theyoungcenter.org/.

43. See figure 7 at United States Office of Refugee Resettlement, "Office of Refugee Resettlement (ORR) Annual Report to Congress" (Washington, DC: U.S. Dept. of Health & Human Services, Administration for Children & Families, Office of Refugee Resettlement, 2015), https://www.acf.hhs.gov/sites/default/files/orr/arc_15_final_508.pdf.

44. Abbie VanSickle, "Overwhelmed Federal Officials Released Immigrant Teens to Traffickers in 2014," *Washington Post*, January 26, 2016, https://www.washingtonpost.com/national/failures-in-handling-unaccompanied-migrant-minors-have-led-to-trafficking/2016/01/26/c47de164-c138-11e5-9443-7074c3645405_story.html?utm_term=.341d94d1df9d.

45. Exec. Order. No. 13768 (January 25, 2017), https://www.whitehouse.gov/presidential-actions/executive-order-enhancing-public-safety-interior-united-states.

46. Lutheran Immigration and Refugee Service and USCCB Migration and Refugee Services, *Post-Release Services: Family Preservation Services for Immigrant Children Released From Federal Custody* (Washington, DC: Lutheran Immigration and Refugee Service & USCCB Migration and Refugee Services, 2014), http://www.usccb.org/about/children-and-migration/upload/LIRS-and-USCCB-Post-Release-Services-FAQs-Final.pdf.

47. Lauren Heidbrink, and Michele Statz, "Parents of Global Youth: Contesting Debt and Belonging," *Children's Geographies* 15, no. 5 (2017): 545–557, Doi: 10.1080/14733285.2017.1284645.

48. Roque Planas, "Children Deported To Honduras Are Getting Killed: Report," *Huffington Post*, August 20, 2014, https://www.huffingtonpost.com/2014/08/20/minors-honduras-killed_n_5694986.html.

49. The Young Center, Subcommittee on Best Interests of the Interagency Working Group on Unaccompanied and Separated Children, *Framework for Considering the Best Interests of Unaccompanied Children* (Chicago, IL: The Young Center, 2016), https://www.gcir.org/sites/default/files/resources/2016%20Young%20Center%20Framework%20for%20Considering%20Best%20Interests%20of%20Unaccompanied%20Children.pdf.

50. Ibid., 5.

51. Laura Meckler, https://www.wsj.com/articles/donald-trump-wants-limits-on-asylum-seekers-in-immigration-talks-1516322665.

BIBLIOGRAPHY

Cavendish, Betsy, and Maru Cortazar. *Children at the Border: The Screening, Protection and Repatriation of Unaccompanied Mexican Minors.* Washington, DC: Appleseed, 2011. http://appleseednetwork.org/wp-content/uploads/2012/05/Children-At-The-Border1.pdf.

Child Welfare Information Gateway. *Determining the Best Interests of the Child.* US Department of Health & Human Services, Children's Bureau, 2013.

Cohen, Judith A. "Practice Parameter for the Assessment and Treatment of Children and Adolescents with Posttraumatic Stress Disorder." *Journal of the American Academy of Child & Adolescent Psychiatry* 49, no. 4 (2010): 414–430.

Conner, Philip. *International Migration: Key Findings from the U.S., Europe and the World.* Pew Research Center, December 2016. http://www.pewresearch.org/fact-tank/2016/12/15/international-migration-key-findings-from-the-u-s-europe-and-the-world.

De Vogue, Ariane, and Tal Kopan. "ACLU Class Action Lawsuit Seeks to Block Immigrant Family Separations." *CNN*, March 9, 2018. https://www.cnn.com/2018/03/09/politics/aclu-lawsuit-separating-immigrant-families/index.html.

Dickerson, Caitlin. "Hundreds of Immigrant Children Have Been Taken From Immigrant Parents at US Border." *New York Times*, April 20, 2018. https://mobile.nytimes.com/2018/04/20/us/immigrant-children-separation-ice.html?login=email&auth=login-email.

Dickerson, Caitlin, and Nixon, Ron. "Trump Administration Considers Separating Families to Combat Illegal Immigration." *New York Times*, December 21, 2017. https://www.nytimes.com/2017/12/21/us/trump-immigrant-families-separate.html.

Ensalaco, Mark, and Linda C. Majka, eds. *Children's Human Rights: Progress and Challenges for Children Worldwide.* Lanham, MD: Rowman & Littlefield Publishers, 2015.

"Figures at a Glance." Graph. The UN Refugee Agency, *UNHCR*. June 19, 2017. http://www.unhcr.org/en-us/figures-at-a-glance.html.

Frydman, Lisa, Elizabeth Dallam, and Blaine Bookey. *A Treacherous Journey: Child Migrants Navigating the U.S. Immigration System.* San Francisco and Washington, DC: Center for Gender & Refugee Studies and Kids in Need of Defense, 2014. http://www.uchastings.edu/centers/cgrs-docs/treacherous_journey_cgrs_kind_report.pdf.

Hart, Benjamin. "Trump Administration Will Separate Parents from Children At Border." *New York Magazine*, May 7, 2018. http://nymag.com/daily/intelligencer/2018/05/trump-administration-to-separate-parents-children-at-border.html.

Heidbrink, Lauren, and Michele Statz. "Parents of Global Youth: Contesting Debt and Belonging," *Children's Geographies* 15, no. 5 (February 8, 2017): 545–557. https://doi.org/10.1080/14733285.2017.1284645.

Hennessy-Fiske, Molly. "This Judge Says Toddlers Can Defend Themselves in Immigration Court." *Los Angeles Times*, March 6, 2016. http://www.latimes.com/nation/immigration/la-na-immigration-judge-20160306-story.html.

Lutheran Immigration and Refugee Service and USCCB Migration and Refugee Services. *Post-Release Services: Family Preservation Services for Immigrant Children*

Released From Federal Custody. Washington, DC: Lutheran Immigration and Refugee Service & USCCB Migration and Refugee Services, 2014. http://www.usccb.org/about/children-and-migration/upload/LIRS-and-USCCB-Post-Release-Services-FAQs-Final.pdf.

Meckler, Laura. "Donald Trump Wants Limits on Asylum Seeker Rights in Immigration Talks." *Wall Street Journal*, January 18, 2018.

Musalo, Karen, Lisa Frydman, and Pablo Ceriani Cernadas. *Childhood and Migration in Central and North America: Causes, Policies, Practices and Challenges*. Center for Gender and Refugee Studies and National University of Lanus, 2015.

Perry, Bruce D. "Childhood Experience and the Expression of Genetic Potential: What Childhood Neglect Tells Us about Nature and Nurture." *Brain and Mind* 3, no. 1 (2002): 79–100.

Pierce, Sarah. *Unaccompanied Child Migrants in U.S. Communities, Immigration, Court, and Schools*. Washington, DC: Migration Policy Institute, 2015. https://www.migrationpolicy.org/research/unaccompanied-child-migrants-us-communities-immigration-court-and-schools.

Planas, Roque. "Children Deported To Honduras Are Getting Killed: Report." *Huffington Post*, August 20, 2014. https://www.huffingtonpost.com/2014/08/20/minors-honduras-killed_n_5694986.html.

Siegel, Daniel. *The Developing Mind: How Relationships and the Brain Interact to Shape Who We Are*. 2nd ed. New York: Guilford Press, 2012.

———. "Toward an Interpersonal Neurobiology of the Developing Mind: Attachment Relationships,"Mindsight," and Neural Integration." *Infant Mental Health Journal* 22, no. 1–2 (2001): 67–94.

Sroufe, L. Alan, Byron Egeland, Elizabeth A. Carlson, and W. Andrew Collins. *The Development of the Person: The Minnesota Study of Risk and Adaptation from Birth to Adulthood*. New York: Guilford Press, 2009.

Steinberg, Laurence, and Elizabeth S. Scott. "Less Guilty by Reason of Adolescence: Developmental Immaturity, Diminished Responsibility, and the Juvenile Death Penalty." *American Psychologist* 58, no. 12 (2003): 1009.

Transactional Records Access Clearinghouse. *TRAC Series on Juveniles and Families in Immigration Court: Representation for Unaccompanied Children in Immigration Court*. Syracuse, NY: Transactional Records Access Clearinghouse, 2014. Accessed March 26, 2018. http://trac.syr.edu/immigration/reports/371.

United Nations High Commissioner for Refugees (UNHCR). "Children on the Run: Unaccompanied Children Leaving Central America and Mexico and the Need for International Protection." Washington, DC, 2014. http://www.unhcr.org/56fc266f4.html.

U.S. Department of Health and Human Services, Office of Refugee Resettlement. "Unaccompanied Alien Children Released to Sponsors By State." Last modified, June 2017. https://www.acf.hhs.gov/orr/resource/unaccompanied-alien-children-released-to-sponsors-by-state.

———. "Children Entering the United States Unaccompanied: Section 1." Last modified January 30, 2015. https://www.acf.hhs.gov/orr/resource/children-entering-the-united-states-unaccompanied-section-1#1.1.

———. "Services Provided." Accessed March 26, 2018. https://www.acf.hhs.gov/orr/about/ucs/services-provided.

———. "Office of Refugee Resettlement (ORR) Annual Report to Congress." Washington, DC: U.S. Dept. of Health & Human Services, Administration for Children & Families, Office of Refugee Resettlement, 2015. https://www.acf.hhs.gov/sites/default/files/orr/arc_15_final_508.pdf.

"US to Stiffen Border Rules and Separate Children from Parents," *Reuters*, May 7, 2018. https://www.theguardian.com/us-news/2018/may/07/us-border-rules-prosecutions-parents-families.

VanSickle, Abbie. "Overwhelmed Federal Officials Released Immigrant Teens to Traffickers in 2014." *Washington Post*, January 26, 2016. https://www.washingtonpost.com/national/failures-in-handling-unaccompanied-migrant-minors-have-led-to-trafficking/2016/01/26/c47de164-c138–11e5–9443–7074c3645405_story.html?utm_term=.f0bf6a525b02.

"The World's Most Dangerous Cities." Graph. Igarape Institute, The Data Team. *The Economist*, March 31, 2017. https://www.economist.com/blogs/graphicdetail/2017/03/daily-chart-23.

Wong, Tom K. "Statistical Analysis Shows that Violence, not US Immigration Policies, is Behind the Surge of Unaccompanied Children Crossing the Border." Center for American Progress, 2014. https://www.americanprogress.org/issues/immigration/news/2014/07/08/93370/statistical-analysis-shows-that-violence-not-deferred-action-is-behind-the-surge-of-unaccompanied-children-crossing-the-border.

The Young Center, Subcommittee on Best Interests of the Interagency Working Group on Unaccompanied and Separated Children. *Framework for Considering the Best Interests of Unaccompanied Children.* Chicago, IL: The Young Center, 2016. https://www.gcir.org/sites/default/files/resources/2016%20Young%20Center%20Framework%20for%20Considering%20Best%20Interests%20of%20Unaccompanied%20Children.pdf.

Chapter 6

The Curious Case of Jane Doe

Susan J. Terrio

In September 2017, a seventeen-year-old teenager fled domestic abuse in her home country in Central America and crossed the US-Mexico border without authorization. After being apprehended by immigration authorities and designated as an "unaccompanied alien child (UAC)" because she was under eighteen, alone, and without legal papers, the young woman, dubbed Jane Doe by her state-appointed guardian and attorneys, was placed in removal proceedings in federal immigration court and detained in a Brownville, Texas, federal shelter under contract to the Office of Refugee Resettlement (ORR). After a medical examination in custody confirmed her pregnancy, Jane Doe immediately requested an abortion.

Jane Doe's request ignited a month-long legal battle between, on the one hand, her guardian and attorneys who argued for her constitutional right to an elective abortion regardless of her legal status and, on the other hand, Trump administration officials who opposed it in court citing a new federal policy that prohibited federal staff from facilitating the access of undocumented minors to abortion services. The litigation began in earnest in the wake of a September 25, 2017 ruling by a Texas family court judge that waived the parental consent requirement and granted Jane Doe the legal authority to terminate her pregnancy. In the weeks following the decision, federal staff used a series of tactics to delay or block her access to an abortion. With the help of her Texas guardian, Jane's Due Process, a local NGO,[1] and ACLU attorneys, Jane Doe brought suit in federal court seeking to exercise her right to end the pregnancy. On October 18, 2017 Federal District Court Judge Tanya Chutkan ordered the government to stop "interfering with or obstructing her access to abortion counseling or an abortion."[2] Despite repeated government appeals of Judge Chutkan's ruling, on October 24, 2017, in a 6–3 decision, a full panel of the US District Court of Appeals for the District of Columbia granted Jane Doe's right to obtain an elective abortion "promptly and without delay."[3] She exercised that right in Texas on October 25, 2017 but remains in federal custody.

By virtue of the vulnerability and immaturity of UACs who are apprehended alone by immigration authorities, the federal government asserts its obligation to become their legal guardian and to detain them for their own protection. Jane Doe's case raises critical questions concerning non-citizens' claims to the constitutional protections of due process, equal protection, and the prohibition on government-compelled speech; access to reproductive services including abortion while in custody; freedom from unjustified government detention; and the state's responsibility for the welfare of the minor child. The divided court opinions issued in the October 24 Court of Appeals ruling turn on the recognition of "aliens" rights, on the one hand, and, on the other, their unique position as "alien juvenile" plaintiffs. We should ask why the medical and family planning services mandated for all UACs in federal custody by the federal government in the Flores Settlement Agreement (FSA) in 1997 and by Congress in the Trafficking Victim Protection Reauthorization Act (TVPRA) in 2008 were not provided to her. What do these debates tell us about the enduring legacy of the 1886 Supreme Court decision Yick Wo v. Hopkins that defined "persons" for the purpose of protection as all those in the territorial United States, including non-citizens? How should we understand the divergent reactions of judges, attorneys, federal staff, and government officials to Jane Doe's insistence on her right to determine her own best interest? Did the situation of a seventeen-year-old immigrant, pregnant and alone, create the kind of empathy usually reserved for Dreamers? Or did it stimulate suspicion of undocumented youth who game an overly generous immigration system?

"I STAND WITH DREAMERS," CHUCK SCHUMER, JANUARY 18, 2018

By January 2018, the vociferous congressional debates over how or if to shield hundreds of thousands of undocumented immigrants brought to the country as children from deportation had largely eclipsed the widespread media coverage of the Jane Doe case in the fall of 2017. While numerous polls demonstrate the overwhelming bipartisan support for the protection of Dreamers and DACA recipients, in contrast, the moral claims of UACs are more easily contested. Until recently, little was reported about the thousands of UACs who were apprehended and detained in federal custody. That changed with the rapid influx of undocumented Central American and Mexican children and families in 2014. That "surge" reopened the debate over border security, heightened fears about unregulated illegal immigration, disproportionately criminalized migrants from El Salvador, Guatemala, and Honduras[4] and hardened public opinion against child migrants. In the summer of 2014, a majority of Americans supported legislation to expel unaccompanied minors without a hearing before an immigration judge.[5] Since then undocumented youth from Central America and Mexico have tended to become newsworthy only when they are depicted as the perpetrators, victims of heinous crimes like murder or rape or when they are separated from their parents.

This selective attention contrasts sharply with the largely sympathetic portrayal of Dreamers or the DACA recipients. If the original sin of the "alien" is unlawful entry and illegal presence in the United States, this sin can, at least partially, be absolved for them.[6] It is their parents, not them, who are blamed for creating their status as undocumented immigrants. Dreamers and DACA recipients claim membership in the national community by virtue of having spent a formative period in their lives inside the country. Indeed, to qualify for this limited protection, Deferred Action for Child Arrivals (DACA) applicants must have arrived *with a parent* before the age of sixteen. They had to prove that they were in school or the military and did not have a record of criminal activity. Their close ties to families, attachment to US communities, educational accomplishments, work ethic, command of English, and embrace of mainstream identities could translate into a moral imperative for protection.

In contrast, UACs like Jane Doe are presumptively guilty, a fact that is confirmed when they cross the border without parents or documents, are apprehended for breaking immigration law, and placed in both mandatory custody and deportation proceedings. Their origin from outside the nation, their separation from family members who are back home or working without papers inside the United States, and illegal entry all weaken their claim to protection. After their apprehension and detention UACs like Jane Doe find themselves in a classically liminal position. They are betwixt and between various classificatory systems, different legal frameworks, and shifting institutional responses. When they leave home alone or with smugglers rather than endure domestic abuse, gang intimidation, or state violence and assert their right to make their own decisions, their behavior mimics the actions of adults and citizens in ways that may be deemed to be threatening and unjustified. Federal authorities may be suspicious of the active agency they demonstrate in the decision to leave home, their resourcefulness in the face of violence, and their resilience in dealing with traumatic experiences.

The case of Jane Doe garnered so much attention in part because she seemed to straddle the boundary separating adolescence from adulthood, claiming, on the one hand, that she was only a seventeen-year-old girl not able to take care of a child and, on the other hand, insisting that only she knew what was best for her.[7] Her case involves contested symbols of moral worth and vulnerability as well as disputed claims to political agency and the right to self-determination for under-aged teenagers. It throws into stark relief the coercive state responses that target undocumented youth, particularly young women, when they transgress normative expectations and move out of prescribed social categories.

FEDERAL CUSTODY FOR UNACCOMPANIED ALIEN CHILDREN

When undocumented children are apprehended at or near the border and designated as unaccompanied alien children, they are put in mandatory federal custody and placed in removal proceedings in immigration courts. The system of privately contracted federal shelters operated by the ORR that Jane Doe entered in September 2017 had significantly improved from its troubled beginnings in the 1980s, when legal aid organizations in California sued the federal government for confining immigrant children and youth in prison-like facilities, then operated by the Immigration and Naturalization Service. After years of litigation, a 1993 Supreme Court decision sustained the government's discretion to detain unaccompanied, undocumented children and to determine the conditions for release but did not resolve the standards of care.[8] In 1997, after prolonged litigation, the government agreed for the first time to establish minimum standards for the humane treatment of minors in custody and to ensure their prompt release in the FSA.[9]

After apprehension, Customs and Border Protection (CBP) or Immigration and Customs Enforcement (ICE) officials from the enforcement branches of immigration conduct initial screenings in order to determine the youth's status as accompanied and unaccompanied. The label of "unaccompanied" is a misnomer because it describes three different populations: the majority of new arrivals who are merely separated from parents or family members already in the United States; children who already live in the United States on their own or with family members and later came to the attention of immigration authorities; and the approximately 10 percent of children who, like Jane Doe, have no relatives able to provide care in the United States.

Since 2008 when I began to conduct research on the ORR system, primary consideration for placement within a network of private, state-licensed facilities and programs has been based on information collected by Border Patrol personnel or ICE agents. This data involves the youth's family history, criminal background, past history in custody and/or gang affiliation. Available bed space, age, gender, geographic location at apprehension, and evidence of psychological trauma were important but secondary considerations. In 2017, when Scott Lloyd was appointed director of ORR, greater attention was placed on security and risk factors, particularly any suspicion or history of gang involvement.[10] Because Jane Doe was a first-time border crosser, was apprehended without parents or a guardian, and had no delinquency or criminal record, she was placed in a large-scale minimum-security shelter in Brownsville, Texas.

Government regulations call for children in immigration custody to be held "in a non-institutional home-like atmosphere of care." They must receive food, shelter, clothing, visitation with family, case management, education, and medical, mental health and family planning services, including emergency interventions. They have the right to be screened for legal relief, to register grievances, and to be released without delay to approved sponsors (family members and other caregivers in the United States) while they are undergoing immigration proceedings—and 95 percent are. But I saw firsthand that custody was not anything like home.[11] All of the closed facilities that I visited between 2009–2012 were organized on a penal or psychiatric model: locked or monitored entry and exit, controlled movement inside, 24-hour internal surveillance and continuous supervision even in the absence of high fences, barred windows, or gated entrances.

Custody Before 2014

Before the influx of 2014 critics pointed to long periods of detention with no set endpoint, particularly for children with special needs, the overuse of secure facilities, rigid behavioral management programs, the use of a detention model organized by security level and the long-standing trend of locating facilities in remote areas to reduce costs or to keep children close to the border and ready for deportation. They also noted procedural and structural problems such as the intensive scrutiny of sponsors, including biological parents and close relatives, a shortage of therapeutic facilities, and the lack of independent oversight to ensure the government's compliance with its own standards.[12]

During their detention children suffered from the challenge of finding competent legal counsel, the uncertainty about winning legal status, the frustration of confinement in closed facilities, the fear of deportation, and the pain of separation from families in the United States. Being locked up for indefinite periods and knowing that government authorities made release decisions created feelings of helplessness among children and youth, many of whom were suffering from trauma, anxiety, and depression. Most of the formerly detained young people I interviewed between 2009 and 2013 understood that custody was intended to separate "good" from "bad" clients. Good clients accepted behavior restrictions, were rewarded with extra privileges, and were fast tracked for release. Problem clients came with checkered pasts like suspected gang affiliations and criminal charges. They challenged authority and created disruptions. At best they were labeled as psychologically unstable and managed with medication. At worst, they were recognized as security, criminal or terroristic threats, detained for longer periods, and transferred to more secure facilities.

Congress has reported incidents of physical and verbal abuse of unaccompanied minors by federally contracted personnel since 2005. The government has closed facilities in Texas, Indiana, and Oregon following internal complaints or legal action by NGOs. However, federal officials have repeatedly failed to hold abusers accountable and have been slow to enact procedures to prevent and report abuse by federal employees. It is significant that investigations conducted from 2004 to 2014 in federal shelters in Texas—including the Brownsville facility—by child welfare licensing personnel documented over 100 serious staff incidents ranging from inappropriate behavior and inadequate supervision to various forms of physical, psychological and sexual abuse.[13]

The "Surge" of 2014

In 2014, an unprecedented 68,000 Central American and Mexican children and youth entered the United States without authorization. After a harrowing journey and border crossing many of them ran to, not away from, immigration authorities. Federal regulations require thorough in-take screenings of new arrivals and intensive scrutiny of prospective sponsors before releasing unaccompanied children and youth from custody. These include a range of background checks, immigration status, a national FBI criminal history and/or a child abuse/neglect and home studies.[14] By early summer of 2014, with an unprecedented influx of new arrivals, the purported protections governing release had all but collapsed. As the influx of unaccompanied children accelerated to 500 a day in July, emergency facilities were opened, average stays were reduced to thirty days, and the release process was accelerated with inadequate vetting of potential sponsors.

Attorneys and advocates began to hear about cases of children falling into situations of exploitation. A Senate investigation was launched in 2014 after the government approved the release of six youths to a human trafficker who forced them to work on an egg farm twelve hours a day, six to seven days a week. The release of their report[15] prompted additional congressional hearings and investigations uncovering the systemic failures of the federal detention system for minors.[16]

Court challenges began to mount. Citing the 1997 FSA, on July 24, 2015, the US Court of the Central District of California held that the US family detention policies and short-term conditions in border patrol stations violated the government standards for the humane treatment and prompt release of undocumented children.[17] In August of 2016, advocates initiated a lawsuit against the government for subjecting unaccompanied minors to "peremptory detention," arbitrary release procedures, and failing to afford them the right to a bond hearing before an immigration judge to determine their eligibility for release.[18]

In response, ORR administrators moved to institute reforms despite facing the continuing challenge of large numbers of referrals. When the number of UACs in custody dramatically increased in 2014, ORR announced plans to open huge facilities in Texas, New Mexico, Colorado and Florida. In response to record numbers of new arrivals in November 2016, bed capacity grew from 7,800 beds in 2015 to nearly 11,500 in 2016.[19] A new and disturbing trend is the opening of what one prominent stakeholder described as "mega facilities in border states" that will house up to 1,000 UACs.[20] As of October 18, 2017, ORR has subcontracted with 136 detention facilities in sixteen states, forty-eight of which were located in the state of Texas. The government has awarded contracts to General Dynamics Information Technology for three large shelters to open in 2018.[21]

TRUMP ADMINISTRATION CHANGES

In contrast to previous directors of ORR who were themselves refugees or had considerable experience working with refugee communities, the Trump administration appointee, Scott Lloyd, lacked such expertise. He joined the agency from the Knights of Columbus, a Catholic fraternal and charitable organization.[22] Lloyd's writings on abortion and contraception reflect his pro-life beliefs. In a 2011 article he argued that contraceptives are the cause of abortion and rallied against population control entities such as Planned Parenthood for spreading misinformation.[23]

Soon after his appointment, Lloyd instituted dramatic changes regarding reproductive services for unaccompanied minors within the agency. He issued a directive prohibiting all federally contracted shelters from facilitating abortion access for unaccompanied minors in their care without the "direction and approval" from the director of ORR—in stark contrast to the policies of US ICE and the Bureau of Prisons (BOP). The new policy required shelters to alert ORR before doing anything to facilitate an abortion.[24] Robert Carey, the director of the Office of Refugee Resettlement from April 2015 to January

2017, described the Trump administration policy as a departure from the Obama administration, when the government only reviewed abortion requests from unaccompanied minors if they were seeking funding for the procedure.[25] Carey explained that minors were allowed to make their own decisions to terminate unwanted pregnancies[26] and that federal funds were approved only for abortions in the case of rape, incest, or a danger to the mother's life.

Government emails included in the ACLU case filings open a window into the administration's new policy.[27] In one email, Lloyd told his staff "the unborn child is a child in our care," implying they were to make medical decisions accordingly.[28] ORR now requires federally contracted shelters to notify the government before allowing a pregnant minor to petition a state court for a waiver of parental consent. Similarly, Lloyd has directed pregnant minors to go to crisis pregnancy centers, which are run by pro-life religious groups whose mission is to discourage abortions.[29] Mr. Lloyd also directed ORR and grantee shelter staff to notify the parents and immigration sponsors of unaccompanied immigrant minors' pregnancies, despite the minors' requests to keep the information confidential. In a recent complaint, attorneys allege that he notified a young woman's prospective sponsor—her adult brother—of her abortion request with advance knowledge that it might jeopardize her release to his care.[30]

Most recently, representatives of the Vera Institute of Justice, a nonprofit that holds a multimillion-dollar contract to provide legal screenings for all UACs in federal custody, instructed all the lawyers in its network not to discuss abortion access, even if minors requested help. They feared doing so would jeopardize their lucrative government contract with ORR.[31]

JANE DOE'S CONSTITUTIONAL RIGHTS?

On October 13, 2017, the American Civil Liberties Union (ACLU) filed suit against the Department of Health and Human Services and its agencies, ACF and ORR, alleging that obstructing Jane Doe's right to terminate her pregnancy violated the First and Fifth amendments to the Constitution by compelling her participation in religiously affiliated counseling and by infringing on her right to privacy and liberty. The suit also charged that the government had violated the FSA's mandate for access to medical and reproductive services in federal custody.[32]

Granting the ACLU's request for an expedited briefing on the case, District Court Judge Tanya Chutkan heard oral arguments on October 18, 2017. Judge Chutkan asked Scott Stewart, a deputy assistant attorney general at the Justice Department, whether he thought illegal immigrants had constitutional rights and whether the 1973 Supreme Court ruling Roe v. Wade, which guarantees a woman's right to an abortion, is still the "law of the land." Stewart said "I'm not going to give you a concession on that, Your Honor," adding that the government views this case differently. He signaled that undocumented minors do not have a constitutional right to an elective abortion *while in federal custody*, unless it is a medical emergency, and added that immigrants here illegally have "minimal" protections in this country.[33] While not challenging her constitutional right to an abortion, Trump administration officials argued that the government may legitimately express a preference for childbirth over abortion for undocumented, detained minors. They further maintained that federal detention did not pose an undue burden on any right to abortion, claiming that Jane Doe could end her predicament by agreeing to return to the Central American country she had fled because of domestic abuse.

The judge was incredulous saying, "This is remarkable," noting that the teen's legal status was irrelevant and that she still had constitutional rights:

> I am astounded by that position. I have to tell you, I'm astounded that the government is going to make this 17-year-old girl who has received judicial authorization for a medical procedure to which she is constitutionally authorized choose between a pregnancy that she does not want to go forward with to term or returning to the country from which she left. Those are her options. And is it your position that that does not constitute a substantial obstacle? She can leave the country or she cannot get her abortion, those are her options?[34]

The Justice Department argued that the government has "strong and constitutionally legitimate interests in promoting childbirth and in not providing incentives for pregnant minors to illegally cross the border to obtain elective abortions while in federal custody."[35] Judge Chutkan countered that the teenager had followed state and federal rules, obtaining a parental consent waiver and permission to have an abortion from a state family court judge in Texas as well as funds to cover the procedure.

Judge Chutkan also addressed actions taken by ORR that potentially violated Jane Doe's constitutional rights: federal workers took the teenager, against her wishes, to get Christian counseling aimed at persuading her not to abort, and also informed her mother about the pregnancy. In her October 18, 2017 ruling, Judge Chutkan issued a Temporary Restraining Order that barred the government from forcing the teen to reveal her abortion decision to anyone or retaliating against her. The judge ordered the government to release Ms. Doe to her state-appointed guardian so that she could get the abortion.[36]

Later that evening, the government appealed her decision to the US Court of Appeals for the District of Columbia and the ORR issued a statement claiming that the ruling "exceeds the US Constitution and sets a dangerous precedent by opening our borders to any illegal children seeking taxpayer-supported, elective abortions." ORR added that "Federal law is very clear on giving the director of the Office of Refugee Resettlement the legal responsibility to decide what is in the best interests of a minor in the unaccompanied alien children program and, in this case, her unborn baby. We cannot cede our responsibility to care for minors and their babies by releasing them to ideological advocacy groups."[37]

In response to the ACLU litigation, Texas and seven other states filed a friend of the court brief supporting the government's position.[38] They argued that "no federal court has ever declared that unlawfully-present aliens without substantial ties to this country have a constitutional right to abortion on demand." They claimed that granting the Temporary Restraining Order would harm the public interest and "create a right to abortion for anyone on Earth who entered the United States illegally."[39]

In court filings and numerous media interviews, Jane Doe's state-appointed guardian and ACLU litigators rebutted this view of federal custody. Susan Hays, the legal director of Jane's Due Process described her "captivity" in a government detention where the staff ignored her medical needs and forced her to go to a crisis pregnancy center staffed by pro-life counselors. "She is being abused both physically, by denying her access to medical care, and emotionally, by the way they are haranguing her and trying to break her down psychologically because she wants an abortion," said Hays.[40]

Brigitte Amiri, the lead attorney for the ACLU explained, "It is clear is [sic] that Scott Lloyd has the full force of the government backing him. It is unconstitutional and cruel to block access and force these young women to go to anti-abortion counseling. They are trying to defend an indefensible position." Based on the ACLU representation of other pregnant, undocumented teenagers in federal detention facing the same challenges, she explained the multistep process used by ORR to prevent elective abortions:

> First they [ORR administrators] try coercion to persuade them not to get an abortion. If that does not work they block access to the services. They contact the parents [in the home country] to exert pressure on the young women [not to abort]. They instruct the shelter staff to obstruct. We have seen cases where the parents in the home country are alerted to the pregnancy and they exert tremendous force on the young women [to change their minds]. They also force them to go to anti-abortion crisis centers and to have ultrasounds and to look at the fetus. They require them to undergo this so-called "counseling." We know that in Jane Doe's case the staff at the Crisis Pregnancy Center prayed over her. We also know that Lloyd has personally visited or called the women in question if they are insisting on ending the pregnancy.[41]

JANE DOE IN ORR CUSTODY

Throughout the month of October, legal representatives, federal authorities and journalists spoke for and about Jane Doe's case. After the October 24 ruling of the Court of Appeals, Jane Doe finally spoke on her own behalf. In a statement published on the ACLU website after her abortion, she thanked the Texas family court judge "who gave me permission to end my pregnancy without my parents' consent." She went on to explain that "the government provides most of my needs at the [ORR-contracted] shelter," but the federal staff "made me see a doctor that tried to convince me not to abort and to look at sonograms [of the fetus]."[42] In a longer interview, a journalist with *Vice News* asked her "what it is like at the shelter?" Her description of the strict rules, monitored movement, and constant surveillance echoes the interviews that I have conducted with formerly detained youth since 2010.[43] She explained,

"Being in this place is something difficult for me because you have no freedom for anything. Not even the freedom to take the time you want to take a shower or the time to go to the bathroom. If you want to do something you have to tell somebody. You can't even hug someone. If you feel sad, all you can do is cry and vent by yourself."[44]

The release process and identification of an approved sponsor for Jane Doe was at the heart of the government's case. The government argued that Jane Doe had the right to obtain an abortion only after her release from custody but cited its statutory obligation to keep her in detention until a suitable sponsor could be found. Agency regulations stipulate that preferred sponsors must be family members or have a social relationship with the child that predated her arrival in the United States.[45] Failing that, ORR regulations permit a non-family sponsor to be chosen after comprehensive vetting. Nonetheless, over the seven weeks that elapsed between her detention and the October 24, 2017 ruling of the Court of Appeals for the District of Columbia, ORR had rejected multiple sponsors.

In a dissenting opinion to the Court of Appeals ruling, Circuit Judge Kavanaugh, joined by Circuit Judges Henderson and Griffith, argued that requiring Jane Doe to continue her pregnancy did not constitute an "undue burden" provided that the sponsorship search is undertaken "expeditiously."[46] In her majority opinion, Judge Patricia Millett forcefully rebutted that view, saying that the government never requested a stay to find a sponsor, never suggested that there was a realistic prospect of finding a sponsor, and never hinted "that a non-family member could be identified, vetted and take custody of Jane Doe."[47] By the end of January 2018 Jane Doe had spent four months in federal custody with no end in sight.[48]

An *LA Times* editorial concluded that the Jane Doe case was not about a minor obtaining an abortion, or about seeking help to obtain abortion services in Texas or about subsidizing, abortions with federal dollars. Rather it was about how "the Office of Refugee Resettlement handles the care of undocumented minors in its custody." The editorial board decried "the conservative ideology forced onto vulnerable young people in federal custody."[49]

ALIEN JUVENILE OR PREGNANT CHILD?

Pregnant Child

The court opinions and public statements on the Jane Doe case reveal the ambiguity surrounding her position as a vulnerable child needing protection, on the one hand, or as a young adult taking responsibility, on the other. In discussing her ordeal, Jane Doe emphasized her vulnerability and immaturity:

> I don't feel capable of being a mature woman or being strong or old enough to take care of it [a child]. I don't feel sure about having a child.

Jane Doe described her need for protection from the heavy-handed and moralistic policies of federal staff that imposed their pro-life values on her:

> [The government] made me see a doctor that tried to convince me not to abort and to look at sonograms. People I don't even know are trying to make me change my mind. I made my decision and that is between me and God.

Her Texas guardian, Rochelle Garza agreed that "she does not want a child. She is a child herself. She cannot have a child and raise it. She is in detention."[50]

On the other hand, Jane Doe laid claim to moral deservedness and the right to determine and act on her own best interest:

> When I was detained, I was placed in a shelter for children. It was there that I was told I was pregnant. I knew immediately what was best for me then, as I do now—that I'm not ready to be a parent.

Invoking a difficult journey alone to the United States from Central America, Jane Doe described her determination to leave behind the abuse she had encountered in her home country, her resourcefulness in the face of violence, and her resilience in dealing with trauma and loss:

> I'm a 17 year-old girl that came to this country to make a better life for myself. My journey wasn't easy, but I came here with hope in my heart to build a life I can be proud of. I dream about studying, becoming a nurse, and one day working with the elderly.

Her seemingly liminal position between childhood and adulthood created categorical confusion—was she a vulnerable child or an accountable adult—and informed sharply diverging positions among the Circuit Court judges regarding her constitutional rights in the United States. In her majority opinion, Judge Millett argued that while the government—to its credit—never suggested that her unlawful status as an unaccompanied minor eliminated her constitutional right to an abortion, it "bulldozed" over other safeguards by categorically blocking exercise of her rights while in detention. In noting that the court decision "rights a grave constitutional wrong by the government," she added:

> Remember, we are talking about a child here. A child who is alone in a foreign land. A child, who after her arrival here in search of safety and after the government took her into custody, learned that she was pregnant.

Judge Willett denounced the circular logic of the government position that "an unaccompanied child has the burden of extracting herself from custody if she wants to exercise the right to an abortion that the government does not dispute she has." She held that "a detained, unaccompanied minor has precious little control over the sponsorship" [and release] process or "the independent ability to overcome obstacles to the exercise of her reproductive freedom."[51] She sarcastically noted that Jane Doe's only options were reduced to finding her own way out of detention ("like some kind of Houdini") or accepting the offer of Voluntary Departure from the immigration judge and return to the abuse she fled in her home country.[52] The *New York Times* journalist Linda Greenhouse argued that as an unaccompanied minor, pregnant, detained, and alone, Jane Doe became an ideal target for the anti-immigrant agenda and pro-life ideology of the Trump administration "because she had the gumption or desperation to flee something even worse."[53]

Alien Juvenile

In her dissenting opinion for the Circuit Court Judge Karen Lecraft Henderson castigated the government for "inexplicably and wrongheadedly failing" to take a position on Jane Doe's constitutional right to an elective abortion. She argued instead that the ORR had placed no undue burden on that alleged right and stated unequivocally:

> Jane Doe is not a U.S. citizen. She is not a permanent resident, legally or otherwise . . . has no connection to the United States, let alone "substantial" connections. Despite her physical presence in the United States, Jane Doe has never entered the United States as a matter of law and cannot avail herself of the constitutional rights afforded those legally within our borders.[54]

She held that "Jane Doe is not a person in the eyes of the Constitution" and is, therefore, not entitled to due process protections. Judge Henderson wrote that it was "highly likely she knew she was pregnant when she attempted to enter the US," suggesting that Jane Doe came to the United States for purely instrumental reasons—to get an abortion because "that procedure is illegal in her home country."[55] She concluded that the majority decision "plows potentially dangerous ground" because it will allow alien minors anywhere in the world to claim the constitutional right to an abortion in the United States.[56]

CONCLUSION

Unaccompanied alien children in federal detention occupy positions that disrupt the binaries of legal and illegal, worthy and unworthy, dependency and autonomy, and the personal and the political. By virtue of their vulnerability and immaturity, UACs must be detained for their own protection. This arrangement assigns the government as their legal guardian and empowers federal ORR staff to make all decisions governing custody and release. Jane Doe's display of agency and insistence on her right to determine her own best interest threatened the dominant humanitarian narrative and new operational policies governing pregnant unaccompanied minors in custody. By demanding justice and her constitutional right to exercise reproductive choice, Jane Doe drew strong censure from conservative media, the DHS attorneys, and dissenting circuit judges who argued that she could end her predicament by returning to her home country. Judge Karen Lecraft Henderson described her as an "alien minor" whose illegal breaching of the US border set a dangerous precedent.

In a November 2017 interview, ACLU attorney Brigitte Amiri cautioned that despite the victory in Jane Doe's case, the "ORR policy still exists and is still being enforced."[57] Scarcely one month later, ACLU was back in court representing another detained minor, Jane Poe, who had been denied permission to terminate her pregnancy despite having been raped. On December 21, 2017, Scott Lloyd wrote:

> How could abortion be in [her] best interest where other options are available, and where the child might even survive outside the womb at this stage of pregnancy? Here there is no medical reason for abortion, it will not undo or erase

the memory of the violence committed against her, and it may further traumatize her. I conclude it is not in her interest.[58]

In the era of Trump, the legal protections that should apply to unaccompanied minors while in custody: humane treatment, effective legal screenings, best interest determinations, prompt release, and access to reproductive services, are increasingly compromised or set aside. In his State of the Union address on January 30, 2018 and in a White House meeting on February 6, President Trump conflated unaccompanied minors with MS-13 gang members and demanded that loopholes in immigration law be closed to prevent "criminals" from entering the United States. This message reflects the increased alignment between the operational priorities of the ORR and the Trump administration regarding the enhanced threat and security risks purportedly posed by this population. As ORR director Scott Lloyd instituted a policy requiring that he personally review and approve the release of any child detained in a secure facility. In a May hearing in New York challenging this policy, Lloyd testified that he based the new policy on news reports about the criminal activity of unaccompanied minors, not on actual trends within federal custody.[59] As a result more unaccompanied minors are subject to secure detention at placement, held for longer periods, and face enhanced scrutiny before release on the mere suspicion of gang affiliation or criminal and delinquent activity. This heightened emphasis on enforcement and the paternalistic imposition of a pro-life agenda on young women in detention is an alarming harbinger of things to come, not only for the treatment of all detained immigrant minors but also for the reproductive rights of US citizen women and girls.

NOTES

1. Jane's Due Process ensures legal representation for pregnant teens in Texas seeking the judicial waiver alternative to parental consent for abortion in cases where parental involvement is unsafe or impossible. Jane's Due Process16_v8-2. pdf.
2. Garza v. Hargan. U.S. District Court for the District of Columbia, 1:17-cv-02122-TSC, filed October 18, 2017.
3. Garza v. Hargan, U.S. Court of Appeals for the District of Columbia, no. 17-5236, filed October 24, 2017.
4. Cecilia Menjivar and Daniel Kanstroom, *Constructing Immigrant Illegality: Critiques, Experiences, and Responses* (New York: Cambridge University Press, 2014), 17.
5. Migration Policy Institute, *Unaccompanied Minor Crisis Has Receded from Headlines But Major Issues Remain*, 2014. https://www.migrationpolicy.org/article/unaccompanied-minors-crisis-has-receded-headlines-major-issues-remain.

6. Leti Volpp, "Civility and the Undocumented Alien," in *Civility, Legality and Justice in America,* ed. Austin Sarat (New York: Cambridge University Press, 2014), 88.

7. ACLU, 10-25-2017, https://www.aclu.org/news/after-month-obstruction-trump-administration-jane-doe-gets-her-abortion.

8. Reno V. Flores 507 US (1993).

9. Flores v. Meese, NO. CV 85-4544-RJK (PX) (C.D. Cal. Filed January 17, 1997).

10. Scott Lloyd, director of the Office of Refugee Resettlement, "Testimony before the Senate Committee on the Judiciary," June 21, 2017.

11. Susan J. Terrio, *Whose Child am I? Unaccompanied, Undocumented Children in U.S. Immigration Custody* (Oakland, CA: University of California Press, 2015).

12. Wendy Young and M. McKenna, "The Measure of a Society: The Treatment of Unaccompanied Refugee and Immigrant Children in the United States," *Harvard Civil Rights-Civil Liberties Law Review* 45 (2010): 252; Terrio, *Whose Child Am I?* 2015; Women's Refugee Commission, *Forced from Home: The Lost Boys and Girls of Central America.* 2012, http: www.womensrefugeecommission.org; Marjorie S. Zatz, and Nancy Rodriguez, *Dreams and Nightmares: Immigration Policy, Youth and Families* (Oakland, CA: University of California Press, 2015).

13. Susan Carroll, "Crossing Alone. Children Fleeing to US Land in Shadowy System," *Houston Chronicle*, May 24 and 29, 2014, https//: www.houstonchronicle.com/News/investigations/article/Crossing-alone-Children-fleeing-to-U-S-land-in-5503127.php.

14. Lutheran Immigration and Refugee Services Round Table Report, *At the Crossroads for Unaccompanied Migrant Children: Policy, Practice and Protection,* 2015, https://bettercarenetwork.org/sites/default/files/At%20the%20Crossroads%20for%20Unaccompanied%20Migrant%20Children%20-%20Policy,%20Practice%20and%20Protection.pdf.

15. United States Senate, "Protecting Alien Children from Trafficking and Other Abuses: The Role of the Office of Refugee Resettlement," Permanent Sub-Committee on Investigations, January 28, 2016, https://www.hsgac.senate.gov/imo/media/doc/Majority%20&%20Minority%20Staff%20Report%20-%20Protecting%20Unaccompanied%20Alien%20Children%20from%20Trafficking%20and%20Other%20Abuses%202016-01-282.pdf.

16. House Judiciary Committee, February 4, 2016; U.S. Senate Judiciary Committee, February 23, 2016.

17. D.C. no. 2:85—cv-04544-DMG-AGR. On appeal, the ninth Circuit Court affirmed the district court's order to enforce the FSA which set nationwide policy for the detention and release of all minors, whether unaccompanied or with an accompanying adult. See Flores v. Lynch 15-56434, July 6, 2016.

18. Case 2:85-cv-04544-DMG-AGR Document 239-1 Filed August 12, 2016, filed by Carlos Holguín and Peter A. Schey at the Center for Human Rights and Constitutional Law and Holly Cooper at the University of California at Davis School of Law.

19. Statistics presented at the Interagency Working Group meeting on unaccompanied children, December 1, 2016.

20. Telephone interview, January 12, 2018.

21. Stakeholder interview, January 10, 2018. GDIT has had contracts with the Office of Refugee Resettlement to provide case management services for detained minors since 2011.

22. Administration for Children and Families, "Scott Lloyd," https://www.acf.hhs.gov/about/leadership/scott-lloyd.

23. Scott Lloyd, "Facts on Abortion: Why You Can't Be Pro-Life and Pro-Contraception," *Ethika Politika*, April 4, 2011, https://ethikapolitika.org/2011/04/04/facts-on-abortion-why-you-cant-be-pro-life-and-pro-contraception/.

24. ACLU, Jane Doe v. Don Wright v. USCCB, October 5, 2017, https://www.aclu.org/sites/default/files/field_document/10.05.17_doc._84_plaintiffs_notice_of_motion_motion_for_tro_pi.pdf.

25. Renuka Rayasam, "Trump Official Halts Abortions Among Undocumented, Pregnant Teens," *Politico*, October 16, 2017, https://www.politico.com/story/2017/10/16/undocumented-pregnant-girl-trump-abortion-texas-243844?lo=ap_a1.

26. Ibid.

27. Hannah Levintova and Pema Levy, "Internal Emails Reveal How the Trump Administration Blocks Abortions for Migrant Teens," *Mother Jones*, November 29, 2017, https://www.motherjones.com/politics/2017/11/internal-emails-reveal-how-the-trump-administration-blocks-abortions-for-migrant-teens/.

28. Emails within ORR, https://www.documentcloud.org/documents/4106150-20170304-ORR-Emails-Re-Abortion-Policies.html#document/p13/a380998.

29. Levintova and Levy, *Mother Jones*.

30. Katie O'Connor, Complaint, Scott Lloyd, director of the Office of Refugee Resettlement, Campaign for Accountability, October 20, 2017, CFA-Complaint-Scott-Lloyd-HHS-IG-10-20-2017-2.pdf.

31. Marimow and Sacchetti, "Immigrant Rights Group Warned," *The Washington Post*.

32. Garza v. Hargan. U.S. District Court for the District of Columbia, 1:17-cv-02122-TSC, filed October 13, 2017.

33. Maria Sacchetti, "U.S. Judge Orders the Trump Administration to Allow Abortion for Undocumented Teen," *Washington Post*, October 18, 2017, https://www.washingtonpost.com/local/immigration/judge-trump-administration-cancannot-block-abortion-for-pregnant-undocumented-teen/2017/10/18/82348e08-b406-11e7-be94-fabb0f1e9ffb_story.html?utm_term=.1931f4675d77.

34. Stacy Sullivan, "Jane Doe Wants an Abortion but the Government is Hell-Bent on Stopping Her," *ACLU*, October 19 and 23, 2017, https://www.aclu.org/blog/immigrants-rights/immigrants-rights-and-detention/jane-doe-wants-abortion-government-hell-bent.

35. Sacchetti, "Trump administration cannot block abortion," *The Washington Post*.

36. Temporary Restraining Order, case 1:17-cv-02122-TSC, document 20, October 18, 2017.

37. Guilia Afuine, "Federal Judge Rules that Pregnant, Undocumented Teen in Texas has Right to Abortion Access," *Texas Tribune*, October 18, 2017.

38. Brief of the State of Texas, et al as amici curiae, Case 3:16-cv-03539-LB Document 96-2, filed 10-10-2017. The state of Texas was joined by Louisiana, Missouri, Nebraska, Ohio, Oklahoma, and South Carolina.
39. Ibid., 6.
40. Afuine, "Undocumented Teen in Texas," *Texas Tribune*.
41. Telephone interview, Brigitte Amiri, January 10, 2018.
42. https://www.aclu.org/news/after-month-obstruction-trump-administration-jane-doe-gets-her-abortion.
43. Terrio, *Whose Child am I?* 116–117.
44. *Vice News*, "Watch Our Full Interview with Jane Doe about her Abortion Battle," October 25, 2017, https://news.vice.com/en_us/article/qvzwnx/watch-we-talked-to-jane-doe-about-her-abortion-battle.
45. Office of Refugee Resettlement, Children Entering the United States Unaccompanied: Section 2," January 30, 2015, https://www.acf.hhs.gov/orr/resource/children-entering-the-united-states-unaccompanied-section-2.
46. Garza v. Hargan, U.S. Court of Appeals for the District of Columbia, no. 17-5236, filed 10-24-2017, dissent, 1.
47. Garza v. Hargan, U.S. Court of Appeals for the District of Columbia, no. 17-5236, filed 10-24-2017, 5.
48. Vasquez, "Trump Official's Obsession Still Shaping Federal Policy." *Rewire*.
49. *LA Times* editorial, October 20, 2017.
50. *Vice News*, Interview with Jane Doe, October 25, 2017, https://news.vice.com/en_us/article/qvzwnx/watch-we-talked-to-jane-doe-about-her-abortion-battle.
51. Garza v. Hargan, U.S. Court of Appeals for the District of Columbia, no. 17-5236, filed 10-24-2017, majority, 6.
52. Ibid., 1–2.
53. Greenhouse, "The Worrisome Future of Abortion Rights," *New York Times*.
54. Garza v. Hargan, October 24, 2017, US Court of Appeals for the District of Columbia Circuit, no 17-5236, dissent, 8.
55. Ibid., 2–3.
56. Ibid., 17.
57. Tina Vasquez, "Trump Official's Obsession with Pregnant Immigrant Minors is Still Shaping Federal Policy," *Rewire*, November 30, 2017, https://rewire.news/article/2017/11/30/trump-officials-obsession-pregnant-immigrant-minors-still-shaping-federal-policy.
58. Lloyd Full Memo, case 1:17-cv-02122-TSC, Document 92-1, filed December 22, 2017.
59. On June 27, 2018, U.S. District Court Judge Paul Crotty in New York issued a preliminary injunction ending an ORR policy of review he termed, "The zenith of impermissible agency actions." NYCLU 2018 *Court Halts Trump Administration Policy Prolonging Detention of Hundreds of Immigrant Children*, June 27, 2018, https://www.nyclu.org/en/press-releases/court-halts-trump-administration-policy-prolonging-detention-hundreds-immigrant.

BIBLIOGRAPHY

Afuine, Guilia. "Federal Judge Rules that Pregnant, Undocumented Teen in Texas has Right to Abortion Access." *Texas Tribune*, October 18, 2017. http://www.kvue.com/news/local/federal-judge-rules-pregnant-undocumented-teen-in-texas-has-right-to-abortion-access/484345458.

Carroll, Susan. "Crossing Alone. Children Fleeing to US Land in Shadowy System." *Houston Chronicle*, May 24 and 29, 2014. https//:www.houstonchronicle.com/News/investigations/article/Crossing-alone-Children-fleeing-to-U-S-land-in-5503127.php.

Greenhouse, Linda. "The Worrisome Future of Abortion Rights." *New York Times*, November 9, 2017. https://www.nytimes.com/2017/11/09/opinion/the-worrisome-future-of-abortion-rights.html?rref=collection%2Fcolumn%2Flinda-greenhouse&action=click&contentCollection=opinion&region=stream&module=stream_unit&version=latest&contentPlacement=7&pgtype=collection.

Levintova, Hannah, and Pema Levy. "Internal Emails Reveal How the Trump Administration Blocks Abortions for Migrant Teens." *Mother Jones*, November 29, 2017. https://www.motherjones.com/politics/2017/11/internal-emails-reveal-how-the-trump-administration-blocks-abortions-for-migrant-teens.

Los Angeles Times Editorial Board, "The U.S. Government Cannot Hold Undocumented Pregnant Teens Hostage When They Want an Abortion." *Los Angeles Times*, October 20, 2017. https://www.latimes.com/opinion/editorials/la-ed-undocumented-teen-abortion-20171020-story.html.

Lutheran Immigration and Refugee Services Round Table Report. *At the Crossroads for Unaccompanied Migrant Children. Policy, Practice and Protection.* 2015. https://bettercarenetwork.org/sites/default/files/At%20the%20Crossroads%20for%20Unaccompanied%20Migrant%20Children%20-%20Policy,%20Practice%20and%20Protection.pdf.

Marimow, Ann, and Maria Sacchetti. "Immigrant Rights Group in Email Says it was Warned not to Mention Abortion to Migrant Teens." *The Washington Post*, February 15, 2018. https://www.washingtonpost.com/local/immigration/attorneys-warned-not-to-mention-abortion-to-immigrant-teens-in-custody-per-email-from-legal-group/2018/02/14/cd0aecc6–0da5–11e8–8890–372e2047c935_story.html?hpid=hp_hp-top-table-low_immigrationabortion-840a%3Ahomepage%2Fstory&utm_term=.af5a5aa86583.

Menjivar, Cecilia, and Daniel Kanstroom, eds. *Constructing Immigrant "Illegality": Critiques, Experiences, and Responses*. New York: Cambridge University Press, 2014.

Migration Policy Institute. *Unaccompanied Minor Crisis Has Receded from Headlines But Major Issues Remain*, 2014. https://www.migrationpolicy.org/article/unaccompanied-minors-crisis-has-receded-headlines-major-issues-remain.

New York Civil Liberties Union. *Court Halts Trump Administration Policy Prolonging Detention of Hundreds of Immigrant Children*, June 27, 2018. https://www.nyc

lu.org/en/press-releases/court-halts-trump-administration-policy-prolonging-detention-hundreds-immigrant.

Rayasam, Renuka. "Trump Official Halts Abortions Among Undocumented, Pregnant Teens." *Politico*, October 16, 2017. https://www.politico.com/story/2017/10/16/undocumented-pregnant-girl-trump-abortion-texas-243844?lo=ap_a1.

Sacchetti, Maria. "U.S. Judge Orders the Trump Administration to Allow Abortion for Undocumented Teen." *Washington Post*, October 18, 2017. https://www.washingtonpost.com/local/immigration/judge-trump-administration-cancannot-block-abortion-for-pregnant-undocumented-teen/2017/10/18/82348e08-b406–11e7-be94-fabb0f1e9ffb_story.html?utm_term=.1931f4675d77.

Sullivan, Stacy. "Jane Doe Wants an Abortion but the Government is Hell-Bent on Stopping Her." *ACLU*, October 19 and 23, 2017. https://www.aclu.org/blog/immigrants-rights/immigrants-rights-and-detention/jane-doe-wants-abortion-government-hell-bent.

Terrio, Susan J. *Whose Child am I? Unaccompanied, Undocumented Children in U.S. Immigration Custody*. Oakland, CA: University of California Press, 2015.

United States Senate, "Protecting Alien Children from Trafficking and Other Abuses: The Role of the Office of Refugee Resettlement," Permanent Sub-Committee on Investigations, January 28, 2016. https://www.hsgac.senate.gov/imo/media/doc/Majority%20&%20Minority%20Staff%20Report%20-%20Protecting%20Unaccompanied%20Alien%20Children%20from%20Trafficking%20and%20Other%20Abuses%202016–01–282.pdf.

Vasquez, Tina. "Trump Official's Obsession with Pregnant Immigrant Minors is Still Shaping Federal Policy," *Rewire*. November 30, 2017. https://rewire.news/article/2017/11/30/trump-officials-obsession-pregnant-immigrant-minors-still-shaping-federal-policy/.

Volpp, Leti. "Civility and the Undocumented Alien." In *Civility, Legality and Justice in America,* edited by Austin Sarat, 69–106. New York: Cambridge University Press.

Women's Refugee Commission. *Halfway Home: Unaccompanied Children in Immigration Custody*. New York, 2009. http: www.womensrefugeecommission.org.

———. *Forced from Home: The Lost Boys and Girls of Central America*. 2012. http: www.womensrefugeecommission.org.

Young, Wendy, and M. McKenna. "The Measure of a Society: The Treatment of Unaccompanied Refugee and Immigrant Children in the United States." *Harvard Civil Rights-Civil Liberties Law Review* 45 (2010): 247–260.

Zatz, Marjorie S., and Nancy Rodriguez. *Dreams and Nightmares: Immigration Policy, Youth and Families*. Oakland, CA: University of California Press, 2015.

Chapter 7

Human Vulnerability and Vulnerable Rights

On Children's Rights and Asylum Politics in Sweden

Elena Namli and Linde Lindkvist

How does human vulnerability relate to human dignity and human rights? Are human rights an instrument of reducing or even overcoming vulnerability in order for human beings to secure their autonomy, agency, and dignity? An affirmative answer to this question is a traditional approach within human rights studies and human rights practices.[1] In this chapter we challenge this view by addressing the situation of unaccompanied minors seeking asylum in contemporary Sweden.

In recent years, a significant proportion of the total number of asylum seekers coming to Sweden have been unaccompanied minors, coming from countries such as Afghanistan, Iraq, Morocco, Somalia, and Syria.[2] These persons are vulnerable because they are human, because they are displaced, and because they are young. If the traditional approach to human rights as a means of reducing vulnerability is plausible, then young asylum seekers should be firmly protected by any society recognizing human rights as a part of its constitutional order. How then can we understand and evaluate the recent developments in Europe in general, and in Sweden in particular, that demonstrate a weakening of human rights protection for some of the most vulnerable human beings?

This weakening is visible on many different levels. A 2016 agreement between the European Union and Turkey—directly aimed at reducing the flow of migrants to Europe through Greece—has forced young asylum seekers from the Middle East to use the much more hazardous path through Northern Africa in order to reach preferred end-destinations like Germany and Sweden. The introduction of stricter border controls and ID requirements in many EU countries has also affected young migrants, many of whom travel without papers. Yet, even those that reach their destination and are able to apply for asylum find themselves in highly exposed situations. A recent study based on interviews with unaccompanied minors in residential care homes across Sweden revealed a profound deficit in their enjoyment of basic human rights, including healthcare, adequate housing, clothing, and personal security. They often face protracted asylum processes, frequently involving intimidating procedures like medical age assessments, language analysis to determine their place of origin, and detailed questioning on traumatic experiences. The outcomes of these processes are also highly uncertain. One girl described what it was like to live in this state of uncertainty: "It's like you're hanging from a rope or something. You have no idea if it's gonna hold, or if it's gonna break. And everything just kinda falls apart."[3]

Sweden is known as a country with a highly developed human rights culture, and is sometimes referred to as "the best country in the world to be a child."[4] This view corresponds with the dominant self-perception of Swedish authorities and Swedish society. But Sweden is also a country sending young refugees back to conflict areas, denying families the right to reunite, and ignoring tremendous suffering of lonely young people. This paradox is obviously of political nature, and it can only be addressed by political means. Yet, we believe that scholars can make valuable contributions and strengthen those political actors who fight for a return to a more humane refugee and human rights politics. In what follows, we offer an analysis of how Sweden deals with unaccompanied minors seeking asylum here, with the particular aim of scrutinizing established views on human vulnerability within European human rights discourse.

Vulnerability is a part of human existence, a substantial dimension of what it means to be human. As several scholars have convincingly argued, the concept of vulnerability challenges any attempt to reduce the question of human dignity to a protection of individual autonomy.[5] Although our aim is not primarily conceptual, we will contribute to the discussion by arguing in favor of a more dialectical understanding of the relation between vulnerability and human rights. We start off with a short presentation of our view of the Swedish case. In the next step we formulate what appears to be a paradox—the Swedish state incorporating the United Nations Convention on the Rights of the Child (CRC) and, simultaneously, enforcing inhumane restrictions on the rights of young asylum seekers. We will proceed by deconstructing the paradox and arguing that these seemingly conflicting trends can be explained as manifestations of two different but interrelated dimensions of the current human rights culture, namely, juridification of human rights protection and reduction of vulnerability to a function of age. In the concluding part of the chapter we offer a critical reflection on the relation between authentic human rights protection and human vulnerability.

TWO CONFLICTING TRENDS?

In 2015, 162,877 persons—mainly from Afghanistan, Iraq, and Syria—applied for asylum in Sweden. This was an all-time high for the Nordic country of roughly 9.5 million inhabitants, and more than double the amount of applications received in the peak year of 1992 following the Balkan crisis.[6] To be sure, this peak was not only a consequence of a general increase of migration to Europe, but also because of the absence of adequate migration structures in many European countries and the failure to establish a common EU framework. Amidst widespread, albeit grossly exaggerated, fears that the Swedish welfare state was facing an imminent collapse, the Minority coalition government—consisting of the Social Democrats and the Green Party—decided to introduce a series of temporary measures, explicitly aimed at reducing the flow of migrants, including stricter border controls and new asylum rules adapted to the minimum levels under EU law. As a consequence, the number of applications fell dramatically to a total of 28,939 in 2016 and 25,666 in 2017.[7]

Of the total corpus of applications in 2015, roughly 22 percent were submitted by unaccompanied minors. 66 percent of these were submitted by persons (mostly boys) from Afghanistan, but many also came from Syria, Somalia, Eritrea, Iraq and Ethiopia. Since then, the proportion of applications by unaccompanied minors has dropped dramatically to around 5 percent in 2017. This is partly because of the general measures to reduce the flow of migrants, including the introduction of short-term residence permits and strict rules on family reunification. But the government has also introduced measures specifically targeting unaccompanied children. The most controversial of these was a July 2016 decision to allow the National Board of Forensic Medicine (an expert body within the Swedish judicial system) to carry out medical age assessments—consisting of dental x-rays and MRIs of the knee joint—in cases where a person is unable to produce other forms of evidence for his or her stated age.

Naturally, this procedure raises a wide range of ethical concerns, some of which have been acknowledged by Swedish authorities. In response to a recent government initiative to introduce age assessments already in the early stages of the asylum process, two independent ethical inquiries were carried out, one by the National Board on Health and Welfare, and another by the Swedish National Council on Medical Ethics. These studies identified a number of ethical issues related to autonomy, integrity, justice, gender equality, and the right use of public resources. However, both reports concluded that as long as we accept a system in which children are entitled to special rights—such as cost-free education and healthcare, guardianship, public counsel, and special accommodation—and in which childhood ends on the day you turn eighteen, there must be some reliable and preferably scientific procedure for age verification. Although recognizing that medical age assessments often produce ambiguous results, and recommending that in such doubtful cases the applicant should normally be categorized as a child, both reports endorsed the basic idea of using age verification techniques as a means of alleviating doubts about the truthfulness of applicants' statements in the asylum process.

It should be noted that these conclusions have been questioned by independent scholars. Legal scholar Gregor Noll cites a 2013 Asylum Procedures Directive in EU Law, requiring member states to treat an applicant as a minor until they are no longer "in doubt concerning the applicant's age." Given that the applicant's "ethnic, socio-economic, and stress profile" are all likely to impact the outcome of radiological age assessments, and given the impossibility of conducting baseline studies on the concerned groups, since that would require solid civil registration systems in the countries of origin, Noll concludes that "properly understood advice from a forensic expert . . . *can never dispel doubt*." "The prevailing doubt," he asserts, should therefore "automatically [trigger] the assumption that the applicant is a child."[8]

In a different tenor, pediatrician Lars H Gustafsson laments that the official ethical analyses of medical age assessments have failed to consider the ethical codes of medical practitioners. One study, carried out by the National Board on Health and Welfare, even indicated that those physicians who object to use medical age assessments often do so because of political convictions or personal beliefs. Such assessments, Gustafsson claims, fail to recognize the purely scientific objections to age assessments, but also how the practice discords with guidelines from the World Medical Association, including a 2016 document stating that "physicians cannot be compelled to participate in any punitive or judicial action involving refugees."[9] But the legal and ethical objections to the use of medical age assessments have so far fallen on deaf ears and the practice is now widespread in Swedish asylum processes.

In parallel to the imposition of stricter asylum rules and intensified efforts to weed out the "false minors" in the asylum process, the minority coalition government in 2016 initiated a seemingly disconnected process of incorporating the UN Convention on the Rights of the Child (CRC) of 1989 into Swedish law. This was coupled with a series of legal reforms intended to improve the "child rights perspective" in several domains, including stronger protection of the best interest of the child and the child's right to be heard in the asylum-seeking process.[10]

The initiative to make the CRC part of Swedish law marked what one scholar refers to as "the culmination of nearly three decades of political and societal efforts to implement the CRC and to strengthen the enforcement of children's rights in Sweden."[11] Although Sweden was actively involved in the drafting of this treaty in the 1980s, and was among the first countries to ratify the Convention in 1990, Swedish legislators have generally been unwilling to yield to the repeated calls for incorporation from the UN Committee on the Rights of the Child, as well as by domestic nongovernmental actors. This was so partly because of the established practice of transformation—by which the content of international agreements is translated into national law through the regular legislative process—and partly because of the held belief that Swedish law is already "in harmony" with the content of the CRC.[12]

While the initiative to incorporate the Convention was hailed by many child rights activists, some scholars expressed doubts about the practical effects this would have. Human rights scholars Anna Lundberg and Jacob Lind argue that simply changing the law is unlikely to change the degree to which children's rights are taken seriously in the asylum process. Based on a range of interviews with officers from the Swedish Migration Board, they conclude that what is lacking is not primarily more child-centered laws and policies. Rather, the reason why children's vulnerability and rights are often neglected in administrative processes more often has to do with insufficient training in the art of communicating with children in exposed situations, and, above all, the lack of time and resources. Lundberg and Lind even suggest that the strategy of creating "more rights through more rules" might in fact lead to the opposite result, further legitimizing and cementing established practices that displace children's rights.[13]

These two processes—stricter migration laws on the one hand, and moves to strengthen the legal protection of children's rights on the other—have been regarded as two conflicting trends, creating a paradox in Swedish human rights politics. At the same time, as the Swedish government is joining the European "race to the bottom" in asylum and refugee politics, it is working to strengthen the country's legal framework for the protection of children's rights.[14]

To some extent, this view of a "human rights paradox" is warranted. At any rate, it is clear that many of the most prominent proponents of incorporation of the CRC are also among the most vocal critics of tighter immigration laws and the targeting of young asylum seekers. The Swedish National Ombudsman for Children, for instance, has dismissed the stricter immigration laws after 2015 as "hostile to children."[15] The CRC is also frequently invoked as a normative tool for pinpointing such deficiencies. Those scholars calling for a heightened attention to professional ethics as a basis for justifying resistance among medical personnel to administrative measures targeting refugees and unaccompanied minors also invoke the CRC as one of their central normative resources.

In what follows, we explore the possibility that these two developments, conflicting as they may seem, are different but interconnected symptoms of two broader trends in Swedish human rights politics: 1) the reduction of human rights to positive law, and 2) the reduction of young people's vulnerability to a function of age.

JURIDIFICATION OF HUMAN RIGHTS AND VULNERABILITY

As already mentioned, in 2016, a Swedish government inquiry called on Swedish lawmakers to consider incorporating the UN Convention on the Rights of the Child into Swedish law. The inquiry states that "Incorporation would mean that officials and decision-makers would have to relate to the CRC differently than today, as the Convention would become applicable as law and could be used as the sole basis for authorities' decisions in cases and matters."[16]

The proposal was preceded by an intense period of lobbying activities by human rights organizations—political as well as civil. Being a domestic law implies possibilities to legal enforcement of the demands of the CRC, and supporters of incorporation believe that the very possibility of using the Convention in courts would give the stipulated rights much stronger status. Opponents of incorporation point to several challenges related to legal processes, such as difficulties to apply the Convention's often abstract and general language in particular cases.[17] Even more important is the objection that highlights the fact that human rights protection under the CRC in many cases is weaker compared to other human rights instruments. As Lena Halldenius and Olof Beckman argue, the CRC in fact limits/conditions rights—including freedom of speech and freedom of religion—that are neither limited nor conditioned in other human rights instruments.[18]

To evaluate the arguments in the Swedish debate on incorporation of the CRC is beyond the scope of this chapter. Our aim is rather to scrutinize the very idea that human rights protection is necessarily strengthened if rights are viewed as primarily legal rights. On both sides of the Swedish debate about the CRC, there is a dominant view that what is needed in order to protect children's rights is a firmer legal status of these rights. We are not questioning the motivations behind the will to strengthen children's rights by focusing on the possibility of legal enforcement. However, there is a tendency to reduce human rights of children to the legal dimension of these rights. The idea that the legal status of the CRC is crucial to protection of children is a form of juridification of rights, which underestimates the importance of moral and political dimensions of human rights.

Moral and political components of rights are suppressed if we regard the criterion of legal enforcement of rights as the main or even the only criterion for the quality of a human rights culture. Juridification of human rights is problematic for any settings of human rights, but even more so for children's rights. Children are especially exposed if we expect them to actively claim their rights in the legal domain. There is a debate among legal scholars and lawyers about different methods to strengthen the child rights perspective in legal proceedings, but there is a consensus about the profound difficulty of securing children's agency, and right to be heard, in the legal domain.[19]

Additionally, children are an exposed group in terms of democratic participation and thus have only limited possibilities to morally and politically question legislation and adjudication. Human rights law, as any other positive law, must be evaluated and developed by means of moral critique and democratic deliberation. As Herbert L. Hart put it, the separation between law as it is and law as it ought to be helps us to minimize "the danger that the existing law may supplant morality as a final test of conduct and so escape criticism."[20] Yet, in order to sustain a democratic and critical culture we should not exaggerate the importance of the legal status of human rights documents. While there are good arguments in favor of different ways of framing human rights obligations as legal obligations, no legal technique can solve all moral and political challenges related to human rights protection.

Human rights, we claim, are essentially three-dimensional, namely moral, political, and legal. It is crucial that human rights are related to concrete and contextual forms of violations of human dignity or risks of such a violation. They are related to different types of socially embedded vulnerability and various forms of injustice. Therefore, protection of human rights demands vital moral and political critique of positive law and social practices. In his famous, although often misread,[21] article on human dignity, Oscar Schachter defends this argument and states that the moral principle of human dignity is the foundation of positive rights precisely because it cannot be reduced to positive law. Schachter writes,

> The general idea that human rights are derived from the dignity of the person is neither truistic nor neutral. It has two corollaries that challenge conceptions prevalent in some societies and ideologies. The first corollary is the idea that basic rights are not given by authority and therefore may not be taken away; the

> second is that they are rights of the person, every person. . . . We can extend and strengthen human rights by formulating new rights or by construing existing rights to apply to new situations.[22]

Human dignity is fundamentally related to humanity that, in turn, is vulnerable existentially as well as socially. The recognition of the fact that neither of these forms of vulnerability can be eliminated is crucial for the proper protection of human dignity. When human rights law and human rights politics are framed, the principle of equal respect for human dignity is much more fundamental than the issue of how to define the legal status of international human rights treaties like the CRC. Any positive law needs specified criteria for application by authorities and for adjudication. A reductive understanding of vulnerability is therefore unavoidable in the domain of positive law. The principle of equal respect of human dignity, however, questions any type of reduction and therefore relativizes every legal solution.

Young asylum seekers are vulnerable for several interrelated reasons. Factors like loneliness, lack of resources and language skills, and the stress of being questioned by authorities during their long and dangerous journey to Europe all interact and amplify one another. Simultaneously, this vulnerability makes the legal agency of children even more difficult. Young persons, mostly boys, find themselves in situations where European states expect them to prove their status of eligibility, both in terms of grounds for asylum and regarding their age. In such a situation, the question of legal status of human rights documents seems to be a relatively marginal issue, precisely because even the most advanced legal ways of dealing with refugees' rights transforms the overall vulnerability into a formalized attribute of adjudication: it becomes a vulnerability that has to be objectively proven rather than be humanely trusted.

In the Swedish case, it is not the status of the CRC but the moral sensitivity of citizens and the professional ethics of medical staff that generate the motivation to question the legally approved X-ray and MRI examination of unaccompanied minors seeking asylum. While legal aspects of the procedure have to do with the level of reliability of the examination's conclusions, the moral aspect of it has to do with the way of dealing with highly vulnerable persons. As already stated, many Swedish physicians question the reliability of these examinations. However, the most important issue, we claim, is not this technical reliability. Any society that looks for techniques to replace fundamental human trust by objective evidence—which cannot be obtained without doubt by the existing technologies—weakens its human rights culture.

The Swedish public has now been exposed to strong testimonies of young persons from countries such as Afghanistan, Iraq, and Syria. They all agreed to medical examinations in a desperate effort of trying to make Swedish authorities trust them. In the spring of 2017, a local TV station broadcasted a short documentary about a young refugee from Afghanistan. The boy—Mushtaq—spoke about life back in Afghanistan and how he lost his family on the dangerous path to Europe. After a year and a half in Sweden, Mushtaq was still expected to prove his age to Swedish authorities. Persons who knew him, including professional social workers, were convinced about him being a child as well as about the authenticity of his story. But the authorities were not. Desperate for further evidence, Mushtaq eventually agreed to undergo a medical age assessment. The documentary testifies to the state's profound distrust of asylum seekers, and how it seeks to handle this through the introduction of medical age assessments. In February 2018, a local newspaper in Uppsala published a letter written by Alireza Khademi, another young refugee from Afghanistan, stressing this point: "The only thing you need to do is to trust us. Give us a chance to contribute to society. Let us stay, we can live together."

This profound lack of trust that minors must first overcome before their case to political asylum is heard is not counteracted by the government's project of incorporating the CRC that does not even regulate children's rights in asylum processes. To the contrary, the incorporation might be used as a legitimization of the governmental politics that withholds trust from the most vulnerable human beings. Instead of focusing on the moral and highly political issue of how to secure dignity and rights of young refugees, the government focuses on its efforts to strengthen the status of the Convention by means of a new legal technique.

We argue that a firm protection of human rights, although necessarily including legal arrangements, must also be framed in terms of political justice and equal respect for human dignity. Such an approach includes a domestic as well as a global dimension and forces the government and the public to discuss their priorities in a transparent manner. One important feature of this transparency would be a need to compare what the Swedish state describes as a risk of welfare state collapse with the challenges that other states, such as Lebanon and Turkey, experience when hosting refugees.

To sum up the discussion so far, we argue that legalistic reduction of human rights is especially problematic when vulnerable human beings such as unaccompanied minors are in need of protection. The idea that the legal status of the CRC is the most important criterion of human rights culture is itself reductionist, underestimating the political and moral dimensions of human rights protection. Therefore, although proponents of incorporating the CRC are often motivationally and normatively opposed to the process of legal limitations of migrants' rights, their arguments might in practice strengthen the legalistic reductionism of human rights and therefore weaken human rights as the main instrument for the protection of vulnerable humanity.

CHILDREN'S RIGHTS AS PART OF THE PROBLEM: VULNERABILITY AS A FUNCTION OF AGE

The UN Convention on the Rights of the Child is widely thought of as a centerpiece in the body of international treaties on human rights that evolved during the second half of the twentieth century. To this date, all members of the United Nations except the United States have ratified it. It also serves as the normative bedrock for a whole plethora of non-state, state, and international actors promoting the practical implementation of children's rights. While there is no unequivocal answer to the question of whether the efforts to implement the CRC have led to real gains in children's social standing and well-being on a global scale, it is evident that the Convention has acquired immense discursive power. After its adoption in the fall of 1989, it has come to dominate our understanding of children's rights as a moral, political, and legal concept. As some critics have remarked, it is now virtually impossible to "think" children's rights outside the framework of the Convention.[23]

Much of the available literature on the CRC calls our attention to the ways in which the Convention's content differs from earlier, non-binding international statements on children's rights. One such difference is the inclusion of language on civil and political rights, such as freedom of information, freedom of religion, and the right to be heard in judicial and administrative procedures. In the negotiations on the treaty, the dominant perception of children in international politics underwent what appeared to be a radical transformation. Children, as Anna Holzscheiter writes, went from being constructed as "mute and helpless objects of charity and protection" to "speaking and, accordingly, also 'reasoning' social agents who should be actively involved in the shaping of their own destiny."[24]

In this regard, the CRC could be read as an assertion that children are capable human beings who should enjoy the same basic human rights as adults. At the same time, the CRC also contains provisions intended to address specific vulnerabilities directly linked to the state of childhood. Some of these—for example, the best-interest principle, and protection against abuse and neglect—had already been recognized in international human rights discourse. Others were more novel, including the right to "survival and development," as well as protection against female genital mutilation and military participation. The Convention also specifies that states are responsible to ensure that children seeking refugee status, accompanied or not, are guaranteed basic rights.

What was also novel about the CRC was its aspiration to launch a universal conception of the "child." Earlier international statements—such as the Geneva Declaration on the Rights of the Child of 1924 or the UN Declaration on the Rights of the Child of 1959—had not entailed any provisions clarifying the boundaries of childhood, simply skipping ahead to a list of goods that children should enjoy in order to "develop physically, mentally, morally, spiritually and socially in a healthy and normal manner and in conditions of freedom and dignity." The CRC follows these earlier instruments in so far as it evades the question of when childhood begins. But the Convention is less equivocal on the question of when childhood ends. While allowing states to define the local age of majority, the CRC nonetheless sets eighteen years as the absolute end-point of childhood. As soon as persons are past that point, they are no longer subjects of children's rights.

Much has been written on the eighteen-year threshold. Historians of childhood have taken great lengths to remind us that for the most part of Western history, the transition of childhood to adulthood was not linked to age but to other criteria, such as maturity, work, class, and sexuality. Critics have also remarked that even though the CRC's definition of childhood avoids the arbitrariness that easily comes with alternative definitions, it paves the way for standardized and decontextualized vulnerability assessments.[25] As Mark Drumbl argues, the principal victims of such sharp boundaries tend to be persons in the gray area between childhood and adulthood: "When law internalizes the chronological watershed of the age of eighteen, and turns to it to contrast the capable adult from the incapable child, law creates an exigent situation for young adults. After all, neuroscience teaches us that, as a matter of age, cognitive functions continue to develop well into the mid-twenties. When the law draws bright-lines, outsiders may become excessively exposed to the very vicissitudes from which law aims to insulate insiders."[26]

The introduction of medical age assessments in Swedish asylum procedures is a clear-cut manifestation of the ways in which a legalized discourse of children's rights risks reducing the complex question of vulnerability, and, as a consequence, the question of rights, to the criterion of age. It is telling that the information about these procedures that Swedish authorities provide to young asylum seekers begins by citing the CRC.[27] The Convention thus becomes one of the main grounds for justifying costly and ethically questionable procedures aimed at determining which individuals should be entitled to children's rights (including cost-free education, healthcare, and legal assistance in the asylum-seeking process).

This problematic feature of child rights discourse is also visible in the debate on the status of the CRC into Swedish law. The 2016 government report—which proposed a full incorporation of the treaty—noted that the CRC both recognizes children as full human beings entitled to the same rights as adults, and as "generally more exposed and vulnerable than adults," something which entitles them to a higher degree of protection and additional rights.[28] While this may be true, such generalized assessments are problematic as grounds for determining a person's actual vulnerability and need of protection.

The initiative to make the CRC part of Swedish law also points to the tendency of considering children's rights as separate from the wider field of human rights. The move to incorporate the UNCRC was not launched as part of a comprehensive, national human rights strategy and involved very limited discussion on what this would mean for Sweden's relation to other specialized human rights instruments, such as the Convention Against all Forms of Discrimination Against Women (CEDAW) or the Convention on the Rights of Persons with Disabilities (CRPD). In recent years, we have also seen how more concrete advances in the area of children's rights—including the introduction of cost-free healthcare and education for asylum seekers under eighteen years—have not been matched by similar gains in the rights of persons over eighteen years. While this may be far from what the advocates of children's rights have intended, the child rights discourse has to a large degree helped to play up the significance of the eighteen-year threshold, establishing age as a one-size-fits-all indicator of young people's vulnerability.

BEYOND VULNERABILITY?

If the above-presented argumentation is right, attempts to strengthen the legal status of the CRC on one hand and the harsher asylum laws on the other do not create a paradox because both are manifestations of a weakening human rights culture. This weakening appears in our analysis as two interrelated forms of reductionism: legalistic reduction of human rights protection and a reductionist understanding of human vulnerability. In the context of this chapter, we were mostly concerned with the reductionist understanding of age as the determinant criterion for the vulnerability of young people. These two forms of reductionism are generally problematic because they downplay the moral and political dimensions of human rights. They are directly dangerous if allowed to be instruments for addressing situation of extremely vulnerable people.

When unaccompanied minors seek asylum in Sweden, the state expects them to prove their personal stories in legal processes. Vulnerability is expected to be objectively confirmed. Politicians defending this view claim that if children are to be firmly protected, it is absolutely necessary to draw a line between children and adults.[29] The Swedish government does not believe that distrusting vulnerable individuals and exposing their bodies to medical age assessment contradicts the very moral basis of human rights. Such an understanding of human rights fails to protect obviously vulnerable people in need of protection, but it also weakens human rights culture. Moreover, legalistic inhumane treatment of young refugees, immoral as it is, demonstrates the vulnerability of human rights law, politics, and morality.

Let us further elaborate on this vulnerability. According to the understanding of human rights that we advocate, young refugees are entitled to be treated with respect for their human dignity. Such treatment includes basic trust and this fundamental trust used to be acknowledged by human rights bodies.[30] Additionally, most of young refugees entering Sweden belong to cultures that highly value hospitality toward the stranger. In both Islam and Judaism, the alterity of God is fundamental, and an encounter with the stranger symbolically signifies an encounter with God. Due to the centrality of the belief in God's incarnation in the human, Christian traditions focus more on the likeness. However, Christian traditions also recognize the Son of God in Jesus as a homeless wanderer.[31]

Human rights culture as it has been framed in Sweden today seems to abandon this deeply human insight. One tragic result of the development is the inhumane treatment of young people who risk losing their confidence in human rights.

Moreover, human rights, if reduced to their technical legal dimensions, themselves become "vulnerable" in several ways. First and most importantly, human rights that peacefully coexist with grave injustices lose their legitimacy and become an empty ideology. Secondly, human rights, if framed by differentiating people, can be used and further corrupted by nationalists and even racists. One example may suffice: one of the most exploited images in current racist propaganda against refugees is one image showing small children from Finland entering Sweden during World War II, a sharp contrast to older young boys from Afghanistan and Syria entering Sweden today. Thirdly, if human rights legitimize inhumane treatment of obviously vulnerable humans, they can contribute to even lower sensitivity to human suffering and a weaker social contract in Swedish society in the long run. Swedish citizens have a high level of social trust and are ready to contribute to social security. Mistrust of people in need of support is fundamentally opposite to the Swedish model of society as the world knows it.

Therefore, we believe that the current situation in Sweden calls for a serious reevaluation of the human rights culture and vulnerability. Such a reevaluation must include the insight that human vulnerability neither can nor should be reduced to what can be incorporated in legal techniques. At the other end of the spectrum, human rights protect vulnerable persons because human rights essentially differ from a ground sentiment that calls for protection. Properly practiced human rights protection does not demand "the pity sentiment" of the majority population. What it does demand is a political and human sensitivity toward violated human dignity, that is, toward undignified human conditions. The dignity of a lonely and terrified person's humanity is violated when mistrust escalates to such a degree that the usage of dental x-rays and MRIs of the knee joint is legitimized before their vulnerability is acknowledged. We do hope that the Swedish situation will change and those who today defend a view on human rights which is fundamentally different from that expressed by refugee politics will reaffirm Sweden's decent human rights culture.

NOTES

1. See, for example, Michael Ignatieff, *Human Rights as Politics and Idolatry* (Princeton: Princeton University Press, 2001).
2. For the latest statistics, see the webpage of the Swedish Board of Migration, https://www.migrationsverket.se/English/About-the-Migration-Agency/Facts-and-statistics-/Statistics.html, accessed February 26, 2018.
3. The Ombudsman for Children in Sweden, "Vi lämnade allt och kom hit': Röster från barn och unga på flykt," Stockholm, 2017, 21, https://www.google.com/url?sa=t&rct=j&q=&esrc=s&source=web&cd=3&ved=0ahUKEwjbxK7xsojbAhXDtVkKHWv7DzMQFghBMAI&url=https%3A%2F%2Fwww.barnombudsmannen.se%2Fglobalassets%2Fdokument-for-nedladdning%2Fpublikationer%2Fvi_lamnade_allting_och_kom_hit_barnombudsmannen_2017.pdf&usg=AOvVaw2Dm8Ft50e-US9JS4Ug7c7J.
4. Cited in Rebecca Thorburn Stern, *Implementing Article 12 of the UN Convention on the Rights of the Child: Participation, Power and Attitudes* (Leiden: Brill Nijhoff 2017), 119.
5. Hille Haker, "Vulnerable Agency: Human Dignity and Gendered Violence," in *Dignity and Conflict: Contemporary Interfaith Dialogue on the Value and Vulnerability of Human Life*, eds. Jonathan Rothschildt and Matthew Petrusek (Notre Dame: University of Notre Dame Press, 2018 forthcoming), 393–436.
6. Swedish Migration Agency, "Nearly 163,000 people sought asylum in Sweden in 2015," accessed December 16, 2017, https://www.migrationsverket.se/English/About-the-Migration-Agency/News-archive/News-archive-2016/2016-01-12-Nearly-163000-people-sought-asylum-in-Sweden-in-2015.html.
7. 10,909 of these were registered as minors, and 2,199 as unaccompanied minors. See the Ombudsman for Children in Sweden, "*Vi lämnade allt och kom hit,*" 12.
8. Gregor Noll, "Junk Science? Four Arguments Against the Radiological Age Assessment of Unaccompanied Minors Seeking Asylum," *International Journal of Refugee Law* 28, no. 2 (2016): 249.
9. Lars H Gustafsson, "Läkaren som statens hjälpreda. Om yrkesetik och mänskliga rättigheter," *Socialmedicinsk tidskrift* 94, no. 5 (2017): 556–564.
10. Ministry of Health and Social Affairs, "Barnkonventionen blir svensk lag," SOU 2016:19 (Stockholm, 2016), 174–181, https://skl.se/download/18.755485c815b6ce426f76ead5/1492591454022/barnkonventionen-blir-svensk-lag-sou-2016_19.pdf.

11. Jonathan Josefsson, "*Children at the Borders*" (PhD dissertation, Linköping University, 2016), 10.

12. For more on the status of the CRC in Swedish law, see Thorburn Stern, *Implementing Article 12,* 123–130.

13. Anna Lundberg and Jacob Lind, "Technologies of Displacement and Children's Right to Asylum in Sweden," *Human Rights Review* 18, no. 2 (2017): 189–208.

14. See, for example, Ulf Bjerled, "Föreslagna flyktinglagarna försämrar integrationen," *Dagens Nyheter,* March 11, 2016; Victor Banke, "Regeringen har tappat känslan för barns rättigheter," *Dagens Nyheter,* March 15, 2016.

15. Cited in Josefsson, "Children at the Borders," 10.

16. Ministry of Health and Social Affairs, "Barnkonventionen blir svensk lag," 54.

17. Anna Singer, "Alla talar om barns rätt," in *Festskrift till Anna Hollander: Rätt, social utsatthet och samhälleligt ansvar* (Stockholm: Norstedts Juridik, 2012), 73–86.

18. Lund University, Department of History, "Yttrande om Barnrättsutredningens slutbetänkande Barnkonventionen blir svensk lag. SOU 2016:19," October 4, 2016.

19. For a recent assessment of the child's right to be heard, see Aoife Daly, *Children, Autonomy and the Courts: Beyond the Right to Be Heard* (Leiden: Brill Nijhoff, 2018).

20. H. L. A Hart, "Positivism and the Separation of Law and Morals," *Harvard Law Review* 71, no. 4 (1958): 597.

21. What we have in mind here is the way Schachter is used in the current American debate on bioethics. Opponents of the usage of human dignity within the field of bioethics used to recapitulate Schachter's view of human dignity as an abstract principle without mentioning that, according to Schachter, precisely this makes the principle valuable to the law.

22. Oscar Schachter, "Human Dignity as a Normative Concept," *The American Journal of International Law* 77 no. 4 (1983): 853.

23. Josefsson, "Children at the Borders," 23.

24. Anna Holzscheiter, *Children's Rights in International Politics: The Transformative Power of Discourse* (Hampshire: Palgrave Macmillan, 2010), 2.

25. David M. Rosen, *Child Soldiers in the Western Imagination: From Patriots to Victims* (New Brunswick: Rutgers University Press, 2015), 177.

26. Mark A. Drumbl, *Reimagining Child Soldiers in International Law and Policy* (New York: Oxford University Press), 17.

27. The National Board of Forensic Medicine, "Medicinska åldersbedömningar i asylärenden," accessed January 16, 2018, https://www.rmv.se/verksamheter/medicinska-aldersbedomningar/medicinska-aldersbedomningar-asylarenden.

28. *Barnkonventionen blir svensk lag,* 91, 260, 478.

29. Annie Reutersköld, "Trots starka kritiken: Sverige fortsätter att åldersbedöma," *Svenska Dagbladet,* January 9, 2018.

30. In March 2010 the United Nations High Commissioner for Refugees published a research report on asylum procedures in Europe. The results of the report confirm that the issue of identity is often given priority at the cost of investigations of refugees' reasons for application. Commenting on the procedure of interviews, the report states that "approximately two-thirds of interview time was dedicated to gathering bio-data and information on the travel route, and only one third of the interview time was dedicated to exploring the reasons for the application. UNHCR was concerned to

note that in some of the interviews observed in these Member States, questioning with regard to the reasons for the application tended to be superficial, formalistic or insufficient to elicit all the facts that are relevant to qualification for international protection. Questioning was often more extended and more probing with regard to the identity of and travel route taken by the applicant." United Nations High Commissioner for Refugees, "Improving Asylum Procedures. Comparative Analysis and Recommendations for Law and Practice," (Brussels, 2010), 39, http://www.unhcr.org/protection/operations/4ba9d99d9/improving-asylum-procedures-comparative-analysis-recommendations-law-practice.html.

31. Elena Namli, *Human Rights as Ethics, Politics, and Law* (Uppsala: Acta Universitatis Upsaliensis, 2014): 147–166.

BIBLIOGRAPHY

Banke, Victor. "Regeringen har tappat känslan för barns rättigheter." *Dagens Nyheter,* March 15, 2016.

Bjereld, Ulf. "Föreslagna flyktinglagarna försämrar integrationen." *Dagens Nyheter,* March 11, 2016.

Daly, Aoife. *Children, Autonomy and the Courts: Beyond the Right to Be Heard.* Leiden: Brill Nijhoff, 2018.

Drumbl, Mark A. *Reimagining Child Soldiers in International Law and Policy.* New York: Oxford University Press, 2016.

Gustafsson, Lars H. "Läkaren som statens hjälpreda. Om yrkesetik och mänskliga rättigheter." *Socialmedicinsk tidskrift* 94, no. 5 (2017): 556–564.

Haker, Hille. "Vulnerable Agency: Human Dignity and Gendered Violence." In *Dignity and Conflict: Contemporary Interfaith Dialogue on the Value and Vulnerability of Human Life,* edited by Jonathan Rothschildt and Matthew Petrusek, 393–436. Notre Dame: University of Notre Dame Press, 2018, forthcoming.

Hart, H. L. A. "Positivism and the Separation of Law and Morals." *Harvard Law Review* 71, no. 4 (1958): 593–629.

Holzscheiter, Anna. *Children's Rights in International Politics: The Transformative Power of Discourse.* Hampshire: Palgrave Macmillan, 2010.

Ignatieff, Michael. *Human Rights as Politics and Idolatry.* Princeton: Princeton University Press, 2001.

Josefsson, Jonathan. "Children at the Borders." PhD dissertation, Linköping University, 2016.

Lundberg, Anna, and Lind, Jacob. "Technologies of Displacement and Children's Right to Asylum in Sweden." *Human Rights Review* 18, no. 2 (2017): 189–208.

Lund University, Department of History. "Yttrande om Barnrättsutredningens slutbetänkande Barnkonventionen blir svensk lag. SOU 2016:19" October 4, 2016.

Ministry of Health and Social Affairs. "Barnkonventionen blir svensk lag." SOU 2016:19, Stockholm, 2016. https://skl.se/download/18.755485c815b6ce426f76ead5/1492591454022/barnkonventionen-blir-svensk-lag-sou-2016_19.pdf.

Namli, Elena. *Human Rights as Ethics, Politics, and Law*. Uppsala: Acta Universitatis Upsaliensis, 2014.

Noll, Gregor. "Junk Science? Four Arguments Against the Radiological Age Assessment of Unaccompanied Minors Seeking Asylum." *International Journal of Refugee Law* 28, no. 2 (2016): 234–250.

Reutersköld, Annie. "Trots starka kritiken: Sverige fortsätter att åldersbedöma." *Svenska Dagbladet,* January 9, 2018.

Rosen, David M. *Child Soldiers in the Western Imagination: From Patriots to Victims*. New Brunswick: Rutgers University Press, 2015.

Schachter, Oscar. "Human Dignity as a Normative Concept." *The American Journal of International Law* 77 no. 4 (1983): 848–854.

Singer, Anna. "Alla talar om barns rätt." In *Festskrift till Anna Hollander: Rätt, social utsatthet och samhälleligt ansvar*. Stockholm: Norstedts Juridik, 2012.

Swedish Migration Agency. "Nearly 163,000 people sought asylum in Sweden in 2015." accessed December 16, 2017. https://www.migrationsverket.se/English/About-the-Migration-Agency/News-archive/News-archive-2016/2016–01–12-Nearly-163000-people-sought-asylum-in-Sweden-in-2015.html.

The National Board of Forensic Medicine. "Medicinska åldersbedömningar i asylärenden." accessed January 16, 2018. https://www.rmv.se/verksamheter/medicinska-aldersbedomningar/medicinska-aldersbedomningar-asylarenden.

The Ombudsman for Children in Sweden. "Vi lämnade allt och kom hit': Röster från barn och unga på flykt." Stockholm, 2017. https://www.google.com/url?sa=t&rct=j&q=&esrc=s&source=web&cd=3&ved=0ahUKEwjbxK7xsojbAhXDtVkKHWv7DzMQFghBMAI&url=https%3A%2F%2Fwww.barnombudsmannen.se%2Fglobalassets%2Fdokument-for-nedladdning%2Fpublikationer%2Fvi_lamnade_allting_och_kom_hit_barnombudsmannen_2017.pdf&usg=AOvVaw2Dm8Ft50e-US9JS4Ug7c7J.

Thorburn Stern, Rebecca. *Implementing Article 12 of the UN Convention on the Rights of the Child: Participation, Power and Attitudes*. Leiden: Brill Nijhoff 2017.

United Nations High Commissioner for Refugees. *Improving Asylum Procedures. Comparative Analysis and Recommendations for Law and Practice.* Brussels, 2010. http://www.unhcr.org/protection/operations/4ba9d99d9/improving-asylum-procedures-comparative-analysis-recommendations-law-practice.html.

Part III

CATHOLIC ETHICS AND CHILD MIGRATION

Chapter 8

Holy Family or Holy Child?

Child Migrants as Vulnerable Agents

Cristina L. H. Traina

Each year the United States Border Patrol apprehends tens of thousands of unaccompanied child migrants at the nation's southern border.[1,2] Simply by exercising the initiative to journey alone to the United States, these children contradict the ideal of sheltered childhood written into most of US law and into middle- and upper-class US culture. They also contradict the Roman Catholic Holy Family narrative that subsumes migrant children into parent-headed families, rather than treating them as individuals. Migrant children force us to confront the fact that children are both vulnerable persons—as the US culture of protected childhood implies—and active agents of their own welfare—as their arrival here attests. Although their need for supportive, reliable adults is certainly one dimension of their age-related vulnerabilities, the shorthand of family-centered migration policy does not suffice to express the respect US policy and Catholic teaching on migration owe to them as communally embedded agents in their own rights. We must move from reflection guided mainly by Holy Family imagery to ethics guided by Jesus's direct invitation to children (Mt 19:14), as well as by the preteen Jesus's own purposeful detour to the Temple (Lk 2:41–51).

RHETORIC THAT CONCEALS

At first glance, children are ubiquitous in Roman Catholic documents on migration. "Children of God" and its close relative, "family of God," appear frequently in recent summaries of Vatican teaching on migration, in the closing prayer of John Paul II's apostolic exhortation *Ecclesia in America*, and in the United States Conference of Catholic Bishops (USCCB) documents *Welcoming the Stranger Among Us* (2000) and *Strangers No Longer* (2003).[3]

In each case, however, the focus is not on the chronological period of childhood but on our shared relationship with God, our common Father, which unites all people in a single human family of mutual love, care, and justice.

To be sure, the tropes "children of God" and "family of God" are indispensable elements of Christian theology, not to mention of a robust, critical, prophetic Christian ethic of migration. Kristin Heyer, among others, has demonstrated this connection.[4] However, in Roman Catholic teaching, documents on migration tend to obscure actual children. They appear mainly as the offspring of migrant parents: children who are either mourning the loss of mothers and fathers who migrated to seek work and left them behind, or juggling confusing conflicts between their migrant families' cultures of origin and the new cultures in which they are being raised. Typically, these documents subsume children in the family that deserves to migrate together or to be reunited when separated.

As Heyer has pointed out, the documents' rhetoric of family conjures the modern Western nuclear family: mother and father protecting their relatively helpless children within the cocoon of the household.[5] The image recalls the Holy Family in flight to Egypt, cited by Pius XII in his 1952 Apostolic Constitution *Exsul Familia Nazarethana*.[6] From this perspective, "the family" is shorthand for parents who care for their children by interacting politically, economically, and socially in the wider world from which they also protect their children. For instance, responding to US migration policies that regularly separate parents from children, the 2011 USCCB document on immigration enforcement calls for "family-based" reforms in immigration policy, and a follow-up 2013 document likewise stresses the need to preserve family unity and the rights of parents to provide for their children without leaving them.[7]

The assumptions in these documents hobble ethical analysis by obscuring some of the agents in their narratives. Here, social and political justice for families is thought to guarantee children's safety and well-being: family unity and welfare imply child welfare. In addition, parents are actors, and children are acted upon, implying that children are never, and never need to be, agents of their own welfare. This language mirrors current American political rhetoric about child migrants, in which, for example, undocumented immigrants who have qualified for the US Deferred Action for Childhood Arrivals (DACA) program are almost uniformly described having been brought to the United States "through no fault of their own," as powerless victims of adult decisions.[8] Of all the recent Catholic documents, only *Strangers No Longer* mentions children as migrant persons in their own rights, once briefly and extremely obliquely—"entire villages . . . depopulated of their young people," which implies that youth migrated without their adult relatives—and once directly—condemning "shameful" US treatment of undocumented, unaccompanied Latin American children apprehended near the border.[9] But even these nods to unaccompanied child migration do not examine undocumented child migrants as the active agents they must be if they are to migrate at all.

To be sure, unaccompanied child migration is a horror and an injustice that is a product of other horrors and injustices we must correct. But until we do, we are accountable to the children who arrive. As citizens of a nation that apprehends tens of thousands of unaccompanied migrant children annually at its southern border alone, American Christians are obligated to reflect honestly both on these children's vulnerabilities and on their special agency. As voters and providers of social services, they must have a sophisticated understanding of these children if they wish truly to help them. As will be clear, child migrants should not be treated exactly as adults. Nevertheless, I argue that unaccompanied child migrants are not merely passive victims of adult decisions or incapable beings whose futures should be determined entirely by others. Rather children, like all persons, are vulnerable agents who pursue the good within circumstantial constraints. Some of children's vulnerabilities are peculiar to their stage of life, and all need to be accommodated, but none erase their agency.

In what follows, I first describe vulnerable agency generally. Then, drawing on previous theorizations of my own and Hille Haker's, I argue that childhood renders unaccompanied migrants vulnerable in specific, human ways that demand accommodation. I fill in some of the details of these vulnerabilities from accounts of child migrants' experiences. Finally, I argue that the clashes among the visions of children's agency implied in children's own accounts and in their treatment in immigration detention and courts reveal the inadequacy of both American liberal developmental visions of childhood and Roman Catholic Christian leaders' eclipse of children by the nuclear family. Rather, child migrants force us to see that migrant children exercise their dignified right to act, if vulnerably, for their own and their families' welfare. As Kate Ward's account of virtue reminds us, they can do so best when not isolated from community in immigration detention or in court.

CHILD MIGRANTS AS VULNERABLE AGENTS

The stories Valeria Luiselli records for refugee children in *Tell Me How It Ends*, the complex, harrowing trips from Honduras to California that Sonia Nazario recounts in *Enrique's Journey*, and the US immigration detention experiences that Susan Terrio analyzes in *Whose Child Am I?* all describe children as intentionally acting to maximize their own and often others' welfare by migrating.[10] First, as Heyer also notes, these children and their families tend not to live or embrace a middle-class liberal ideal of nuclear family. Rather, their families are large, complex networks of blood and social kin that both transcend the nuclear model and compensate for some of the fractures that poverty and conflict inflict on nuclear households.[11] Even when migrating alone, child migrants see their own decisions as corporate and see themselves as supported by and responsible for the support of these extended family networks.

Second, whether escaping gangs or abusive families, attempting to reunite with migrant parents, or hoping to work to provide for family members at home, these children are active subjects of their own welfare. Sometimes parents themselves, they are described by US Office of Refugee Resettlement workers as "not kids" and "long past parenting."[12] Because they have strategized long, dangerous trips (often without the aid of an adult coyote) for clear, complex ends, they do not fit neatly into a liberal, paternalistic vision of children as subject to the guidance and control of adults who act "in their best interests" and meter new adult responsibilities out to them gradually. They demand treatment as full, dignified agents who, despite needing support to develop their capacities, are in charge of themselves.

These children's lives reveal universal truths of childhood and agency that the liberal, nuclear family model of childhood obscures. As I have argued elsewhere, *all* children are embedded and interact in networks of social, familial relationships, encountering law and social institutions constantly and directly, rather than only indirectly, through the buffering influences of adults around them. Their age, their inability to give fully articulate reasons for their considered actions, and their incomplete autonomy do not remove their agency in this complex world, even when they render it more challenging.[13] Indeed, except for age, the qualities that qualify their agency characterize adult agents to various degrees.[14]

The other side of children's embedded, relational agency is their openness to their social and physical environs, a vulnerability that shapes them and also makes them susceptible to particular kinds of harms.[15] Like all migrants, unaccompanied migrant children are vulnerable to death, amputation, de facto enslavement, sexual assault, indefinite custody, and deportation, to name a few of the dangers. But some of their vulnerabilities are pegged to or magnified by age. In particular, children have short histories: their experiences are limited, which makes them vulnerable to particular kinds of exploitation. They have long futures: especially given their deeply impressionable stage of life, both the true benefits and the deep harms they experience in childhood are likely to reverberate for decades in their lives and in their networks.[16] For instance, childhood sexual abuse can lead to a lifetime of destructive relationships, with harsh consequences for one's own children.[17] In what follows, I loosely engage Hille Haker's tripartite vision of ontological, structural, and moral vulnerability to articulate the ways in which migrant children's particular vulnerabilities inflect their agency without erasing it.

MODES OF VULNERABILITY

If vulnerability is to be useful in ethics, it cannot remain generic. A moral anthropology must describe the particular ways in which human beings are open to the world, as well as describe the mutually entailed benefits and dangers of that openness. Haker distinguishes three connected, interdependent realms of human vulnerability. Ontological vulnerabilities arise because we are biological organisms inhabiting an environment beyond our control, an environment that not only affects but forms us as persons. Structural vulnerabilities—which are primarily negative in Haker's telling—arise when socially powerful groups put other socially recognized groups (identified, e.g., by gender, sexual orientation, religion, nationality, race or ethnicity) in institutional jeopardy; their marginalization limits their scope of action in the world. Moral vulnerability is the risk that moral integrity will be harmed so that one is unable to form or maintain a consistent moral identity, so that one becomes unable to see oneself both as truly unique and as a member of the common human community. Another way to put this is that a person with an intact moral identity can safely "be oneself" in social relations and does not need to dissemble by holding a dual identity.[18] Further, moral vulnerability entails being shaped morally, for good or ill, by surrounding circumstances and people. For instance, a preteen from Chiapas in search of community could adopt the ethics of the violent gangs that prey on passengers of northbound freight trains without experiencing a conflict between his social and personal, universal and unique conceptions of the self.[19] His moral wound is a true moral harm even if it does not divide his identity.

Ontological Vulnerability

The vulnerability of being an organism in the world both inspires migration and besets the journey, especially for undocumented migrants. Youth only magnifies this vulnerability. In general, survival drives the decision to migrate. Adults often migrate to support children at home, and children may migrate to join them. But children may migrate to support their families at home too, or to flee danger or debilitating poverty. Terrio tells stories of children escaping the possibly fatal threats of gangs and domestic abuse, seeking basic support for themselves and their families at home or hoping to end the Catch-22 choice, for example, between eating and getting an education.[20] Journeys through Mexico to the southern border of the United States, too, are fights for survival: avoiding abandonment, kidnappers, gangs, traffickers, rapists, and the police; holding on to money and phone numbers; finding food, water, and shelter; keeping clear of the wheels and couplings of freight cars, and of tree branches and low tunnels that can sweep one off the top of the cars; surviving the heat of the desert.[21] Although the need for food, water, and clothing can be a point of connection—in the past, some residents of Veracruz and Oaxaca made a ministry of feeding freight train riders, even convincing engineers to slow down to make it easier for them to toss goods to passengers—basic survival is more a point of anxiety for these children than an opportunity.[22]

Children's particular susceptibilities exaggerate the ontological vulnerabilities of all migrants whose survival forces them toward the United States. Their small size means they are easily ignored, outrun, or overpowered; they are also more susceptible to dehydration, illness, and lack of food. In need of protection, or simply companionship, they are vulnerable to older children or adults who victimize them through extortion, smuggling, and sexual abuse, particularly if they need money to pay coyotes or continue their journeys.

Some children are naïve not only about their companions on the journey but also about their chances. Terrio describes one Mexican children's shelter director who soberly reminded a group of children heading north of the likelihood of their deaths on the journey and the unlikelihood of their ever returning home; asked whether they still wanted to ride the train, all the children eagerly raised their hands.[23] For others, youth coexists with circumstances that erode what we think of as "natural" developmental naiveté. Terrio also recounts children's chilling pragmatism, demonstrated in calculated decisions to migrate, wagering certain physical death or social marginalization at home against only possible death or injury on the journey.[24] The circumstances of their short pasts are so oppressive that they bet on their long futures: they may succeed in reaching the United States and making a claim for asylum, or they may arrive and escape detection. In this case, children's political and economic situations, products of forces much larger than they, put them in the most vulnerable position possible: risking death to live.

Children who migrate demonstrate profound, persevering agency in the face of danger. Sonia Nazario's subject Enrique, for example, made eight attempts simply to survive the trip from Guatemala through the province of Chiapas without detection, and he succeeded only after a gang beating that marred him for life. A choice between certain and likely death calls forth a kind of agency than no one, child or adult, should face. Thus ontological vulnerability points to structural failures in home-country politics, international economic conditions, and US immigration systems, all of which marginalize children differently than they marginalize adults.

Structural Vulnerability

Structural vulnerabilities belong to groups that are susceptible to systematic marginalization and disempowerment; only systematic structural supports can protect them against this marginalization. Undocumented Latin American immigrants to the United States are by definition not just structurally vulnerable, but structurally marginalized. Not only are they migrating to escape untenable political and economic situations, but they also have few presumptive legal rights in the United States; they are not fully aware of the processes through which they might be able to request asylum; and they are often deported before they have the chance to make that case. Language barriers increase their structural vulnerability.

Their relative lack of experience and knowledge makes unaccompanied children even more vulnerable structurally than adults, in ways that make them susceptible to transgressions of their human rights. For instance, children are less likely than adults to know how to protest their treatment in the "Icebox," an Immigration and Customs Enforcement (ICE) holding facility where unaccompanied children have been subjected to frigid temperatures and fed frozen sandwiches after being apprehended by the US Border Patrol.[25] This disadvantage is compounded by institutional impediments that also stymie their agency: procedures that are inadequate to their legal purposes, conflicts of jurisdiction and philosophy among government institutions that deal with child migrants, and gaps in the structures. Unaccompanied children will suffer systemically until structural protections adequate to their specific needs are in place.

Valeria Luiselli's *Tell Me How It Ends* illustrates the first problem, inadequate procedures to the systemic protections offered. Luiselli, a native Spanish speaker, volunteered to interview undocumented, mostly unaccompanied children whose eligibility for legal representation in immigration court depended on their giving answers to standard interview questions that touched on criteria that could trigger an asylum case.[26] (This is a further structural vulnerability: children must go to court without a lawyer to prove that they merit legal representation.) Although the questions were too abstract for most children to comprehend or to answer usefully, Luiselli was forbidden to interpret the questions or steer the answers, and the children were to reply without the help or even the supportive presence of adult family members or guardians. One interview proceeded this way:

How did you travel here?
A man brought us.
A coyote?
No, a man.

Was he nice to you?
Yes, he was nice, I think.
And where did you cross the border?
I don't know.
Texas? Arizona?
Yes! Texas Arizona.[27]

In this case, Luiselli called on the child's mother to fill in some details, breaking protocol in the interest of accuracy. The structural problem is that the procedures created to protect children who may need legal representation in an asylum case cannot reliably produce the information needed to reach the judgment. The situation resembles the skit in which a blindfolded person acts as the hands for another person who is guiding her orally. Yet this is not comedy, but a decision of legal justice in which the default result is deportation.

Susan Terrio's analysis of interviews and policy reveal conflicts in structures and expectations that, ostensibly intended to protect unaccompanied children as a vulnerable group, actually jeopardize children's situations at every turn. To find shelter and begin their asylum process, unaccompanied children turn themselves in to the Border Patrol, which turns them over to ICE, which attempts to justify their deportation before turning a fraction of them over to the Office of Refugee Resettlement (ORR). In contrast to ICE's presumptions about children's criminality, ORR's goal is to care for them during their immigration hearing process in ways that are compatible with "the best interests of the child," but security and liability rationales tend to yield detention in prison-like facilities with rigorous behavior codes rather than release to relatives. For example, Fernanda described strict limits on time for hygiene, as well as rules against not just touching but approaching within arms' length of another child, as well as against running or sending messages to other children in the facility. All behavior irregularities (like waking in the night) were noted, and children were warned that ORR staff reports of rule violations would harm their cases in court.[28] What is more, the uncertain calendars of asylum proceedings create anxiety among older children who, when they "age out" at eighteen, are shipped summarily to adult detention centers where they may need to start their cases over again. In addition, ORR's efforts to conform the unaccompanied children to middle class, white American templates of childhood devalue the adult capacities for self-reliant strategizing that the children developed on their difficult journeys to the border, not to mention dishonor their worries about providing for their families or paying off coyotes. For example, Terrio reports children who have been looking out for themselves being shoehorned into a strict schedule of adult-led formal education, organized recreation, field trips, and supervised social events with the objective of helping them recover a childhood they may never have had.[29] To be sure, solo migrant children have suffered unjustly, but their treatment in ORR facilities should build on the strengths they have acquired in their sufferings, not devalue them. Terrio all but concludes that conflicting goals within and among agencies and in the courts create no-win situations for unaccompanied children: they are alternately viewed as incompetent or as fully accountable, as innocent and victimized or as criminal, as informed and savvy or as ignorant and needing to be "managed."[30]

Gaps in children's immigration detention and hearing systems make for arbitrary and unjust differences in process. A "fast track" created for evaluating young children's immigration cases has stressed courts, pro bono attorneys, and volunteers like Luiselli so severely that outcomes have seemed, and probably are, random.[31] Throughout her book, Terrio notes instances of confidential information being shared inappropriately among agencies as well as failures to share information within agencies, both to children's disadvantage. Novario frankly admits that the Honduran teenager whose odyssey is the focus of her book would never have succeeded in gaining residency were it not for his extraordinary good luck in being represented by two diligent pro bono attorneys; had others not found him representation, or had the representation been less energetic, his case would have failed.[32] In short, the structural conflicts in some realms and the lack of clear structure in others make children's journey through the legal system more like a random lottery than a clear process of justice, giving them little opportunity to engage knowledgeably or effectively on their own behalf. This is especially ironic because they could not have arrived in immigration courts without having exercised their initiative insistently and strategically. To be sure, versions of many of these difficulties plague adult migrants as well, but ironically, their ostensible legal responsibility for themselves at least tempers the ambiguities children experience.

Structural problems reverberate ontologically as well. Terrio notes that the indefinite calendar for detention and deliberate withholding of information about their cases led many children to decline psychologically, with detrimental effects on their behavior and their chances for remaining in the United States.[33] Structural issues can cause moral conflicts, too, for both children and their advocates, as well as deeper wounds in moral identity and moral formation. In all these cases children must operate within structures ostensibly set up to protect their particular vulnerabilities that instead expose them systematically to fresh dangers and conflicts.

Moral Vulnerability

Because people do much of the work of forming their identities, relationships, and moral compass in childhood, moral violence harms them even more deeply than it harms adults. Children's vulnerability is not just a matter of their current impressionability and susceptibility to manipulation; moral violence can scar them for the long term, multiplying its effects in their long futures.

Most of the moral violence of migration and application for residency erupts from structural vulnerabilities. Nazario writes of girls who try to discourage rape on their journey through Mexico by passing as boys or writing "Tengo SIDA" ("I have AIDS") on their chests.[34] Some children must decide whether to accept residency with strings: U visas, which reward applicant victims' cooperation in solving a crime and could expose them to retaliation by neighbors, or SIJS visas, which acknowledge children's abuse, abandonment, or neglect by relatives at home but forbid the children to sponsor any relatives for immigration later.[35] Terrio tells many stories of children who want to escape the dehumanizing conditions of detention centers for the homes of extended family living in the United States but face judgments that these families are inadequate (by white middle-class US standards) to host them, or feel guilty that they will overburden or endanger their families, or are refused by them. Advocates, too, suffer moral dilemmas: Luiselli constantly worries about how much she should press for information on possible experiences that might qualify children to stay in the United States, especially given that the children themselves are usually unaware of the criteria, which she is not permitted to share with them. Members of the aid group No More Deaths have been arrested for supplying migrants with water, clothing, and medical care.[36]

These structurally imposed dilemmas signal harm to children's moral agency in both ways described above. With respect to identity, immigration detention contradicts and fractures the selves that children form in the process of traveling to the United States. Their journeys demand that they develop laser focus, perceptiveness, perseverance, creativity, resilience, collaboration, and canniness. In the process of attempting to support unaccompanied children by compensating for their vulnerabilities, the conflicting goals of US immigration enforcement and refugee protection systems frequently end up disrespecting children's hard-won, self-motivated, self-responsible agency in the world by reducing them to objects of others' decisions about their "best interests." To make matters worse, children's best bets for gaining legal standing often depend on their presenting themselves as sympathetic victims, passive sufferers of violence or neglect. In detention, their caretakers' practices of withholding information about their cases and treatment and their demands that they behave as victims and docile subjects also contradict their legitimate vision of themselves as strong, thoughtful actors.[37] Terrio's account of one ORR staff member's matter-of-fact description of immigration detention practices sums up the problem: "We give them choices and freedom so that they *think* they have control."[38] Further, evaluation and decision processes, especially the SIJS visa process, contradict children's identities as responsible members of interdependent families (whom children often cannot safely contact or claim because they are also undocumented) at the same time that it punishes their unwanted isolation.[39] In this way, the processes fracture the very sense of a connected, integrated self that may have inspired them to travel to the United States alone in the first place. Finally, as all three authors illustrate vividly, the same children who are treated in detention as non-agents who must be represented and guided by others are expected to function in court as adults, with few or no structural accommodations for their youth.

Not surprisingly, children with strong grasps on their own goals—particularly older children—have some resources to resist this fracturing of their identity. For instance, children in detention may consciously adopt docility and cooperation as tactics to achieve their goals of legal residency. Terrio recounts one case of a detained teen who modeled such strategic behavior specifically to help new residents in their own efforts.[40] Still, such tactics reinforce rather than resolve the mismatch between children's own self-concepts and the many identities imposed on them by their unavoidable interactions with coyotes, Border Patrol agents, ICE and ORR employees, and judges. Although opportunities to tell their own stories may help children to integrate their identities as foreigners, family members, migrants, and seekers of permanent residency, these opportunities do not relieve the conflicts and stresses that fracture identity to begin with.[41]

Certainly some of the detention systems' conflicting treatment of children unfolds from the psychic wounds caused by their real traumatization: rapes, beatings, robberies, injuries, abandonment, trafficking, and other offenses. In this necessary work, the line between humane treatment for damages caused by trauma and consequent claims about children's debilitation that can be used to circumscribe children's agency or dismiss children's desires is not always clear, producing another opportunity for identity fracture and silencing.[42] But such trauma also causes other kinds of moral harm: damage to children's relationships and to their sense of moral integrity. When children left behind by parents migrating for work make the strenuous trip to reunite with them, often years later, their parents are ensconced in new lives and, often, new families. The children often have a difficult time overcoming the hurt, mistrust, and resentment caused by their sense that they were abandoned by parents who led happier lives without them even while supporting them financially from a distance, and by their own displacement by often much younger, still very dependent siblings.[43] Luiselli and Terrio both describe children who are wracked by guilt that relatives in the United States must support them, or that relatives at home or in the United States paid for their travel, or that they may "out" undocumented US family members who take them in, or that their detention or the schooling that is a condition of their release from detention prevents them from working to support their families at home financially.

The children's feelings of distress and guilt point to the unjust circumstances that force children into survival and loyalty choices they should not have to make. Choosing to leave immigration detention for the community of extended family can mean choosing to endanger another person. Choosing to be sheltered by gang members on "La Bestia" (The Beast), the Mexican northbound freight train, can mean choosing to betray a fellow traveler or at least to risk owing the gang members a possibly violent favor. Choosing survival after kidnapping might entail choosing to run drugs or turn tricks for a border gang. Unaccompanied migrant children constantly find themselves in situations in which virtuous behavior can cost them or get them killed, and in which sheer survival can demand bald consequentialism.[44] Not only do the dreams they hold of "the good life" become mutually unrealizable, but their visions of themselves as good persons fracture. At ages at which people are especially in need of moral formation from adults and older peers, the influence they actually receive can warp children's moral sense. As a consequence they cannot maintain an integrated moral identity. For example, to be loyal members of their undocumented American families may paradoxically demand that they protect those families by forgoing living with them or even contacting them.

The accounts of unaccompanied children often soft-peddle their susceptibility to moral harm, perhaps so they will remain sympathetic to readers. Nazario's inventories of Enrique's many bad decisions and questionable actions pass without comment or are filed under addiction, a category of psychological illness rather than moral failing. Luiselli tells the story of Manu, who bravely filed a police report against a gang in Honduras and then made the dangerous journey to the United States after gang members killed his best friend, only to find the same gang operating in his new American high school.[45] Manu's moral integrity may have survived the harrowing journey and the gang pressures at both ends of it, but clearly the moral compasses of the immigrant gang members who accosted him in Hempstead, New York were broken. Many children do not transcend the forces that batter them on the journey north, in detention, and in their new homes.

Returning to the Holy Family imagery with which we began, we see that its usual interpretation obscures moral vulnerability when it could illumine the problem compassionately. Given the proclivity of religious leaders to cite the Holy Family as the prototypical migrant family seeking safety and a good life for its child (Mt 2:16–23), it is telling that they seem not to address Mary and Joseph's own survival. Rather than risking exposure by warning other families of the approaching slaughter of baby boys, they slip out of Bethlehem undetected under cover of darkness. When Herod's death makes it safer to return to Israel, they avoid Judea, where Herod's son rules, and steer toward Nazareth. But they could not have returned to Bethlehem had they wanted to; their betrayal of their neighbors would have made them unwelcome. In short, dire circumstances drive even the Christian poster family of migration to throw their neighbors under the bus in order to preserve their own lives, and they suffer the consequences of that moral failure in their exclusion from their former community.

A less quantifiable loss is the fracturing of moral identity that results from children's isolation from moral communities, a loss also reflected in the gospel accounts of Mary and Joseph's wanderings: separated from family, they had only dreams as their guides. Migrant children often begin and even more frequently finish their northward journeys on their own. The slow pace of assessment and the immigration courts isolates children from families and friends in the United States and delays their formation of connections in their potential new communities. ORR staffs' regimented practices and the uncertainties of each child's schedule of departure prevent children from forming intimate, sustaining relationships in detention.

Yet as Kate Ward argues, moral community is the key to surviving bad moral luck with one's moral identity intact. Using the work of Emily Townes, Melanie Harris, and Rosita deAnn Mathews, Ward has pointed out that persons who are marginalized or oppressed can find refuge and support for their moral growth in community, which "holds members accountable for their own individual good, the good of the community and the good of the world at large" and supports them in finding strategies (as Townes would say) for dancing "with a twisted hip"—wounded, but with support and with moral integrity.[46] The apprehension, detention, and asylum processes could be moments of moral reintegration for migrant children. But in the accounts cited here, they exacerbate the problem by intentionally isolating the children from family and from each other.

The moral harms of desperate migration are real. Because of children's inevitable vulnerability as moral agents in formation, these harms fall harder on children, especially unaccompanied children, and reverberate longer into their futures than into adults' futures. To be sure, the harms may be cushioned by migrating or remaining in place with family, but only if that family is supportive, is supported by legal status, and can provide for children's needs.

CONCLUSION

Although all human beings are ontologically, structurally, and morally vulnerable, unaccompanied migrant children's age and separation from their families magnify their vulnerabilities at all levels. Addressing this heightened risk through the lens of traditional Christian family ethics does not erase it. The problem is not only that migrant children's families are often already fractured and in any case take shapes that vary greatly from nuclear families. And it is not only that both migration routes and US systems for refuge, asylum, and permanent residence "protect" children by fracturing their identities and removing their communities of support and much of their agency. It is also that migrant children share in the general condition of human ontological, structural, and moral vulnerability, which the nuclear family cannot remove from them or entirely compensate; indeed it is because parents are vulnerable in the same ways that families split up to survive. The solution for ethics is not to subsume children's agency in their parents' initiative but to describe children's vulnerability with the goal of promoting their agency and flourishing directly. In particular, ethics must condemn the current inescapable dilemmas caused by the detention and asylum systems that at best fracture migrant children's moral identities and at worst tempt them to bend their identities toward violence to escape the pressure of incessant compromise.

For these reasons our scriptural imagery should not end with the flight into Egypt, which can obscure both "Egypt's" responsibility for the situation in Israel and the separate, if interdependent, personhood of the child Jesus, not to mention the Holy Family's own moral compromises. It must continue with the invitation of Mt 19:14, "let the little children come to me," which addresses children on their own accounts, independent of the first-century forces that reduced them to political and ethical ciphers. And it must reflect deeply on the boy Jesus of Lk 2:41–51, who fulfilled his calling by going alone to the Temple on his own account, despite his parents' departure, acting on his own and yet within his larger religious community.

Christian ethics can contribute constructively to policy debates on child migration only when it addresses children as ontologically, structurally, and morally vulnerable persons in themselves and as members of wider moral communities, rather than as passive members of idealized nuclear families. And it can do so only when it acknowledges that situations of brutal poverty and violence—for which northern countries' policies bear significant responsibility—have fractured the families they do have and forced them and their families to take life-threatening, often morally compromising risks simply to survive.

Thus the first, immediate responsibility for northern hemisphere Christians is to press for comprehensive hospitality that respects migrant children as moral persons—hospitality that assembles the missing ontological, structural, and moral supports that drive them north, in a way that also honors the virtues of self-reliance and self-assertion that they have cultivated on their journeys and that mends the wounds they have inevitably also suffered. At the very least, migrant children must not be held in cages, in frigid temperatures, without adequate food and water, lacking means to contact friends and family, or without access to information about status and procedures in language they can understand. They must not be separated from their traveling companions without important cause, and they must not be forbidden to comfort each other.[47]

Our second responsibility is to press for the reversal of the policies of our own nations that fracture children's lives in their home countries, preventing their ontological, structural, and moral needs from being met in place. Heyer argues for parents' rights to provide for their children in their home countries, arguing for "the right not to have to migrate."[48] Christian ethics must add that this right to flourish in place applies to children not derivatively, but directly. The first line of defense for children's vulnerable agency is energetic efforts by rich countries to promote genuine economic, legal, and political security elsewhere. For instance, failure to offer adequate economic aid to Central American nations while deporting undocumented Central Americans who have developed gang connections in the United States seeds international gang networks, driving gang victims' migration to the United States in a relentless stream.[49] Only when northern nations embrace their identity as powerful, accountable actors in international political and economic systems will crisis migration flows slow.

NOTES

1. Thanks to Amanda Gvozden for research on US legal and constitutional treatments of childhood and to Molly Greening, Hille Haker, and the reviewers at Lexington Books for helpful comments. All remaining shortcomings are mine.

2. William A. Kandel, *Unaccompanied Alien Children: An Overview*, Congressional Research Service, January 18, 2017, https://fas.org/sgp/crs/homesec/R43599.pdf.

3. Pope John Paul II, Apostolic Exhortation *Ecclesia in America*, January 22, 1999, http://w2.vatican.va/content/john-paul-ii/en/apost_exhortations/documents/hf_jp-ii_exh_22011999_ecclesia-in-america.html; United States Conference of Catholic Bishops (USCCB), *Welcoming the Stranger Among Us: Unity in Diversity*, November 15, 2000, http://www.usccb.org/issues-and-action/cultural-diversity/pastoral-care-of-migrants-refugees-and-travelers/resources/welcoming-the-stranger-among-us-unity-in-diversity.cfm; and USCCB, *Strangers No Longer Together on the Journey of Hope*, January 22, 2003, http://www.usccb.org/issues-and-action/human-life-and-dignity/immigration/strangers-no-longer-together-on-the-journey-of-hope.cfm.

4. Kristin E. Heyer, *Kinship Across Borders: A Christian Ethics of Immigration* (Washington, DC: Georgetown University Press, 2012).

5. Heyer, *Kinship,* 81–89.

6. Pope Pius XII, *Exsul Familia Nazarethana*, August 1, 1952. http://www.papalencyclicals.net/pius12/p12exsul.htm.

7. Fr. Thomas Betz, OFC, "Catholic Social Teaching on Immigration and the Movement of Peoples," Migration and Refugee Services/Office of Migration Policy and Public Affairs, n.d.http://www.usccb.org/issues-and-action/human-life-and-dignity/immigration/catholic-teaching-on-immigration-and-the-movement-of-peoples.cfm.; The United States Conference of Catholic Bishops, "The Catholic Church's Position on Immigration Reform," August 2013, http://www.usccb.org/issues-and-action/human-life-and-dignity/immigration/churchteachingonimmigrationreform.cfm.

8. This rhetoric has echoed a tweet by US president Donald Trump about migrants who "have been in our country for many years through no fault of their own." Andrew Prokop, "Trump is now tweeting that DREAMers are wonderful and should be allowed to stay in the US." *Vox*, September 14, 2017, https://www.vox.com/policy-and-politics/2017/9/14/16306658/trump-daca-deal-tweets.

9. USCCB, *Strangers No Longer*, paras. 46, 82.

10. Valeria Luiselli, *Tell Me How It Ends: An Essay in Forty Questions* (Minneapolis: Coffee House Books, 2017); Sonia Nazario, *Enrique's Journey*, revised and updated (New York: Random House, 2014); Susan J. Terrio, *Whose Child Am I? Unaccompanied, Undocumented Children in U.S. Immigration Custody* (Oakland, CA: University of California Press, 2015).

11. Heyer, *Kinship*, 81–89.

12. Terrio, *Whose Child*, 151.

13. Cristina L. H. Traina, "Children and Moral Agency," *Journal of the Society of Christian Ethics* 29, no. 2 (2009): 20–21.

14. The latter often arise in a legal setting: when is an adult competent or incompetent to stand trial? See, for example, Patricia A. Zapf and Ronald Roesch, "Evaluation of Competence to Stand Trial in Adults," in *Forensic Assessments in Criminal and Civil Law*, eds. Ronald Roesch and Patricia A. Zapf (New York: Oxford, 2012), 17–31. Explorations of children's competency in court touch similar issues, as well as their linked right to legal representation, which, measured by vulnerability, should be inversely proportionate to their putative competency for trial. See for example Jonathan O. Hafen, "Children's Rights and Legal Representation—The Proper Roles of Children, Parents, and Attorneys," *Notre Dame Journal of Law, Ethics & Public Policy* 7, no. 2 (1993): 423–463; Joseph B. Sanborn, Jr., "Juveniles' Competency to Stand Trial: Wading through the Rhetoric and Evidence," *Journal of Law and Criminology* 99, no. 1 (2009): 135–213; and M. Aryeh Somers, "Children in Immigration Proceedings: Child Capacities and Mental Competency in Immigration Law and Policy," practice advisory produced for the Vera Institute of Justice's Unaccompanied Children Program (May 2015). The latter document lays out examples of the arbitrary, contradictory age threshold guidelines that lead to the conflicting practices Terrio decries. In 2015, former immigration judge Jack H. Weil created a stir by seeming to argue that undocumented children do not need legal representation. Rather, a patient judge can, during an immigration hearing, train unrepresented three- and four-year-olds well enough in immigration law to make a fair judgment between relief and deportation. Weil's claim caused scandal in the press and in scholarship. But on a theoretical level his point deserves greater attention. Unaccompanied immigrant children are truly agents with unique histories acting on their own behalf (albeit

vulnerable agents deserving legal representation) whose circumstances deserve as much, if not more, attention than adults.' Deposition of the honorable Jack H. Weil in the case of J.E.F.M. v. Loretta E. Lynch, United States District Court, Western District of Washington at Seattle (October 15, 2015); see page 161 for an example of the claim that unrepresented preschoolers can receive a fair asylum hearing if the judge is patient and has adequate resources in family members, friends of the court, and community members. Thanks to Amanda Gvozden for her research on these points.

15. Hille Haker argues that vulnerability, or openness to being shaped by surrounding influence, is a prerequisite for moral agency; it is a site of positive formation as well as a site of danger. See Hille Haker, "Vulnerable Agency: Human Dignity and Gendered Violence," in *Dignity and Conflict: Contemporary Interfaith Dialogue on the Value and Vulnerability of Human Life*, eds. Jonathan Rothschildt and Matthew Petrusek (Notre Dame: University of Notre Dame Press, 2018), 397–398. I assume this vision of human formation and focus on vulnerability's risks to agents and agency.

16. See Cristina L. H. Traina, "Children's Situated Right to Work." *Journal of the Society of Christian Ethics* 31, no. 2 (2011): 160; idem, "Vulnerable Agency: Children's Rights and the Law," *Societas Ethica*, Bad Boll, Germany (August 2016), 18–19.

17. See Cristina L. H. Traina, *Erotic Attunement: Parenthood and the Ethics of Sensuality between Unequals* (Chicago: University of Chicago Press, 2011).

18. Haker, "Vulnerable Agency," 398–399; 410–411; 401–402.

19. For an example in Augustine's *Confessions*, see Traina, "Children and Moral Agency," 32.

20. Terrio, *Whose Child,* throughout the book but especially 19–25.

21. Terrio, *Whose Child*, 26–40; see also Nazario, *Enrique's Journey.*

22. Nazario, *Enrique's Journey,* 103–119.

23. Terrio, *Whose Child,* 31.

24. Ibid., throughout, but especially 20–41.

25. Luiselli, *Tell Me How It Ends,* 20–22.

26. See, for instance, ibid., 61.

27. Luiselli, *Tell Me How It Ends,* 55–56.

28. Terrio, *Whose Child,* 116.

29. Ibid., 110.

30. Ibid. The paragraph summarizes central themes of the book, focusing on discussions that occur especially on 42–75 and 161–192. I have not elaborated on the further tension (on one hand) and lack of coordination (on the other) between family reunification and immigration proceedings.

31. According to the American Civil Liberties Union, courts ordered deportation for 85 percent of children who had no legal representation but allowed nearly 75 percent of children with legal counsel to remain in the United States. American Civil Liberties Union, "The Fair Day in Court for Kids Act (H.R. 4646 / S.2540)" April 27, 2016, https://www.aclu.org/fact-sheet/fair-day-court-kids-act-factsheet.

32. Nazario, *Enrique's Journey,* 270–271.

33. Terrio, *Whose Child*, for example 123, 125, 149.

34. Nazario, *Enrique's Journey,* 78.

35. See, for example, Terrio, *Whose Child,* 87.

36. Rory Carroll, "Eight Activists Helping Migrants Cross Brutal Desert Charged by US Government," *The Guardian*, January 24, 2018, https://www.theguardian.com/us-news/2018/jan/24/us-immigration-activists-arizona-no-more-deaths-charged. Thanks to Hille Haker for this reference.

37. Terrio, *Whose Child*, 118.

38. Ibid., 107, emphasis added.

39. Ibid., 113. Luiselli's interviews and Nazario's account confirm this pattern.

40. Ibid., 147.

41. Ibid., 51–52. Nazario's and Luiselli's books are also testaments to the importance of children's forming their identities through telling their own stories. For many, life after migration is a matter of developing an answer to the complex question "Why did you come to the United States?" that gives their journey meaning and transmits something of their identities to their listeners (Luiselli, 55).

42. Terrio, *Whose Child,* 114.

43. Novario, *Enrique's Journey*, 278, 282.

44. For further theorization of burdened virtues and moral failure, see Lisa Tessman, *Burdened Virtues: Virtue Ethics for Liberatory Struggles* (New York: Oxford University Press, 2005) and Lisa Tessman, *Moral Failure: On the Impossible Demands of Morality* (New York: Oxford University Press, 2015). See also Kate Ward's critical theological retrieval, below.

45. Luiselli, *Tell Me How It Ends*, 70–75, 80–83.

46. Kate Ward, "Toward a Christian Virtue Account of Moral Luck," *Journal of the Society of Christian Ethics* 38, no. 1 (2018): 131–145, at 140, 139. The latter quote comes from Emily M. Townes, "To Be Called Beloved: Womanist Ontology in Postmodern Refraction," in *Womanist Theological Ethics: A Reader*, eds. Katie Cannon, Emilie Maureen Townes, and Angela D. Sims (Louisville, KY: Westminster John Knox Press, 2011), 202.

47. See, for instance, Joel Rose, "Doctors Concerned About 'Irreparable Harm' To Separated Migrant Children," National Public Radio (June 15, 2018), https://www.npr.org/2018/06/15/620254326/doctors-warn-about-dangers-of-child-separations; Camila Domonoske and Richard Gonzalez, "What We Know: Family Separation And 'Zero Tolerance' At The Border," National Public Radio (June 19, 2018), https://www.npr.org/2018/06/19/621065383/what-we-know-family-separation-and-zero-tolerance-at-the-border; and US Senator Elizabeth Warren's 1:30 p.m., June 26, 2018 Facebook post documenting her visit to a holding facility in McAllen, Texas.

48. Heyer, *Kinship Across Borders*, 27.

49. See, for example, Terrio, *Whose Child,* 20.

BIBLIOGRAPHY

American Civil Liberties Union. "The Fair Day in Court for Kids Act (H.R. 4646/S.2540)." April 27, 2016. https://www.aclu.org/fact-sheet/fair-day-court-kids-act-factsheet.

Betz, Fr. Thomas, OFC. "Catholic Social Teaching on Immigration and the Movement of Peoples." Migration and Refugee Services/Office of Migration Policy and Public Affairs, n.d. http://www.usccb.org/issues-and-action/human-life-and-dignity/immigration/catholic-teaching-on-immigration-and-the-movement-of-peoples.cfm.

Carroll, Rory. "Eight Activists Helping Migrants Cross Brutal Desert Charged by US Government." *The Guardian*, January 24, 2018. https://www.theguardian.com/us-news/2018/jan/24/us-immigration-activists-arizona-no-more-deaths-charged.

Domonoske, Camila, and Richard Gonzalez. "What We Know: Family Separation And 'Zero Tolerance' At The Border." National Public Radio (June 19, 2018). https://www.npr.org/2018/06/19/621065383/what-we-know-family-separation-and-zero-tolerance-at-the-border.

Hafen, Jonathan O. "Children's Rights and Legal Representation—The Proper Roles of Children, Parents, and Attorneys." *Notre Dame Journal of Law, Ethics & Public Policy* 7 no. 2 (1993): 423–463.

Haker, Hille. "Vulnerable Agency: Human Dignity and Gendered Violence." In *Dignity and Conflict: Contemporary Interfaith Dialogue on the Value and Vulnerability of Human Life,* edited by Jonathan Rothschildt and Matthew Petrusek, 393–436. Notre Dame: University of Notre Dame Press, 2018.

Heyer, Kristin E. *Kinship Across Borders: A Christian Ethics of Immigration.* Washington, DC: Georgetown University Press, 2012.

Kandel, William A. *Unaccompanied Alien Children: An Overview*. Washington, DC: Congressional Research Service. January 18, 2017. http://www.nnirr.org/drupal/sites/default/files/uac_overview_january_2017_r43599.pdf.

Luiselli, Valeria. *Tell Me How It Ends: An Essay in Forty Questions.* Minneapolis: Coffee House Books, 2017.

Nazario, Sonia. *Enrique's Journey,* revised and updated. New York: Random House, 2014.

Pope John Paul II. *Ecclesia in America.* January 22, 1999. http://w2.vatican.va/content/john-paul-ii/en/apost_exhortations/documents/hf_jp-ii_exh_22011999_ecclesia-in-america.html.

Pope Pius XII. *Exsul Familia Nazarethana.* August 1, 1952. http://www.papalencyclicals.net/pius12/p12exsul.htm.

Prokop, Andrew. "Trump is now tweeting that DREAMers are wonderful and should be allowed to stay in the US." *Vox*, September 14, 2017. https://www.vox.com/policy-and-politics/2017/9/14/16306658/trump-daca-deal-tweets.

Rose, Joel. "Doctors Concerned About 'Irreparable Harm' To Separated Migrant Children." National Public Radio (June 15, 2018). https://www.npr.org/2018/06/15/620254326/doctors-warn-about-dangers-of-child-separations.

Sanborn, Joseph B. Jr. "Juveniles' Competency to Stand Trial: Wading through the Rhetoric and Evidence." *Journal of Law and Criminology* 99 no. 1 (2009): 135–213.

Somers, M. Aryeh. "Children in Immigration Proceedings: Child Capacities and Mental Competency in Immigration Law and Policy," Vera Institute of Justice's Unaccompanied Children Program, May 2015.

Terrio, Susan J. *Whose Child Am I? Unaccompanied, Undocumented Children in U.S. Immigration Custody*. Oakland, CA: University of California Press, 2015.

Tessman, Lisa. *Burdened Virtues: Virtue Ethics for Liberatory Struggles*. New York: Oxford University Press, 2005.

———. *Moral Failure: On the Impossible Demands of Morality*. New York: Oxford University Press, 2015.

Townes, Emily M. "To Be Called Beloved: Womanist Ontology in Postmodern Refraction." In *Womanist Theological Ethics: A Reader*, edited by Katie Cannon, Emilie Maureen Townes, and Angela D. Sims, 183–202. Louisville, KY: Westminster John Knox Press, 2011.

Traina, Cristina L. H. "Children and Moral Agency." *Journal of the Society of Christian Ethics* 29, no. 2 (2009): 19–37.

———. "Children's Situated Right to Work." *Journal of the Society of Christian Ethics* 31, no. 2 (2011): 151–167.

———. *Erotic Attunement: Parenthood and the Ethics of Sensuality between Unequals*. Chicago: University of Chicago Press, 2011.

———. "Vulnerable Agency: Children's Rights and the Law." Societas Ethica, Bad Boll, Germany, August 2016.

United States Conference of Catholic Bishops. "The Catholic Church's Position on Immigration Reform." August 2013. http://www.usccb.org/issues-and-action/human-life-and-dignity/immigration/churchteachingonimmigrationreform.cfm.

———. *Strangers No Longer Together on the Journey of Hope*. January 22, 2003. http://www.usccb.org/issues-and-action/human-life-and-dignity/immigration/strangers-no-longer-together-on-the-journey-of-hope.cfm.

———. *Welcoming the Stranger Among Us: Unity in Diversity*. November 15, 2000. http://www.usccb.org/issues-and-action/cultural-diversity/pastoral-care-of-migrants-refugees-and-travelers/resources/welcoming-the-stranger-among-us-unity-in-diversity.cfm.

Ward, Kate. "Toward a Christian Virtue Account of Moral Luck." *Journal of the Society of Christian Ethics* 38, no. 1 (2018): 131–145.

Weil, the Hon. Jack H. Deposition in the Case of J.E.F.M. v. Loretta E. Lynch, United States District Court, Western District of Washington at Seattle. October 15, 2015.

Zapf, Patricia A., and Ronald Roesch. "Evaluation of Competence to Stand Trial in Adults." In *Forensic Assessments in Criminal and Civil Law*, edited by Ronald Roesch and Patricia A. Zapf, 17–31. New York: Oxford, 2012.

Chapter 9

Toward a Moral Response to Unaccompanied Minors in the US Context

Kristin E. Heyer

Significant changes for immigrant youth wrought by President Donald Trump during the first years of his presidency directly reflect his campaign rhetoric that casts immigrants and refugees as threats to the United States.[1] Trump campaigned on promises to deport undocumented immigrants and secure the border with Mexico, a country he charged with sending its criminals, drug dealers, and rapists to the United States. The administration's internal enforcement measures and accompanying rhetoric have fanned the flames of nationalism, sowed fear in immigrant communities and eroded civic life. Increased enforcement measures have contributed not only to upticks in detentions of noncriminal migrants and border deaths, but also to heightened mental health risks in immigrant communities and threats to familial well-being on both sides of the border.

As resistance to such measures has underscored, these moves threaten to harm already vulnerable asylum seekers and divide families of mixed immigration status. They also endanger the nation's deepest values and its standing in the world. In the name of safeguarding national security, further militarization of the border treats symptoms rather than causes of migration. The US government already spends more on federal immigration enforcement than on than on all other principal federal criminal law enforcement agencies combined.[2] Moreover, since 2008 the United States has witnessed a dramatic decline in border crossings, though a growing percentage of border crossers have originated in the Northern Triangle countries of Central America fleeing pervasive violence and seeking not to evade arrest, but request political asylum.[3]

Since 2014, more than 200,000 unaccompanied minors have come to the United States, the majority arriving from Honduras, Guatemala, and

El Salvador, which remain plagued by organized crime and the world's highest murder rates.[4] Beyond food insecurity and family reunification, escalating violence increasingly fuels migration from these Central American communities. Migrants from El Salvador, Guatemala, and Honduras cite forced gang recruitment and extortion as reasons for leaving home.[5] Given that homicides have only increased as Central American governments have implemented "iron fist" policing since 2003 (authoritarian responses to violent crime rates)—in Honduras, for example, about seventy youth have been murdered per month in recent years—many minors feel they have no other option than to flee home. Thirty percent of Central American youth are neither employed nor in school.[6]

In his 2018 State of the Union address, President Donald Trump urged Congress to close "glaring loopholes in our laws" that he charged gang members take advantage of to "enter the country as unaccompanied alien minors."[7] However, the administration's newly adopted measures have already attempted to alter the legal landscape for unaccompanied minors entering the United States. For example, citing the threat of gangs like the one featured in his address, El Salvador's MS-13, President Trump has "moved to restrict special legal protections that help unaccompanied minors gain asylum, rewritten guidelines for judges in deportation proceedings involving children and opted not to renew funding for a program that had helped thousands secure legal aid."[8] Whereas the backlog of cases in immigration court reached nearly 90,000 children in August 2017, the Department of Justice decided not to renew approximately $4.5 million in funding for Justice AmeriCorps, a program created three years ago that helped provide legal services to nearly 7,000 unaccompanied minors, citing the "loss of key leadership and inadequate performance" among the reasons for not renewing the funding.[9] The administration also formally terminated the Obama-era program granting Central American minors a two-year renewable "parole" if they did not win refugee status but had a parent already legally present in the United States.[10]

The administration has also adjusted other internal policies to counter inherited "catch and release" practices it feared would encourage unaccompanied minors to risk crossing the border, such as prosecuting sponsors (usually parents) and pursuit of "the most serious, readily provable offense" leading to federal prosecution for illegal entry rather than mere deportation. When parents are detained for federal prosecution in this way, family separation results.[11] Whereas President Trump's rhetoric suggests Central American youth migrating to the United States are chiefly male gang members, roughly one-third of unaccompanied minors in 2017 were female.[12] Targeting Salvadoran girls for sexual violence, coerced relationships, and gang membership has left young women with little option but to flee; moreover "only a fraction of unaccompanied minors apprehended since 2011 have confirmed gang ties."[13]

A look back at the recent peak of unaccompanied migration to the United States in 2014 sheds some light upon the background of the current rhetoric about security and "illegal immigration." This chapter will attempt to scrutinize dominant narratives about unaccompanied minors' migration against a backdrop of broader diversionary rhetoric; it will help to recontextualize their migration by noting historical and structural contexts of migration; and it will offer resources from Catholic migration ethics in terms of its attention to social sin and structural justice by way of response.

RECONTEXTUALIZATION: THE RECENT HISTORY

The resonance of candidate Trump's anti-immigration rhetoric may have its roots in the recent history concerning the uptick in border crossing of unaccompanied minors in particular. A 2014 United Nations High Commissioner for Refugees study of more than four hundred unaccompanied minors found widespread experiences of violence or threats by organized-crime groups, including gangs, drug cartels, or by state actors in countries of origin (48 percent); recruitment or exploitation by human smuggling organizations (39 percent); and abuse at home (22 percent).[14] As a result, the number of unaccompanied children crossing the US border doubled annually from 2011 to 2014. Smuggling networks profited from these lower risk passengers who frequently turn themselves in upon crossing. After a steady decline in 2016, in November of 2017 the number of unaccompanied minors taken into custody rose 26 percent.[15]

When an estimated 63,000 unaccompanied minors crossed into the United States between October 2013 and July 2014, the uptick (nearly twice the year prior) was alternately framed as a humanitarian or security crisis, adding fuel to the flame of fear-based arguments in the wider national debate about undocumented immigration. Of the group, more than 50,000 minors migrated from El Salvador, Guatemala, and Honduras. A 2013 UN Refugee Agency survey indicated that despite the threats of unscrupulous coyotes and myriad risks and costs of the journey north, the possibility that children would win asylum status via slow deportation hearings, or evading authorities, were preferable for many families to the threats of violence at home.[16] Whereas some minors were placed in Health and Human Services shelters, many were put into the care of family members already living in the United States while they awaited their hearings; during that period, they could enroll in public schools.[17] By way of initial response, the Obama administration intensified enforcement and detention efforts and promoted public information campaigns in sending countries to discourage outflows.[18] The government opened emergency detention centers on military bases, "provided emergency legal counsel to children, accelerated the processing and deportation of migrants [and] provided Central American countries with $255 million for repatriation and reintegration programs."[19]

Whereas the relative dip in child and family arrivals in the fall of 2014 indicated that the regional migration had been resolved, more recent information indicates that Northern Triangle migration pressures endure. Mexican deportations of Central Americans have markedly increased since the country implemented *Programa Frontera Sur* in 2014, with little deterrent effect and reports of exacerbated human rights violations of migrants in transit through Mexico to the United States. For example, migrants have been targeted for kidnapping by criminal gangs and extortion by government officials.[20] Critics worry that the plan "outsources" the US "war on migrants" and that "the model of ramping up resource extraction, militarization, and privatization threatens to worsen inequality[21] and spur a wave of human rights violations without solving the root causes of the crisis."[22] Unless underlying conditions change, given enduring family ties across the borders, lengthy backlogs in US courts and adaptive smuggling networks, Central American flows of migrants—including of unaccompanied minors—will likely persist.[23]

Given that these underlying conditions, such as the world's highest murder rates, deaths linked to drug trafficking and organized crime, and endemic poverty continue to endure in Northern Triangle countries from which minors flee, new policies and practices across the region and new considerations in the field of Christian ethics must address the particular needs of children on the move.[24] With the Trump administration's drastic reductions in the number of refugees the United States will receive and its suspension of Temporary Protected Status for several affected countries, among them El Salvador with over 260,000 beneficiaries, the United States risks turning its back on the vulnerable "children from neighboring countries who show up at our border with no parents and no place to turn."[25] As Sonia Nazario worries, we may well leave those who survive the journey to make their own asylum case in court alone, that is, without legal representation, as six in ten unaccompanied children presently do. She recounts watching "a 7-year-old stand before a judge, shaking like a leaf, because anything he said could send him hurtling back to the danger he just fled."[26] Many unaccompanied minors bear legitimate claims that could lead to legalization if they were able to navigate the nation's complex immigration and asylum laws; roughly 40 percent are "potentially eligible for some kind of relief from deportation."[27] Over the past five years, young defendants with legal representation "won 85 percent of their cases in immigration court, while those without a lawyer lost 87 percent of their cases."[28]

Whereas the dominant narratives either reduce the causes of the minors' entry to lax executive orders or misleading promises of smugglers or violence and lack of economic opportunity in their countries of origin, rarely does political analysis extend to the histories of unequal relationships between sending countries and the United States, such as its military presence in Honduras[29] and El Salvador.[30] The narratives that have framed unaccompanied minors' presence and ignored historic and structural relationships reflect the broader context of undocumented immigration in the United States, which is also marked by diversionary myths and a focus on individual lawbreakers instead of acknowledging broader structural responsibility. Reducing immigration matters to the "illegality" of minors who cross borders alone eclipses transnational actors responsible for violent conflict, economic instability, or climate change from view, much less blame. Recent administrations' enforcement strategies have focused on symptoms rather than causes of migration. The measures are framed by narratives that perpetuate myths about responsibility for irregular migration and genuine threats to national security reflective of enduring interpretive lenses.[31]

THE POWER OF RHETORICAL FRAMING: NARRATIVES OLD AND NEW

Despite significantly beefed up fortification, the increase in arrivals of unaccompanied minors in 2014 rekindled fears of a "border out of control." Fewer than forty-eight hours after the nation collectively chanted "U.S.A.!" for the national soccer team in the 2014 World Cup, a smaller group of Americans in Murrieta, California, coupled the same rally cry with chants of, "Return to sender," "Save our children from diseases," and "Bus illegal children to White House." The protesters employed the slogan to turn back busloads of Central American youth destined for a new detention center in their community.[32] Whether in such overtly jingoistic and racialized framing of young newcomers as particular threats, or subsequent language pitting the innocence of DACA recipients or Dreamers against the culpability of their undocumented parents, narratives shape thought and frame responses. They also help to sustain an amnesia about historic ties and to obscure social responsibilities.

The language surrounding the 2014 unaccompanied minor arrivals underscored a growing "crisis" in light of a "surge" of minors entering the country. Media images included "photos of children lying about on floors, crowded behind prison bars, or overflowing into hallways of detention facilities," further focusing attention on the dangerously porous border.[33] As David Hernandez has pointed out, such framing in terms of "crisis" and "surge" served those on either side of the immigration debate, "demonstrating an unenforced and out-of-control border for anti-immigrant forces, a cruel and rushed detention apparatus for migrant advocates, and the urgent need for comprehensive immigration reform for the Obama administration." For example, Department of Homeland Security attorneys contended that Central American refugees represented a security threat that would encourage trafficking, and that they should be treated en masse (denied bond and release) rather than as individuals. Such prosecutorial decisions led to accelerated court processes intended to deter further migrations by hastening deportations, not prioritizing just adjudication of asylum claims.[34] Moreover, the federal government's lack of preparedness to process and provide custody arrangements for unaccompanied children as required by law magnified the sense of "crisis."

In response, two competing narratives emerged, primarily blaming "push" or "pull" factors for the crisis. Whereas a focus on "push" factors in sending countries ostensibly leads to a humanitarian frame and in many cases determining refugee categorization, the Obama administration adopted the "pull" factor narrative and consequent deterrence-based responses. Despite its expansion of border enforcement funding, information campaigns and deportation "outsourcing," such practices have not had a deterrent effect—the numbers of unaccompanied minors only temporarily dropped in 2015. If the crisis is instead "humanitarian in nature and regional in scope," the "push" narrative has explanatory value and the migrant "surge" represents, rather, a refugee flow.[35] The "crisis" and "surge" language and adoption of the "pull" frame allowed the US government and public to avoid the reality of the violence in Northern Triangle countries, its legal obligations toward refugees, and to prescind from serious consideration of its complicity in the flows or broader obligations in justice.[36]

More broadly, the function of such framing rhetoric helps perpetuate dominant narratives that have long framed immigration debates in the United States, despite rhetoric about liberty and hospitality celebrated beneath the Statue of Liberty. Policy debates have typically remained focused on social costs and security threats, in ways consonant with tropes that were amplified during the 2016 presidential campaign and continued following Trump's election. Its policy debates remain framed by a law-and-order lens, which casts unauthorized immigrants as willful lawbreakers, posing national security threats, including the young migrants turning themselves in to authorities upon arrival. Trump's internal enforcement steps follow from the politics of exclusion peddled throughout his campaign, when appeals to economic and cultural anxieties were often cloaked in nativist rhetoric. Such ongoing portrayals of undocumented immigrants and asylum seekers reflect false assumptions and facile analyses of complex challenges.

Trump billed his initial immigration order as a measure to "Make America safe again," following from the law-and-order mantle he adopted to distinguish his candidacy. The administration's continued efforts to conflate unaccompanied minors' entrance with gang activity perpetuates this trope, yet recent studies indicate that higher rates of immigration correlate with lower rates of violent and property crime.[37] The rule of law rightly occupies a privileged place in the United States, yet a lack of accountability that marks Border Patrol procedures and the lack of due process afforded to immigrant detainees belie this rationale.[38] The Department of Homeland Security's significant backlogs and priority "rocket" dockets in immigration courts give rise to concerns that the removal system is both inefficient and lacking in adequate safeguards. As noted, young migrants from the Northern Triangle countries flee homicide capitals where gang members murder with impunity—hence the threat driving many such migrants is precisely the breakdown of the rule of law at home.

Another script from Trump's migration platform casts newcomers as economic threats, a perception historically fueled in times of economic downturn.[39] Beyond studies that show immigrant laborers provide a net benefit to the US economy—recent estimates indicate that DACA beneficiaries alone would contribute $460.3 billion to the US gross domestic product over the next decade[40]—the detention industry profits off of irregular migrants, further confounding the "economic threat" frame. Like counterparts in Britain and Australia, the US government increasingly employs multinational security companies, which have turned immigration enforcement into a growth industry. The upsurge in privatized detention has been accompanied by record profits as well as by lawsuits based on documentation of widespread abuse and neglect. Share prices for GEO group and Corrections Corporation of America rose over 100 percent in the wake of the 2016 election, given the president's avowed commitment to increase incarceration of immigrants. The administration has called for nearly doubling the number of immigrants detained to 80,000/day, and in April the White House approved plans to construct a $110 million detention center operated by GEO near Houston.[41] Detainees in GEO's Adelanto Detention Center in California staged a hunger strike and a sit-in in the summer of 2017 to protest unsanitary conditions and poor medical care; three had died in the previous three months.[42] The burgeoning "immigrant industrial complex" raises questions about the significant financial stakes in the broken immigration system, diminished public oversight and accountability. Human rights groups indicate that detention has neither deterred asylum seekers nor expedited deportation and is becoming a profitable end in itself. Unaccompanied minors detained in private facilities have faced overcrowded conditions, lack of adequate medical care and food, and abuse.[43]

The Trump administration has connected economic anxieties with anxieties over cultural shifts, shaping a particular vision of "America First" that casts newcomers as threatening to a nation's identity. Tapping into the related anti-immigrant sentiment has provoked the demonization of racial, ethnic, and religious minorities. Bias-related hate crimes surged following the election.[44] Where appeals to nostalgia or anxieties about rapid cultural and demographic changes may have remained more hidden or coded in the recent past, Trump's sympathy with white nationalists has brought overt racist and xenophobic fears into the open. His vulgar characterizations of migrants originating in Haiti and African nations in January 2018 further confirm this conflation. Representations of the outsider as a social menace have been reinvented in moments of national crisis, with the general pattern evidencing xenophobia's productive function in the national imaginary. Portrayals of immigrants as public charges or a dangerously porous border have long shaped US society's collective imagination.

Fear of difference—even of very young children crossing a border and offering themselves to authorities—is relatively easy to mass-market, and it shapes society's imagination in powerful ways. Hence operative lenses shaping the immigration debate can mask realities and can become surrogates for other cultural and political concerns. Christian ethics can help unmask the interests and values that drive immigration policy and its impact on unaccompanied minors in particular (when cast as a "surge" to be feared, "pulled" by misunderstandings of lax loopholes). Encounters with all migrants, including minors, signal significant dissonance between these exclusionary frameworks and the inhumane impact of recent rhetoric and measures alike. At his border mass in Ciudad Juárez on the occasion of his visit to the United States in 2016, Pope Francis bid listeners to measure the impact of forced migration not in numbers or statistics but with concrete names and stories, evoking a counter-narrative to those dominating the airwaves:

> They are the brothers and sisters of those expelled by poverty and violence, by drug trafficking and criminal organizations. Being faced with so many legal vacuums, they get caught up in a web that ensnares and always destroys the poorest. Not only do they suffer poverty but they must also endure these forms of violence. Injustice is radicalized in the young; they are "cannon fodder," persecuted and threatened when they try to flee the spiral of violence and the hell of drugs, not to mention the tragic predicament of the many women whose lives have been unjustly taken.[45]

Attentiveness to such three-dimensional experiences beyond caricatures or statistics can help unmask operative narratives. Probing the complex realities behind deceptive sound bites also expands consideration beyond individuals who cross borders to consider the global contexts that compel migration.

STRUCTURES OF INTERDEPENDENCE

Restrictive measures and reductive rhetoric do not convey a sense of the complex roles that historic relationships, transnational politics and economic globalization play in contemporary migration, including the patterns of unaccompanied minors on the move. Understanding immigration as "individual actions of emigrants" or asylum seekers, wherein individuals are the primary site for enforcement and responsibility, has become increasingly incompatible with transnational politics and economies.[46] Developments in social sciences and migration ethics help reorient analyses away from stopgap efforts (in the face of "surges") and toward contextual assessments of what patterns of migration reveal and demand. Understanding the geopolitical structures and systems that generate and sustain migration impact culpability and warranted responses alike.

Addressing the plight of child migrants during a UN Human Rights Council panel in June of 2017, Archbishop Ivan Jurkovic, Vatican observer to UN agencies in Geneva, not only condemned policies that criminalize and detain child migrants as "an insult to human dignity" and having "lifelong consequences on a child's development," but also detention models themselves as "wrongly absolv[ing] the international community from responsibilities that it regularly fails to fulfill." He called upon the international community to step up its efforts to address root causes of child migration—war, violence, corruption, poverty and environmental disasters—and to take a "farsighted approach" to integral human development for the "hundreds of millions of children who are living in appalling conditions."[47] This approach signals not only a "push" frame of interpretation, but it also points to the contexts in which child migration occurs, the harmful limitations of deterrent detention-only approaches, and the shared responsibility for just resolutions. These contexts are often marked by historic ties and structural interdependence.

Typically, established communities and migrants are "bound together by history, politics and economics even before the act of migration bridges the distance of geography."[48] Dynamics of employer recruitment, for example, tend to be shaped by prior bonds impacted by colonialism, military invasions, or economic ties. Saskia Sassen also highlights the increasing significance of today's "multiplying global imaginaries, which are partly a function of Western economic and media dominance and have their own way of constructing bridges."[49] In the case of the United States, mass migration in the 1960s ensued amid expanded economic and military activity in Asia and the Caribbean and its critical role in the development of a world economic system. Both helped create conditions that mobilized people into migrations as well as the formation of unintended bridges to the United States. Sassen argues these patterns indicate that measures thought to deter emigration from developing countries, such as foreign investment or the promotion of export-oriented growth, "seem to have had precisely the opposite effect, at least in the short and middle run."[50] Miguel De La Torre emphasizes the ongoing legacy of nineteenth- and twentieth-century US foreign policy, expansionism, and neoliberal economic strategies—with attendant narratives—in generating migration flows from Latin America.[51]

Sassen's latest research links deeper dynamics of debt servicing, extraction, and land grabs to new migratory flows.[52] She argues that given "predatory" forms of advanced capitalism, opaque transnational networks, and a global governance system geared to aiding corporations, migration is far more complex an issue than one concerning nationalism versus globalism or different political theories of migration and national sovereignty.[53] Concerned with emergent migrations, she traces how such factors have expelled communities from their habitats: in the case of Central American minors entering the United States, she probes root causes behind proximate violence broadly construed, to rapidly escalating urban violence due to the destruction of small holder rural economies resulting from land grabs and mining. Getting to the roots of such violence—without simply blaming corrupt police and criminalized traffickers or keeping gang violence "local" without interrogating its transnational dimensions and origins—traces systemic migration flows to their sources. In view of President Trump's focus on the threats posed by MS-13 and other transnational gangs he believes further infiltrate the country via unaccompanied minors' migration, this context-attentive approach illuminates MS-13's origins in Los Angeles during the 1980s by refugees from El Salvador's civil war, "fueled in part by Washington," and the role of US deportations in its exportation to El Salvador.[54]

If dominant narratives keep the cause of violence and subsequent migration flows "local" and de-humanize newcomers according to convenient (and increasingly abhorrent) scripts, I suggest the Christian tradition's commitments shape a different story, a (counter)narrative of our common humanity, our kinship, with implications for a just immigration ethic. This ethic does not offer a meek narrative that condones open borders or an ethic of hospitality by way of charity toward vulnerable children, but a tradition steeped in human rights, a relevant notion of structural sin, and summons to shared responsibility and social justice. Christian understandings of what it means to be human radically critique pervasive exploitation and prevailing immigration paradigms that enable exclusion and abet division.

RESOURCES FROM CATHOLIC MIGRATION ETHICS

Whereas a Catholic immigration ethic is rooted in biblical injunctions to welcome the stranger, it is also borne of the tradition's teachings on universal human rights, the understanding of the political community as oriented to serve the common good, and its global rather than nationalistic perspective.[55] Its notion of social sin significantly extends responsibility for irregular migration beyond individuals who cross borders or overstay visas alone. A consideration of the social sins at play in the dynamics of irregular migration illuminate our complex complicities in injustice and the need for robust solidarity with refugees and migrants. The Catholic social tradition is rooted in a scriptural vision of the person as inherently sacred and made for community. Its principles of economic and migration ethics protect not only civil and political rights, such as freedom of conscience, but also more robust social and economic rights and responsibilities. These establish a persons' right not to have to migrate, or fulfill human rights in their homeland (a right to remain or to migrate by choice rather than necessity). They also establish a person's right to migrate if they cannot support themselves or their families in their country of origin.[56] Hence, in situations where individuals face desperate poverty or pervasive gang violence, the magisterial tradition supports the right to migrate so they can live free from credible fears of violence or severe want.

Beyond its foundation in human rights, the Catholic right to migrate is also rooted in the tradition's commitment to the universal destination of created goods, that is, the idea that goods of the earth are generally intended for everyone.[57] Whereas the social tradition recognizes the right of sovereign nations to control their borders, this right is understood not to be absolute; its temperance by conditions of social justice warrants protection for many who remain within US borders or seek entry. In the case of blatant human rights violations, the right to state sovereignty is relativized by the tradition's primary commitment to protecting human dignity (whether in its teachings on humanitarian intervention or migration). More than a decade ago, the US and Mexican bishops urged both nations to address root causes of and legal avenues for migration in their joint pastoral letter. They noted the need to develop the economies of sending nations like Mexico and reduce family visa backlogs. By contrast, border enforcement has remained the primary focus of US migration politics, even as it has failed to resolve the problem of a significant undocumented presence within the United States.

Whereas the narrative of willful lawbreakers or burdensome outsiders frames the rationale behind the responses to the recent entry of unaccompanied minors, the Catholic tradition's emphasis on serving the global common good contextualizes the individual acts of migrants or refugees and underscores social dimensions of justice, interdependence, and complicity with push and pull factors alike. Transnational actors responsible for violent conflict, economic instability, or climate change are eclipsed from view, much less blame. Pope Francis has repeatedly emphasized solidarity with migrants, whether in his first visit outside Rome as Pope to the island of Lampedusa, or his lived example returning from Lesbos with refugee families. He has lamented a "globalization of indifference" that leads to the tragedies of migrants' manipulation and their deaths. His attention to the anesthetizing effects of such indifference illuminates the structures and attitudes that harm immigrants in terms of social sin.

Distinct elements of social sin—dehumanizing trends, unjust structures, and harmful ideologies—shape complex dynamics that perpetuate inequalities and influence receptivity to outsiders. Whether in forms of cultural superiority or profiteering, social inducements to personal sin in the immigration context abound. Social sin indicates how powerful narratives casting immigrants as security threats or "takers" influence our personal roles in collective actions or inaction that impact migration (such as votes in a presidential election or Congressional failures to pass a clean DACA bill or comprehensive reform). Hence, socioeconomic and political structures that lead to minors' undocumented immigration are frequently connected to the ideological blinders that obstruct hospitality to immigrants. For example, the primacy of deterrence has institutionalized security concerns rather than concerns for human rights or family unity in US immigration laws; the nation's economic interests have been institutionalized in uneven free trade agreements. When concerns about national identity are distorted by xenophobia and fear, anti-immigrant sentiment and ethnic-based hate crimes surge.

Internalized ideologies make persons susceptible to myths. When bias hides or skews values, it becomes more difficult to choose authentic values over those that prevail in society. Given such unreflective dimensions of social sin, a Catholic ethic not only calls for defending human rights and providing hospitality to strangers, but also unmasking the complex structures and ideologies that abet personal complicity, preventing justice for migrating unaccompanied minors and the members of their families who are often of mixed status. Viewing immigration through the lens of individual culpability alone obscures these multileveled, subtle dynamics at play. These entrenched, intertwined patterns of social sin require repentance from idolatries that marginalize and disempower those beyond our immediate spheres of concern and borders—including the aforementioned false narratives governing perceptions of migrant children. From repentance and conscientization we are called to alter practices to become more characterized by interdependence in solidarity. These shifts can occur through personal encounters and relationships that provoke new perspectives and receptivity. At the broader systemic level, nations must understand themselves as collectively responsible for the shared challenges posed by child refugees compelled to cross borders. Given these multilayered dimensions of social sin, Christian migration ethics entails not only negotiating relative duties of reception, but also addressing more diffuse and complex structures and ideologies that abet complicity in injustice and apathy. Portraying immigration through a lens of individual culpability alone obscures these multileveled, subtle dynamics at play.[58]

Pope John Paul II forwarded solidarity as the key virtue demanded in a globalized era of de facto interdependence: the social face of Christian love. David Hollenbach has proposed institutional solidarity as a necessary means of moving patterns of global interdependence from ones marked by domination and oppression to ones marked by equality and reciprocity. Institutional solidarity demands the development of structures that offer marginalized persons—including young persons—a genuine voice in the decisions and policies that impact their lives. It demands the inclusion of comprehensive sets of stakes at the decision-making table, structures of institutional accountability and transparency, and empowered participation (subsidiarity).[59] Eliciting conversion from patterns of unjust complicity calls communities beyond intermittent outreach ministry or legislative advocacy, though both remain important. The witness of churches or other institutions who provide sanctuary to vulnerable minors on the move would be strengthened by prophetic conscientization efforts that foster repentance from complicity in patterns of social sin.

Catholic groups often root outreach to unaccompanied minors in biblical imperatives of hospitality to the stranger or human dignity claims or a liberationist option for the poor and vulnerable. For example, the United States Conference of Catholic Bishops' Department of Migration and Refugee Services is the largest refugee resettlement agency in the world, and one of two agencies authorized by the US Department of State to resettle unaccompanied refugee children offering foster care, family reunification, and other culturally competent services since 1980.[60] Beyond the importance of hospitality and compassion for the vulnerable, however, understandings of social sin underscore susceptibility to dominant rhetoric that conflates gang member with young refugees, or indifference to the contexts generating minors' flows. These dynamics invite a response that does not begin and end with charitable outreach and refuge—the importance of which is not to be underestimated in the face of urgent need—but that extends to the responsibility to unmask misleading narratives, resist harmful policies, and recontextualize minors' migration, each of which issues social responsibilities for receiving countries like the United States, given complicity in generating sending conditions through foreign policy and economic practices. Understanding minors arriving as kin, rather than "schemers" or threats, demands that we confront the realities of violence in Northern Triangle countries and our robust obligations in international justice. At the very least it requires that we receive refugees at this time of increasing need, not reduce our resettlement ceiling to its lowest cap since Congress created the Refugee Resettlement Program in 1980.[61]

In closing, the harms wreaked by dominant rhetoric framing unaccompanied minors as security threats or political pawns violate fundamental standards of justice and indicate the urgency of prophetic truth-telling.[62] An approach rooted in repentance from complicity in generating displacement can help reframe the debate about Central American minors' arrivals. Christian commitments to universal human rights, unmasking social sin, and restorative justice can help focus our moral responsibilities to those fleeing violence and other insecurities embedded in relational histories of unequal interdependence. A recognition by the US government of the humanitarian crisis generating most of the Northern Triangle unaccompanied minor flows, on the way to a fuller sense of restoration, would at least enable us as a nation to adjudicate their significant need for refugee protections and employ (or in some cases reinstate) measures to ensure refugees are not returned to persecution in these countries.[63] Moving forward, moral and policy considerations of our responsibilities to unaccompanied minors should also combat diversionary and false rhetoric, provide counsel for minors making asylum claims, enable careful deliberation of said claims rather than fast-tracking or outsourcing enforcement, and work to enact meaningful comprehensive immigration reform that does not trade family reunification for merit-based points or sacrifice safeguards for those fleeing violence. The first refugee family fleeing Herod invites Christians to a solidarity with unaccompanied minors in need that avoids the lure of exculpating rhetoric and facile solutions alike.

NOTES

1. I am grateful for the research assistance of Lindsay Marcellus. Portions of this chapter are adapted from Kristin E. Heyer, *Kinship Across Borders: A Christian Ethic of Immigration* (Washington, DC: Georgetown University Press, 2012) and Heyer, "Internalized Borders: Immigration Ethics in an Age of Trump," *Theological Studies* 79, no. 1 (March 2018): 146–164.

2. Doris Meissner, Donald Kerwin, Muzaffar Chishti, and Claire Bergeron, *Immigration Enforcement in the United States: The Rise of a Formidable Machinery* (Washington, DC: Migration Policy Institute, 2013), 9.

3. Robert Warren and Donald Kerwin, "The 2,000 Mile Wall in Search of a Purpose: Since 2007 Visa Overstays have Outnumbered Undocumented Border Crossers by a Half Million," *Journal on Migration and Human Security* 5, no. 1 (March 2017): 124–136.

4. Office of Refugee Resettlement, "Facts and Data," March 1, 2018, available at https://www.acf.hhs.gov/orr/about/ucs/facts-and-data.

5. Cara Labrador Rocio, and Danielle Renwick, "Central America's Violent Northern Triangle" Council on Foreign Relations Backgrounder, January 18, 2018, available at https://www.cfr.org/backgrounder/central-americas-violent-northern-triangle.

6. National Jesuit Conference and the Washington Office on Latin America, "Myths and Facts on the Central American Migration Surge," accessed June 24, 2014 at http://www.jesuits.org/Assets/Publications/File/Myths%20and%20Facts%20on%20Central%20American%20Migration%20Surge.pdf.

7. President Donald J. Trump, "State of the Union Address," January 30, 2018, available at https://www.whitehouse.gov/briefings-statements/president-donald-j-trumps-state-union-address.

8. Nicole Einbinder, "How the Trump Administration is Rewriting the Rules for Unaccompanied Minors," *Frontline,* February 13, 2018, https://www.pbs.org/wgbh/frontline/article/how-the-trump-administration-is-rewriting-the-rules-for-unaccompanied-minors.

9. Ibid.

10. David Nakamura, "Trump Administration Ends Obama-era Protection Program for Central American Minors," *Washington Post*, August 16, 2017, https://www.washingtonpost.com/politics/trump-administration-ends-obama-era-protection-program-for-central-american-minors/2017/08/16/8101507e-82b6-11e7-ab27-1a21a8e006ab_story.html?utm_term=.c4921fd0bd63.

11. Sarah Pierce, Jessica Bolter, and Andrew Selee. *Trump's First Year on Immigration Policy: Rhetoric vs. Reality* (Washington, DC: Migration Policy Institute, 2018), 4–5.

12. ORR, "Facts and Data."

13. Molly O'Toole, "El Salvador's Gangs are Targeting Young Girls," *The Atlantic*, March 4, 2018, https://www.theatlantic.com/international/archive/2018/03/el-salvador-women-gangs-ms-13-trump-violence/554804/?platform=hootsuite.

14. United Nations High Commissioner for Refugees, "Children on the Run: Unaccompanied Children Leaving Mexico and the Need for International Protection" (Washington, DC: UNCHR, March 12, 2014).

15. Nick Miroff, "To Curb Illegal Border Crossings, Trump Administration Weighs Separating Kids from Parents," *Chicago Tribune*, December 21, 2017, http://www.chicagotribune.com/news/nationworld/politics/ct-trump-immigrants-parents-children-20171221-story.html.

16. Danielle Renwick, "The U.S. Child Migrant Influx," *Council on Foreign Relations* (August 28, 2014), https://www.cfr.org/backgrounder/us-child-migrant-influx.

17. Ibid.

18. Marc R. Rosenblum and Isabel Ball, "Trends in Unaccompanied Child and Family Migration from Central America," Fact Sheet, *Migration Policy Institute,* January 2016, https://www.migrationpolicy.org/research/trends-unaccompanied-child-and-family-migration-central-america.

19. David M. Hernandez, "Unaccompanied Child Migrants in 'Crisis': New Surge or Case of Arrested Development?" Harvard Journal of Hispanic *Policy* 27 (2014): 11.

20. Jan-Albert Hootsen, "Jesuit Groups Cal Trump's Border Wall a Distraction as Migrants Suffer," *America*, October 12, 2017, https://www.americamagazine.org/politics-society/2017/10/12/jesuit-groups-call-trumps-border-wall-distraction-migrants-suffer.

21. Heather Gies, "Big US Aid for Central America Will Worsen Inequality," *teleSUR*, January 13, 2016, https://www.telesurtv.net/english/news/Expert-Big-US-Aid-for-Central-America-Will-Worsen-Inequality-20160113-0037.html.

22. teleSUR, "Mexico Does U.S. Dirty Work Detaining Central American Children," *MintPress News*, October 25, 2016, available at http://www.mintpressnews.com/mexico-does-us-dirty-work-detaining-central-american-children/221756.

23. Rosenblum and Ball, "Trends in Unaccompanied Child and Family Migration from Central America."

24. See Rodrigo Dominguez-Villegas, *Strengthening Mexico's Protection of Central American Minors in Transit* (Washington, DC: Migration Policy Institute, 2017).

25. Sonia Nazario, "Trump's Cruel Choice: Who Gets to Stay?" *New York Times*, October 27, 2017, https://www.nytimes.com/2017/10/27/opinion/sunday/dreamers-children-immigration-congress.html.

26. Ibid.

27. Annie Chen and Jennifer Gill, "Unaccompanied children and the U.S. immigration system: challenges and reforms." *Journal of International Affairs*, 68, no. 2 (2015): 115–133.

28. Warren Richey, "Alejandra, Age 7, is Facing a Judge Alone. Is that Due Process?" *Christian Science Monitor*, November 1, 2016, https://m.csmonitor.com/USA/Politics/2016/1101/Alejandra-age-7-is-facing-a-judge-alone.-Is-that-due-process.

29. Joseph Nevins, "How U.S. Policy in Honduras Set the State for Today's Mass Migration," *The Conversation*, October 31, 2016, https://theconversation.com/how-us-policy-in-honduras-set-the-stage-for-todays-mass-migration-65935.

30. Gene Palumbo and Azam Ahmed, "El Salvador Again Feels the Weight of Washington Shaping its Fate," *New York Times*, January 9, 2018, https://www.nytimes.com/2018/01/09/world/americas/el-salvador-trump.html?mtrref=www.facebook.com&gwh=FF3B2401E646C7984A78378075F898D8&gwt=pay.

31. See Kristin Heyer, "Reframing Displacement and Membership: Ethics of Migration," *Theological Studies* 73, no. 1 (March 2012): 188–206 and "The Politics of Immigration and a Catholic Counternarrative: A Perspective from the United States," *Asian Horizons* 8, no. 4 (December 2014): 719–737.

32. Matt Garcia, "The Thousands of Children Fleeing Central America Have Nothing to Do With Our Ongoing Debate Over Immigration," *Zócalo*, July 10, 2014, http://www.zocalopublicsquare.org/2014/07/10/whats-happening-at-the-border-is-a-humanitarian-crisis-not-a-political-one/ideas/nexus/.

33. Hernandez, "Unaccompanied Child Migrants in 'Crisis,'" 11.

34. Ibid.

35. Karen Musalo, and Eunice Lee, "Seeking a Rational Approach to a Regional Refugee Crisis: Lessons from the Summer 2014 'Surge' of Central American Women and Children at the US-Mexico border." *Journal on Migration and Human Security* 5, no. 1 (2017): 137–179.

36. Ibid.

37. For more, see https://www.americanimmigrationcouncil.org/research/criminalization-immigration-united-states.

38. Legal reform reports have criticized aspects of the US immigration laws at odds with this complement of features: their retroactivity, inconsistent application,

lack of proportionality, procedural unfairness (e.g., the effects of availability of legal counsel), and failure to comport with basic due process norms. See Donald Kerwin, "Rights, the Common Good, and Sovereignty in Service of the Human Person," in *And You Welcomed Me: Migration and Catholic Social Teaching*, eds. Donald Kerwin and Jill Marie Gerschutz (Lanham, MD: Lexington, 2009), 111.

39. Trump courted the "disaffected downwardly mobile as a key voting bloc," and some developments diminishing job security contributed to their captivity beyond this economic scapegoating. See Kenneth Himes's discussion of the plight of the "precariat" and the atomization of the work place in "The State of Our Union," *Theological Studies* 78, no. 1 (2017): 148–149, 160.

40. Tom K. Wong, Greisa Martinez Rosas, Adam Luna, Henry Manning, Adrian Reyna, Patrick O'Shea, Tom Jawetz, and Philip E. Wolgin, "DACA Recipients' Economic and Educational Gains Continue to Grow," *Center for American Progress*, August 28, 2017, https://www.americanprogress.org/issues/immigration/news/2017/08/28/437956/daca-recipients-economic-educational-gains-continue-grow.

41. Michelle Sainato, "Private Prison Industry Lobbying, Profits Soar Under Trump," *The Observer*, October 27, 2017, http://observer.com/2017/10/geo-group-private-prison-industry-profits-soar-under-trump.

42. Leslie Berestein Rojas, "Detainees Start Hunger Strike at Adelanto Immigrant Detention Center," *KPCC*, June 13, 2017, http://www.scpr.org/news/2017/06/13/72892/detainees-start-hunger-strike-at-adelanto-immigran.

43. Anna C. Manuel and Connie de la Vega, "Detention of Unaccompanied Minors in Private Facilities," Report, *Human Rights Advocates*, May 2016, www.humanrightsadvocates.org/wp-content/uploads/2016/07/HRC-28-Children-and-Private-Detention-Centers.pdf; Melissa Del Bosque, "As Feds Lock Up More Immigrant Families, Abuse Allegations Grow," *Texas Observer*, November 4, 2014, http://www.texasobserver.org/growing-number-abuse-cases-immigrant-family-detention-facilities.

44. Hatewatch Staff, "Post-Election Bias Incidents Up To 1,372; New Collaboration with ProPublica," *Southern Poverty Law Center*, February 10, 2017, https://www.splcenter.org/hatewatch/2017/02/10/post-election-bias-incidents-1372-new-collaboration-propublica.

45. Pope Francis, Homily in Cuidad Juárez, Apostolic Visit to Mexico, February 17, 2016, https://w2.vatican.va/content/francesco/en/homilies/2016/documents/papa-francesco_20160217_omelia-messico-ciudad-jaurez.html.

46. Saskia Sassen, *Globalization and Its Discontents: Essays on the New Mobility of People and Money* (New York: The New Press, 1998), 6–8.

47. Junno Arocho Esteves, "Vatican: Failure to Protect Child Migrants an Insult to Human Dignity," *Catholic News Service, "Top Stories"* June 12, 2017, https://cnstopstories.com/2017/06/12/vatican-failure-to-protect-child-migrants-an-insult-to-human-dignity.

48. Silas W. Allard, "Who Am I? Who Are You? Who are We? Law, Religion, and Approaches to an Ethic of Migration," *Journal of Law and Religion* 30, no. 2 (June 2015): 325.

49. Saskia Sassen, "The Making of Migrations," in *Living With(out) Borders: Catholic Theological Ethics on the Migrations of Peoples*, eds. Agnes Brazal and María Teresa Dávila (Maryknoll, NY: Orbis Press, 2016), 12.
50. Ibid., 13.
51. Miguel De La Torre, *The U.S. Immigration Crisis: Toward an Ethics of Place* (Eugene, OR: Cascade Books, 2016), 151–152.
52. Saskia Sassen, "Three Emergent Migrations: An Epochal Change," *SUR File on Migration and Human Rights,* 13, no. 23 (2016): 29–41.
53. Saskia Sassen, "A Massive Loss of Habitat: New Drivers for Migration," *Sociology of Development* 2, no. 2 (2016): 211.
54. O'Toole, "El Salvador's Gangs are Targeting Young Girls."
55. Portions of this section are developed from my "A Catholic Ethic for Immigration: Attending to Social Sin and Solidarity," *Health Progress* 98, no. 4 (July/August 2017): 31–34.
56. United States Conference of Catholic Bishops and *Conferencia del Episcopado Mexicano*, "Strangers No Longer: Together on the Journey of Hope" (Washington, DC: USCCB, 2003).
57. Second Vatican Council, *Gaudium et spes* (1965) no. 69, http://www.vatican.va/archive/hist_councils/ii_vatican_council/documents/vat-ii_const_19651207_gaudium-et-spes_en.html.
58. For discussions of twentieth-century Christian elaborations of collective egotism and how social sin can help unmask operative disvalues that harden resistance to a Christian immigration ethic, see Kristin Heyer, "Radical Solidarity: Migration as a Challenge for Contemporary Christian Ethics," *Journal of Catholic Social Thought* 14, no. 1 (2017): 90–91.
59. David Hollenbach, *Common Good & Christian Ethics* (Cambridge University Press, 2002), 225.
60. See http://www.usccb.org/about/children-and-migration/index.cfm for an overview of services offered by the US Conference of Catholic Bishops' Migration and Refugee Services and its advocacy on unaccompanied minors' behalf.
61. Phillip Connor, "U.S. Resettles Fewer Refugees Even as Global Number of Displaced People Grows," October 12, 2017, *Pew Research Center: Global Attitudes and Trends,* http://www.pewglobal.org/2017/10/12/u-s-resettles-fewer-refugees-even-as-global-number-of-displaced-people-grows.
62. For a meditation on theological vocation as truth-telling see M. Shawn Copeland, "Racism and the Vocation of the Christian Theologian," *Spiritus* 2, no. 1 (2002): 15–29.
63. Karen Musalo and Eunice Lee, "Seeking a Rational Approach to a Regional Refugee Crisis, "Journal on Migration and Human Security Volume 5 Number 1 (2017): 137–179.

BIBLIOGRAPHY

Allard, Silas W. "Who Am I? Who Are You? Who are We? Law, Religion, and Approaches to an Ethic of Migration." *Journal of Law and Religion* 30, no. 2 (June 2015): 320–334.

Arocho Esteves, Junno. "Vatican: Failure to Protect Child Migrants an Insult to Human Dignity." *Catholic News Service, "Top Stories,"* June 12, 2017.

Brazal, Agnes, and María Teresa Dávila, eds., *Living With(out) Borders: Catholic Theological Ethics on the Migrations of Peoples*. Maryknoll, NY: Orbis Press, 2016.

Chen, Annie, and Jennifer Gill. "Unaccompanied Children and the U.S. Immigration System: Challenges and Reforms." *Journal of International Affairs*, 68, no. 2 (2015): 115–133.

Connor, Phillip. "U.S. Resettles Fewer Refugees Even as Global Number of Displaced People Grows." *Pew Research Center: Global Attitudes and Trends*, October 12, 2017. Available at http://www.pewglobal.org/2017/10/12/u-s-resettles-fewer-refugees-even-as-global-number-of-displaced-people-grows/.

Copeland, M. Shawn. "Racism and the Vocation of the Christian Theologian." *Spiritus* 2, no. 1 (2002): 15–29.

Del Bosque, Melissa. "As Feds Lock Up More Immigrant Families, Abuse Allegations Grow." *Texas Observer,* November 4, 2014.

De La Torre, Miguel. *The U.S. Immigration Crisis: Toward an Ethics of Place.* Eugene, OR: Cascade Books, 2016.

Dominguez-Villegas, Rodrigo. *Strengthening Mexico's Protection of Central American Minors in Transit.* Washington, DC: Migration Policy Institute, 2017.

Einbinder, Nicole. "How the Trump Administration is Rewriting the Rules for Unaccompanied Minors." *Frontline*, PBS, February 13, 2018. Available at https://www.pbs.org/wgbh/frontline/article/how-the-trump-administration-is-rewriting-the-rules-for-unaccompanied-minors.

Garcia, Matt. "The Thousands of Children Fleeing Central America Have Nothing to Do With Our Ongoing Debate Over Immigration." *Zócalo*, July 10, 2014.

Hernandez, David M. "Unaccompanied Child Migrants in 'Crisis': New Surge or Case of Arrested Development?" *Harvard Journal of Hispanic Policy* 27 (2014): 11.

Heyer, Kristin E. *Kinship Across Borders: A Christian Ethic of Immigration.* Washington, DC: Georgetown University Press, 2012.

———. "Reframing Displacement and Membership: Ethics of Migration." *Theological Studi* 73, no. 1 (March 2012): 188–206.

———. "The Politics of Immigration and a Catholic Counternarrative: A Perspective from the United States." *Asian Horizons* 8, no. 4 (December 2014): 719–737.

———. "Radical Solidarity: Migration as a Challenge for Contemporary Christian Ethics." *Journal of Catholic Social Thought* 14, no. 1 (2017): 97–104.

———. "A Catholic Ethic for Immigration: Attending to Social Sin and Solidarity," *Health Progress* 98, no. 4 (July/August 2017): 31–34.

———. "Internalized Borders: Immigration Ethics in an Age of Trump." *Theological Studies* 79, no. 1 (March 2018): 146–164.

Himes, Kenneth. "The State of Our Union." *Theological Studies* 78, no. 1 (2017): 147–170.

Hollenbach, David. *Common Good & Christian Ethics.* Cambridge: Cambridge University Press, 2002.

Kerwin, Donald, and Jill Marie Gerschutz, eds. *And You Welcomed Me: Migration and Catholic Social Teaching.* Lanham, MD: Lexington, 2009.

Manuel, Anna C., and Connie de la Vega. "Detention of Unaccompanied Minors in Private Facilities." Report, *Human Rights Advocates,* May 2016, www.humanrightsadvocates.org/wp-content/uploads/2016/07/HRC-28-Children-and-Private-Detention-Centers.pdf.

Meissner, Doris, Donald Kerwin, Muzaffar Chishti, and Claire Bergeron. *Immigration Enforcement in the United States: The Rise of a Formidable Machinery.* Washington, DC: Migration Policy Institute, 2013.

Miroff, Nick. "To Curb Illegal Border Crossings, Trump Administration Weighs Separating Kids from Parents." *Chicago Tribune,* December 21, 2017.

Musalo, Karen, and Eunice Lee. "Seeking a Rational Approach to a Regional Refugee Crisis: Lessons from the Summer 2014 'Surge' of Central American Women and Children at the US-Mexico Border." *Journal on Migration and Human Security* 5, no. 1 (2017): 137–179.

Nakamura, David. "Trump Administration Ends Obama-era Protection Program for Central American Minors." *Washington Post,* August 16, 2017.

National Jesuit Conference and the Washington Office on Latin America. "Myths and Facts on the Central American Migration Surge." http://www.jesuits.org/Assets/Publications/File/ Myths%20and%20Facts%20on%20Central%20American%20Migration%20Surge.pdf.

Nazario, Sonia. "Trump's Cruel Choice: Who Gets to Stay?" *New York Times,* October 27, 2017.

Nevins, Joseph. "How U.S. Policy in Honduras Set the State for Today's Mass Migration." *The Conversation,* October 31, 2016.

Office of Refugee Resettlement. "Facts and Data." March 27, 2018. https://www.acf.hhs.gov/orr/about/ucs/facts-and-data.

O'Toole, Molly. "El Salvador's Gangs are Targeting Young Girls." *The Atlantic,* March 4, 2018.

Palumbo, Gene and Azam Ahmed. "El Salvador Again Feels the Weight of Washington Shaping its Fate." *New York Times,* January 9, 2018.

Pierce, Sarah, Jessica Bolter, and Andrew Selee. *Trump's First Year on Immigration Policy: Rhetoric vs. Reality.* Washington, DC: Migration Policy Institute, 2018.

Pope Francis, Homily in Cuidad Juárez, Apostolic Visit to Mexico, February 17, 2016. Available https://w2.vatican.va/content/francesco/en/homilies/2016/documents/papa-francesco_20160217_omelia-messico-ciudad-jaurez.html.

President Donald J. Trump. "State of the Union Address." January 30, 2018. https://www. whitehouse.gov/briefings-statements/president-donald-j-trumps-state-union-address.

Renwick, Danielle. "The U.S. Child Migrant Influx." *Council on Foreign Relations,* August 28, 2014.

Richey, Warren. "Alejandra, Age 7, is Facing a Judge Alone. Is that Due Process?" *Christian Science Monitor,* November 1, 2016.

Rocio, Cara Labrador, and Danielle Renwick. "Central America's Violent Northern Triangle." Council on Foreign Relations Backgrounder, January 18, 2018. https://www.cfr.org/backgrounder/central-americas-violent-northern-triangle.

Rojas, Leslie Berestein. "Detainees Start Hunger Strike at Adelanto Immigrant Detention Center," *KPCC,* June 13, 2017. Available at http://www.scpr.org/news/2017/06/13/72892/detainees-start-hunger-strike-at-adelanto- immigran.

Rosenblum, Marc R., and Isabel Ball. "Trends in Unaccompanied Child and Family Migration from Central America." *Migration Policy Institute*, January 2016.

Sainato, Michelle. "Private Prison Industry Lobbying, Profits Soar Under Trump." *The Observer*, October 27, 2017.

Sassen, Saskia. *Globalization and Its Discontents: Essays on the New Mobility of People and Money.* New York: The New Press, 1998.

———. "Three Emergent Migrations: An Epochal Change." *SUR File on Migration and Human Rights* 13, no. 23 (2016): 29–41.

———. "A Massive Loss of Habitat: New Drivers for Migration," *Sociology of Development* 2, no. 2 (2016): 204–233.

Second Vatican Council, *Gaudium et spes.* 1965. http://www.vatican.va/archive/hist_councils/ii_vatican_council/documents/vat-ii_const_19651207_gaudium-et-spes_en.html.

United Nations High Commissioner for Refugees. "Children on the Run: Unaccompanied Children Leaving Mexico and the Need for International Protection." Washington, DC: UNCHR, March 12, 2014.

United States Conference of Catholic Bishops and *Conferencia del Episcopado Mexicano*. "Strangers No Longer: Together on the Journey of Hope." Washington, DC: USCCB, 2003.

Warren, Robert, and Donald Kerwin. "The 2,000 Mile Wall in Search of a Purpose: Since 2007 Visa Overstays Have Outnumbered Undocumented Border Crossers by a Half Million." *Journal on Migration and Human Security* 5, no. 1 (March 2017): 124–136.

Chapter 10

Justice as Responsibility to Child Migrants

Tisha M. Rajendra

"Everything that is happening to us is tangled up with the United States. We can't untie ourselves," writes Salvadoran journalist Óscar Martínez.[1] This book is about children who find themselves in the most perilous and desperate of circumstances. Whether crossing seas or deserts, whether in immigration detention or living in the lawless conditions of a refugee camp, these children inhabit a no-man's-land in which the institutions that are ordinarily responsible for protecting and providing for children are either absent, unable, or unwilling to do so. Thus, while these children have rights under international law, they have no one to protect or guarantee such rights. Unaccompanied child migrants are thus extraordinarily vulnerable to assault, to human traffickers, and to disappearance.

While many theories of justice focus on the rights of these children, the question of the responsibilities to protect and defend the rights of *particular* people has gone unanswered.[2] This is, perhaps in part, because those of us who have spent our lives within stable liberal democracies take it for granted that the nation-state is the ultimate guarantor of human rights.[3] But the children who exist in the no-man's-land of responsibility cannot take a well-functioning nation-state for granted. This chapter introduces an account of justice, *justice as responsibility to relationships*, that starts with questions not of who is owed what, but with questions of *who* has the responsibility to provide for unaccompanied child migrants and *where* such responsibilities come from.[4] In my account, justice involves discerning what is owed through an examination of particular narratives about relationships. Because justice as responsibility to relationships focuses on the particular nature of specific relationships, a universal account of who has responsibilities toward which particular migrants is not possible. This chapter focuses on unaccompanied child migrants from El Salvador and Guatemala who come to the United States fleeing gang violence.[5] Part 1 outlines the concept of justice as responsibility for relationships. Part 2 narrates the history of the origins of gang violence in El Salvador and Guatemala, arguing that this history is intimately tied to the foreign and immigration policies of the United States during the Cold War to the 1990s. Part III reflects on how these historical injustices decades in the past impact present-day relationships and thus responsibilities.

JUSTICE AS RESPONSIBILITY TO RELATIONSHIPS

Justice as responsibility to relationships (hereafter justice as responsibility) stands in contrast to two accounts of responsibility: universal obligation and benevolence. Universal obligation is the approach to the rights of migrants taken by instruments of international law, such as the 1951 UN Refugee Convention and the later 1967 Protocol. Both instruments specify that the rights of refugees are to be guaranteed by contracting states in the following manner: if an asylum claim is granted based on a well-founded fear of persecution, an asylee must be treated the same as nationals in claiming the protection of their rights from the state that has granted asylum. The duties to protect the rights of asylees are universally binding upon contracting states. In other words, there is no mention of particular relationships or particular histories in these documents. That is as it should be, for one purpose of international refugee law is to specify minimal rights that can be universally claimed. However, these duties of international law are inadequate to protect the full spectrum of the human rights of refugees, precisely because under international law, there are limits to what can be demanded of sovereign states.

The first limitation becomes clear when we consider that a refugee is, by definition, someone who is "outside of the country of his former habitual residence" (Article 1). The protections granted by the convention therefore only apply to those who either have been expelled from their countries of residence, or who have managed to flee the persecution they experienced there. Those who are left behind, either internally displaced within their states or those unable to flee anywhere, do not enjoy any such protection from contracting states.

The second limitation is that while contracting states are obligated to protect refugees within their territories, nothing in international refugee law obliges them either to accept refugees from other states or to provide assistance to asylees in other contracting states. In other words, while there are significant duties to refugees once they are in the territory of a contracting state, there are no duties if they are not. Although 148 of the UN's 193 member states are parties to either the 1951 Refugee Convention, the 1967

Protocol or both, member states vary widely in their abilities to provide for and protect refugees.

Thus, while in theory the duties of contracting states to refugees already in their territory are quite expansive, in practice, they are inadequate to protect the rights of unaccompanied child migrants. This may well be the best that is possible under international law, which must specify universal (if often unenforceable) legal norms. But depending on a particular context, a country's responsibilities to child migrants may very well exceed the legal minimum.

The other standard account of responsibilities to child migrants is rooted in the Christian norm of hospitality, depicted in New Testament texts such as the parable of the Good Samaritan (Lk. 10:25–37) and Matthew 25. In the parable, a Samaritan, a traditional enemy of the Jews, stops to care for a grievously wounded Jew lying beside the road. In Matthew 25, Jesus speaks of a time when people will be judged according to whether they fed the hungry, welcomed the stranger, clothed the naked, and cared for the sick. Both of these passages are interpreted as ethical mandates to care for needy strangers. In other words, the very helplessness, vulnerability, and otherness of the stranger demand a response of care. Like the obligations embedded in international law, Christians hold that the norm of hospitality is universally binding and has no account of responsibilities based on particular relationships. Unlike international law, this norm is not based in a contractual obligation, but in a religious account of responsibilities to all vulnerable peoples.

But the norm of hospitality, too, falls short as an account of responsibilities to child migrants, in much the same ways as the universally binding norms of international law: it cannot tell us what responsibilities there may be to child migrants who are every bit as vulnerable, but not in our immediate orbit. Nor can it tell us our responsibilities to those children who would migrate if they had the resources to do so, and are currently suffering under terrible conditions.

In response to the shortcomings of both universal obligation of human rights and the religious norm of hospitality, justice as responsibility proposes that justice is meeting the responsibilities that particular, unchosen relationships impose. Fellow citizens may have responsibilities to one another, but they may also have responsibilities to non-citizens, either migrants in their midst, or citizens of other, even distant, countries. Such responsibilities may very well take the form of universal obligation based on the legal minimum of international law. At other times, this responsibility might look more like the norm of hospitality owed to the most vulnerable strangers. In cases where there are no preexisting relationships between persons, the norms of universal obligation and charity may fulfill responsibilities. However, according to theorists of migration, the encounter between citizens and non-citizens rarely takes place without preexisting relationships. More often, migration occurs in contexts characterized by particular histories and particular systemic vulnerabilities to one another.[6] Discerning what responsibilities we have to which groups of people becomes the critical task of justice as responsibility to relationships.

This task would seem to depend on examining the nature of the relationship itself. After all, we have responsibilities to our own children that we do not have to other people's children. We may have responsibilities to our elderly parents that differ substantially from the responsibilities that we have either to our children or to the elderly in general. However, as philosopher Margaret Urban Walker points out, these correlations between kinds of relationships and kinds of responsibilities are not assigned only by biological relationships. They are instead mediated through a complex set of social practices that are reinforced by social narratives.[7] Thus, while twenty-first-century Americans find it obvious, for example, that parents are primarily responsible for a child's well-being, this is so because our practices of assigning a child to a nuclear family who has this primary responsibility is supported by our social narratives about ideal mothers who care for children and ideal fathers who provide for their wives and children.[8]

Determining a just distribution of responsibility therefore depends on an examination of our social narratives to identify both the nature of our relationships and what kinds of responsibilities might emerge from these relationships. However, it is possible for one society to have a variety of different and conflicting narratives. False narratives lead to false accounts of our responsibilities.

Corrections of these false narratives may lead to more just distributions of responsibilities. While it is never simple to identify and examine the social narratives at work behind accounts of what seem obvious, turning to the narratives about relationships between entire political communities makes the task infinitely more complex. In order to determine the responsibilities of U.S. citizens to Central American child migrants, we must examine our narratives and go in search of truer narratives than the ones we hear.

A NARRATIVE OF FAILURES OF RESPONSIBILITY: THE UNITED STATES AND CENTRAL AMERICA

What I call narratives here are stories that attempt to order and make sense of some part of human reality. Narratives can take the form of master narratives, or ideologies—grand, totalizing narratives that attempt to order and make sense of reality as a whole. But narratives can also be smaller and more localized stories. While ideologies ignore or destroy all alternative readings of reality, narratives that contradict one another can co-exist. For example, "Immigrants are lazy" and "Immigrants take our jobs." They cannot both be true, and yet we can find versions of both of these narratives in the speeches of one political party, or at times, one politician.

Narratives can help illuminate reality. They can emphasize ethically salient features of ourselves and our relationships in ways that highlight overlooked responsibilities. They can bring to light obscure histories, interdisciplinary resources, and forgotten perspectives that help us better understand our responsibilities. I call such narratives *truer* narratives, rather than true narratives because by their very nature, narratives are incomplete. Narratives must make sense as stories; they cannot be just lists of facts or sequences of events. As such, they must draw our attention to certain people, events, facts, and processes and de-emphasize or even omit others. Reality is so complex and multifaceted that no one narrative can capture the fullness of reality. However, narratives can either be truer narratives that illuminate reality and reveal responsibilities or false narratives that obscure both reality and our responsibilities.

In contrast to truer narratives, false narratives are often built on shaky foundations of false and misinterpreted data masquerading as facts. At times, false narratives can be completely ahistorical. They amplify the voices of the powerful by dismissing or ignoring completely the perspectives and experiences of the weak. False narratives often become dominant precisely because such narratives reinforce the interests of the powerful. In this historical moment in the United States, we are living through the public dissemination of a particularly vicious and false account of US responsibility to non-citizens: that U.S. citizens have no responsibilities at all to non-citizens, not even to those who have lived in the United States for decades. This account of responsibility is grounded in a false narrative: they are strangers to us, criminals who enter the country without our invitation or consent. A distinct but similar account of responsibility is being disseminated about refugees, even those who are children: While they may be legitimately fleeing for their lives, we are under no obligation to make their problems our problems. They may be, so the narrative goes, gang members or terrorists. We are under no obligation to risk our security to help a stranger who may threaten us.

The only way to accurately understand responsibility for child migrants (in this case) from El Salvador and Guatemala is to both interrogate false narratives and propose truer narratives. While no one narrative can communicate the full truth of the relationship between the United States and El Salvador and Guatemala, my intent here is to aim for a narrative that reveals, rather than conceals, central, ethically relevant features of a relationship.

The story that follows is a story of unintended consequences. It is the story of how both U.S. foreign policy and immigration policy led to the arrival of child migrants at the southern border. This story, like all other stories, does not reveal every detail of the relationship between these countries. Rather, I seek to present a truer narrative that captures the ethically salient features of the relationship. Like all narratives, this one begins not at the beginning, but *in media res*, with the Cold War era intervention of the United States in Central America. Of course, this intervention itself has a story and a history. I emphasize the features of the story that pertain to the current migration from El Salvador and Guatemala to the United States.

During the Cold War, the government of the U.S. embarked on a quest to eradicate communism in the Western Hemisphere. In Latin America, this quest often took the form of interventions into the affairs of these sovereign countries, deposing democratically elected leaders, and installing or propping up military dictators by providing them financial and tactical support.[9] El Salvador and Guatemala were both sites of the U.S.'s proxy war against communism. In Guatemala, the CIA deposed the country's democratically-elected leftist leader and handed the country to a military dictator.[10] In both El Salvador and Guatemala, the support provided by the United States to military dictatorships enabled the governments to arm themselves against their own people, resulting in protracted civil wars.

The "first-round" of migration from El Salvador and Guatemala to the U.S. was thus the result of U.S. intervention in the civil wars in those countries—interventions that, far from being morally neutral, supported repressive governments that murdered, tortured and disappeared hundreds of thousands of civilians. Thousands of civilians fled for their lives, often to the U.S. This migration of peoples to the very country that was intervening in theirs was not a coincidence. According to migration theorists, migrations are not responses only to poverty and unemployment.[11] Instead, economic factors have to be "activated" by some kind of action on the part of the host country.[12] Quasi-colonial interventions, such as US intervention into the political affairs of the countries of Latin America, often start mass migrations back to the country that intervened.[13]

Although Salvadorans and Guatemalans in the U.S. unquestionably met the criteria for asylum under both U.S. and international law, 97% of them were not accorded asylee or refugee status. Instead, the Reagan administration deemed them economic migrants who were ineligible for asylum protections. This was, of course, a political move, for to admit that they were political refugees would have angered the military dictatorships allied with the Reagan administration. Refugee policy was bent to foreign policy goals, and the U.S. immigration courts became another front of the Cold War.[14]

While some of these migrants found asylum in Canada, others remained in the U.S. without legal status until legislation passed in the 1990s, enabling them to apply for Temporary Protected Status, and then, finally, permanent residency.[15] But their troubles did not end when they received their green cards. With the passage of the 1996 Illegal Immigration Reform and Immigrant Responsibility Act, minor, non-violent crimes became deportable offenses for anyone without the protection of citizenship. As a result of this legislation, almost one million people were deported in the following ten years.

Many of these deportees were Salvadoran and Guatemalan refugees who had arrived in the U.S. as children. Their undocumented status meant that they were often cut off from some of the social benefits and opportunities offered to citizens and legal immigrants. Some of these immigrants, as vulnerable youths, joined gangs in an attempt to find a place for themselves in American society. These immigrants, some fraction of whom were gang members, were ripped from their families and the only communities they had ever known and deported to the countries that they had left as children. When they arrived in El Salvador and Guatemala, they found countries still scarred from civil wars that were unable to provide the social support they would have needed to healthily reintegrate into their societies. The result of the toxic combination of time in inhumane U.S. prisons, the trauma of deportation itself, and the lack of services in Central America was that deported gang members established gangs in their new locations.[16] In other words, U.S. deportation policy transformed street gangs into multinational crime operations. In fact, two of the largest and deadliest gangs of Central America, Mara 18 and MS-13, bear the names of the streets in Los Angeles where they originated. Once established in El Salvador and Guatemala, the gangs grew. Even deportees previously unaffiliated with gangs often joined upon arrival, "becoming victimizers to avoid being victimized."[17]

Of U.S. deportation policy, Salvadoran journalist Óscar Martínez writes, "With the logic of an ape, they decided the problem could simply be booted to the other side of the border. [The United States] acted like a scared child who closes his eyes in the hope that what frightens him will simply disappear."[18] But instead of disappearing, gangs in Central America have ripped through the social fabric of these countries, turning parts of them into war zones. In 2015, El Salvador had the highest murder rate of any country not at war. The child migrants who arrive at the U.S. border are often fleeing such gangs. The unaccompanied child migrants at the border include traumatized children whose parents have been murdered in front of them, young girls fleeing enslavement by drug lords, and young boys whose families made the impossible choice to send them to the U.S. rather than see them join gangs. Such stories would move even the hardest of hearts. However, U.S. immigration courts often do not grant refugee protections to those who are persecuted by gangs, and these asylees often find themselves deported.[19]

Unaccompanied children from El Salvador and Guatemala arrive at the southern border as a part of a cycle of unintended consequences that started in the 1980s. This cycle repeats itself in some ways today, with the immigration courts refusing in many cases to accord refugee status to Central Americans fleeing gangs. There are, however, also new factors at play: the expansion of immigration detention means that some of these migrants end up imprisoned, often for years, before being deported back to Central America. Others manage to evade the immigration authorities and become undocumented; some of those undocumented persons are eventually apprehended and deported. The consequences of these new practices have yet to be manifested; however, the lessons of the past suggest that these new deportations will have similar unintended consequences as the first migration and deportation cycle, which will impact the United States at some future date. The lessons of the past might help us foresee what these consequences may be, and to prepare for them. However, we cannot learn from the past unless we understand how the past connects to our present moment, not just as a matter of understanding migrations of peoples, but as a matter of understanding how failures of responsibilities of the past leads to our present moment.

RESPONSIBILITY TO HISTORICAL INJUSTICE

Justice as responsibility requires that we understand our responsibilities by examining the nature of the relationship—in this case, the relationship between Americans and unaccompanied child migrants. What kinds of responsibilities emerge from the specific narrative above? Here, I consider four kinds of responsibilities that may stem from historical injustice: 1) responsibilities to relationship 2) responsibilities to the narrative 3) liability responsibility 4) responsibilities to social structures. These four categories of responsibility in practice overlap with one another and intersect with one another.

Responsibilities to Relationships

The first insight in applying justice as responsibility is that the primary responsibility is to other persons. In contrast to other theories that emphasize responsibilities to social structures or reforming social structures, justice as responsibility posits that the primary responsibility is to the other agents in the narrative, both the child migrants who are actually at the southern border and to the children and parents who remain in their home countries. Americans have responsibilities to both groups because both groups figure in the narrative. Responsibilities to social structures and to make reparations for past injustice stem from this primary responsibility to other persons.

The second insight of the primacy of relationships is the recognition that these unchosen, inherited relationships are the moral starting point for meeting our responsibilities. In other words, if Americans knew in the 1980s what they know now about the consequences of their foreign and immigration policies, they might very well have made different choices. Perhaps they would have elected a different government with different attitudes about the supposed threat of communism in Latin America. Perhaps they would have supported different immigration reform policies or been more vociferous in opposing harsh immigration laws. Even though these policy decisions were not made with the full knowledge and foresight, the relationships that result from these decisions form the moral starting point of justice today. Thus, Americans can and do have responsibilities that result from inherited, unchosen relationships that form the moral context of political decisions. Foreign and immigration policy decisions will continue to impact these relationships whether or not they are acknowledged or considered.

The third insight is that these relationships—between persons and between peoples—occur in a context marked by the interdependence of regions. Óscar Martínez writes, "Everything that is happening to us is tangled up with the United States. We can't untie ourselves."[20] Martinez indicates that while many Salvadorans might wish to cut Central America off from the draw of the United States and from the US consumer market for illegal drugs, they cannot. Similarly, while many Americans may wish to close the borders and develop policies that put "America first" with no regard for anyone else, the historical record shows that such policies have unintended consequences that will almost certainly affect them in the future. This interdependence of regions means that just like the policies of the past, the policies of the present and future will have unintended—though perhaps this time foreseen—consequences that Americans will also bear.

While the relationship between Americans and El Salvadorans and Guatemalans is characterized by an interdependence rooted in the past that will continue on for the foreseeable future, this interdependence is not an interdependence of equals, but an interdependence marked by discrepancies in both power and vulnerability. A larger, wealthier country with a more powerful military, the United States has disproportionate power compared to the peoples of Central America and especially to the child migrants from Central America. Similarly, while all peoples are vulnerable and while Americans are certainly vulnerable to the peoples of Central America, their vulnerability is dwarfed by the vulnerability of Central Americans to the unintended consequences of American laws and policies. This asymmetry in power and vulnerability also forms the moral starting point for a consideration of responsibilities and means that most of the responsibilities for child migrants falls on Americans.

Responsibilities to Narrative

An accurate assessment of responsibilities depends on accurate narratives. However, accurate narratives do not just fall out of the sky. Because all narratives are socially constructed and reproduced, challenging false narratives and replacing them with truer narratives is its own responsibility, and one that also comes from the relationships to others. The relationship between the narratives and our own responsibilities to challenge false narratives is circular. Without more accurate narratives, we cannot challenge false narratives. But we will not go looking for more accurate narratives unless we have already conceded that our narratives might be false. This problem has no easy solution, and indeed is one reason that false narratives become entrenched. One partial answer is that we must recognize the limitations of our narratives and have a kind of humility about them. The relationship between narratives and responsibilities involves its own responsibility of recognizing the limitations of narratives and interrogating them.

Replacing false narratives with truer ones is somewhat more complicated. There is not one, all-encompassing narrative that fully illuminates the reality of any relationship. In order to make sense as a story, all narratives must necessarily omit some details and highlight others. Having only a single story, even the one I have told here, risks silencing some voices and some perspectives and in doing so, entrenching a false account of responsibilities.[21] For this reason, Iris Marion Young insists that "the politics of historical narrative should make room for plural stories…"[22] In other words, it is only in "political contest, debate, and the acknowledgement of diverse perspectives on the stories and the stakes"[23] that we can begin to accurately discern our responsibilities. However, it is not enough to make room for a variety of narratives without attending to the power dynamics that result in some narratives erasing others.

We must seek out alternate narratives that challenge the interests of the powerful that are found precisely among the powerless and even the dead. Though we can no longer hear the voices of the dead civilians of the Salvadoran and Guatemalan civil wars, we can hear the stories of the survivors and review the historical record. We can also hear the stories of the child migrants themselves, their families and of Central Americans who live with gang violence.

False narratives can also be challenged with evidence from a wide variety of academic fields. Sociologies and anthropologies of migration, histories of the Cold War in Latin America and the study of the child migrants themselves all have a role to play in interrogating narratives and challenging them where they are false. An examination of narratives will highlight the stories of interdependence between Americans and Central Americans, examining the specifics of how the two groups are vulnerable to each other and in what ways while acknowledging the asymmetrical nature of both power and vulnerability.

Liability Responsibility

Once we recognize that there is a relationship and we seek out and identify truer narratives, we must still specify the kinds of responsibilities that emerge from specific narratives that describe the relationship. One kind of responsibility that can emerge from the past is rooted in what Iris Marion Young has termed "liability responsibility," which attempts to isolate individual responsibility for a specific harm. However, historical injustice, Young writes, often evades liability responsibility because often those who actually committed the harms are long dead. A better model, she writes, is her "social connection" model of responsibility, in which those who do not have liability responsibility for historical injustice are still responsible for reforming unjust social structures that are rooted in the past.[24]

However, there are instances in which liability responsibility may apply to historical injustice: corporate actors who still persist today, such as businesses and governments, may be held liable for historical injustices even when they occurred long ago.[25] But governments do not have liability for all or even most historical injustices. For example, Young does not think that the U.S. should be have liability-responsibility for slavery, because the actions of the U.S. government have been more ambiguous since the beginning of the Civil War. After all, she writes, the U.S. government emancipated the slaves, passed civil rights legislation, and currently enforces some measure of ongoing civil rights protections.

The ambiguity of government responsibility does not complicate the task of assigning liability responsibility for U.S. participation in the civil wars of Latin America. To be sure, there are many other agents who can also be held liable for the atrocities of the civil wars. However, the U.S. government is still liable for its role in these wars, as the right-wing dictatorships that it enabled may not have been able to unleash the scale and scope of these atrocities without the help of the U.S.

Since the end of the Cold War, the US government has not adequately accepted liability responsibility. During his presidency, Bill Clinton formally apologized for the U.S. role in supporting the repressive regime in Guatemala.[26] This was the closest any US president has come to even verbally accepting liability-responsibility for US intervention in any Latin American country. Even Clinton's verbal acceptance of liability responsibility was not matched by any offer of reparations to the Guatemalan people. Instead, Clinton offered US support for the reconciliation and pledged not to repeat the mistakes of the past.[27] In other words, while Clinton did apologize for the US role in the Guatemalan civil war, he framed US responsibility in terms of forward-looking responsibilities to aid the reconciliation process rather than backward-looking responsibilities for reparations. Neither Clinton nor any other US president has issued any such apology to El Salvador.[28]

The US avoidance of liability-responsibility for Cold War atrocities in Central America enables it to avoid forward-looking responsibility as well. For example, even as Clinton was issuing his apology to Guatemala, the US government was in the midst of implementing the 1996 Immigration Law that resulted in the deportations of thousands of Guatemalans.[29] The insistence on forward-looking responsibility combined with an avoidance of liability-responsibility made it possible to not fully come to terms with the damage done to the peoples of Central America. In other words, the evasion of liability responsibility reinscribes a narrative that undercuts any forward-looking responsibilities.

In contrast, an admission of liability responsibility carries with it not the responsibility to make reparations for the deaths of hundreds of thousands, which is not possible, but the responsibility to make reparations to the peoples for the destruction of their societies. Accepting liability responsibility might mean at minimum investing in the rebuilding after the trauma of war. In other words, while there is no place in international law for specific responsibilities to aid particular peoples who are experiencing humanitarian crises, justice as responsibility to relationships does have a role for this kind of specific responsibility, In the case of Central America, the liability-responsibility for Cold War era atrocities was never met; instead, it was compounded by false narratives that hid the interdependence of two peoples and inaccurately suggested that unwanted non-citizens could be deported without consequence to Americans. The failure to rebuild these countries after the end of the years of military dictatorships and war was a failure not only of forward-looking obligations to social structures, but of the responsibility to make amends based on liability responsibility. While Young wants to make a clear distinction between liability and social connection models of responsibility for historical injustice, in this case they are not so easily detached from one another. Failure to address liability responsibility in this case led to the deeper entrenchment of false narratives and the structures of injustice that such narratives support.

In this case, the US government does owe to the countries of El Salvador and Guatemala (and other Latin American countries) reparations and support for the damage done to those countries during their years of military dictatorships and civil wars. Liability responsibility also dictates explicit acknowledgement of wrongdoing on the part of the US government and formal apologies. Such acknowledgements of wrong-doing prevent reparations from being cloaked under the guise of "foreign aid."

Responsibility to Social Structures

While there is liability responsibility for reparations and apology on behalf of the US government, Americans also have the kind of forward-looking responsibility that Young describes to reform social structures so that they are more just. Social structures include political and legal institutions, laws, policies, and practices that determine the fate of tens of thousands of child migrants every year. While individual Americans can and do provide for child migrants through the provision of various kinds of aid, this individual provision is insufficient in the face of U.S. immigration and asylum laws and policies that fail to protect the human rights of child migrants.

For example, the fact that even children are not guaranteed legal representation for their asylum claims in US immigration court is a characteristic of an unjust social structure. A young child cannot be expected to understand US asylum law and argue that s/he meets the criteria for a successful asylum claim. The very system is structured in a way that makes successful asylum claims contingent upon the generosity and benevolence of citizens who donate their time and resources to supporting child asylees. And yet, the beneficence and generosity of small groups of citizens is not enough to meet the need for legal representation and support of every child migrant. Under the current system, some child migrants with valid asylum claims will be forced to go without representation and will likely be deported.

In this example, aspects of US asylum law are premised on a false narrative of American independence and isolation from the underlying causes of child migration. The narrative posits that Americans owe little to child migrants other than the minimal protections of asylum law. While the execution of and practices surrounding asylum law are inadequate even to the stated minimal goals of asylum law, perhaps these inadequacies go unchallenged because of a pervasive narrative that asserts that because Americans are not responsible for the conditions that cause child migration from the Northern Triangle, they are also not responsible for the child migrants themselves.

Thus, responsibilities to child migrants and responsibilities for challenging false narratives are inseparable from responsibilities to reform social structures. Americans cannot fulfill their responsibilities to child migrants on an individual basis without attending to the structural injustices in the immigration system that render child migrants vulnerable to harm. Reforming social structures also involves challenging the false narratives upon which they are premised. The narrative of the relationship between Americans and Central

Americans does not only lead to the responsibility to reform immigration laws and policies, but also includes the responsibility to reform structures that characterize the immigrant labor market in the United States. Americans also have the responsibility to press for changes to labor laws, unions, and workplaces that protect immigrant workers regardless of their status.

CONCLUSION

Like the chain of unintended consequences of US foreign and immigration policy, the various responsibilities that emerge from historical injustices intersect with and layer on top of one another. They are separable from one another only in theory. In practice, responsibilities to challenge false narratives leads to concrete responsibilities both to the Salvadoran and Guatemalan child migrants themselves and to the social structures that keep them in positions of vulnerability.

While justice as responsibility to relationships posits that specific responsibilities emerge from specific narratives about relationships, that does not mean that there are no responsibilities in the absence of specific relationships. Responsibilities to child migrants based on their vulnerability, their proximity, and the ability of a host country and its citizens to help still exist in the absence of complicated histories of relationship, as in the case of the Syrian refugees who have made their way to France and the United Kingdom.

International refugee law is in no way dispensable and in fact can work in tandem with justice as responsibility. However, justice as responsibility can address the gaps in protection of human rights left by international law. While the international laws that apply to refugees only concern those who have managed to flee their home countries, justice as responsibility to relationships can also address both the liability-responsibility for causing human rights atrocities and the forward-looking responsibility to address conditions that drive refugee migrations.

Similarly, justice as responsibility to relationships sees child migrants not as isolated agents, but as embedded within their families, communities, and entire relationships of interdependence that characterize regions. Thus, justice as responsibility to relationships can also address responsibilities to those left behind: those who will migrate at some point in the future and those who would migrate if they had the resources to do so.

While Americans have many specific responsibilities to unaccompanied child migrants from Central America based on historical relationships, even in the absence of such relationships, Americans would still have minimal obligations based on international law. Currently, the United States is fulfilling neither its minimal obligations nor its relational responsibilities. Here, justice as responsibility to relationships gives guidance to individuals and groups who live in contexts in which fulfilling responsibilities under present circumstances is impossible. American individuals, churches, and immigration advocacy groups can start interrogating false narratives and replacing them with truer narratives. They can form relationships with immigrant communities and amplify their narratives so that they carry weight in the public sphere. They can press for structural change to immigration laws and policies. And even when structural change is impossible or unlikely, the responsibility remains to meet the needs of child migrants on an ad-hoc basis whenever possible.

NOTES

1. Oscar J. Martínez, *A History of Violence: Living and Dying in Central America*, trans. John B. Washington and Daniela Ugaz (New York: Verso Books, 2016), xxi.

2. While Onora O'Neill has insisted that the discourse of children's rights is inadequate without a corresponding focus on the perfect and imperfect obligations to protect those rights, O'Neill ultimately recommends that such imperfect obligations be institutionalized. She is silent on the question of which particular persons and institutions have obligations to which particular children. Onora O'Neill, "Children's Rights and Children's Lives," *Ethics* 98, no. 3 (1988): 445–463.

3. Onora O'Neill, *Bounds of Justice* (Cambridge: Cambridge University Press, 2000), 154.

4. I first developed justice as responsibility to relationships in Tisha M. Rajendra, *Migrants and Citizens: Justice as Responsibility in the Ethics of Immigration* (Grand Rapids, MI: Wm. B. Eerdmans, 2017).

5. Honduras is the third country of Central America's "Northern Triangle." Like El Salvador and Guatemala, Honduras is plagued by gang violence and is a sending country of unaccompanied child migrants. Due to space restrictions, I have not included Honduras in this consideration of narratives of relationships because Honduras's relationship with the United States is different enough from El Salvador's and Guatemala's.

6. Rajendra, *Migrants and Citizens*, Ch. 2.

7. Ibid., Ch. 6.

8. Ibid., 121–122.

9. See Stephen G. Rabe, *The Killing Zone: The United States Wages Cold War in Latin America*, 2nd ed. (Oxford: Oxford University Press, 2016).

10. Stephen Schlesinger, "Ghosts of Guatemala's Past," *New York Times*, June 3, 2011, http://www.nytimes.com/2011/06/04/opinion/04schlesinger.html.

11. See for example Ronald Skeldon, *Migration and Development: A Global Perspective* (London: Addison-Wesley Longman Higher Education, 1997); Saskia Sassen, *Guests and Aliens* (New York: New Press, 1999), xiv; Douglas S. Massey

and others, *Worlds in Motion: Understanding International Migration at the End of the Millennium* (Oxford and New York: Oxford University Press, 2005), 8, 10.

12. Saskia Sassen, "The Making of Migrations," in *Living With(out) Borders: Catholic Theological Ethics on the Migration of Peoples,* eds. Agnes M. Brazal and María Teresa Dávila, (Maryknoll, NY: Orbis Books, 2016), 20.

13. Saskia. Sassen, *Losing Control? Sovereignty in an Age of Globalization* (New York: Columbia University Press, 1996), 71, 76.

14. Susan Gzesh, "Central Americans and Asylum Policy in the Reagan Era," *Migration Information Source*, April 1, 2006.

15. Ibid.

16. Daniel Kanstroom, *Aftermath: Deportation Law and the New American Diaspora* (Oxford: Oxford University Press, 2012), 151–154.

17. Margaret H. Taylor, and T. Alexander Aleinikoff, *Deportation of Criminal Aliens: A Geopolitical Perspective* (Washington, DC: The Inter-American Dialogue, 1998).

18. Martínez, *A History of Violence: Living and Dying in Central America,* xx.

19. Sebastian Amar and others, "Seeking Asylum From Gang-Based Violence in Central America: A Resource Manual," Capital Area Immigrants Rights (CAIR), August 2017.

20. Martínez, *A History of Violence: Living and Dying in Central America,* xxi.

21. Rajendra, *Migrants and Citizens*, 128.

22. Iris Marion Young, *Responsibility for Justice* (Oxford and New York: Oxford University Press, 2011), 182.

23. Ibid.

24. Ibid., Ch. 7.

25. Ibid., 175–177.

26. John M. Broder, "Clinton Offers his Apologies to Guatemala," *New York Times,* March 11, 1999, http://www.nytimes.com/1999/03/11/world/clinton-offers-his-apologies-to-guatemala.html.

27. John M. Broder, "Clinton Offers his Apologies to Guatemala," *New York Times,* March 11, 1999, http://www.nytimes.com/1999/03/11/world/clinton-offers-his-apologies-to-guatemala.html.

28. While Barack Obama did express a kind of qualified regret over the US involvement in Argentina's dirty war, his words did not come close to any acceptance of liability responsibility. Julie Hirschfield Davis, "Obama Expresses Regret for U.S. Policies During Argentina's Dirty War," *New York Times*, March 24, 2016, https://www.nytimes.com/2016/03/25/world/americas/obama-argentina-dirty-war.html.

29. John M. Broder, "Clinton Offers his Apologies to Guatemala," *New York Times,* March 11, 1999, http://www.nytimes.com/1999/03/11/world/clinton-offers-his-apologies-to-guatemala.html.

BIBLIOGRAPHY

Amar, Sebastian, Amy Fairchild Haer, Shaunna Bailey, and Abraham Jacob. "Seeking Asylum From Gang-Based Violence in Central America: A Resource Manual."

Capital Area Immigrants Rights (CAIR), August 2017. http://www.unhcr.org/uk/585a96a34.pdf.

Gzesh, Susan. "Central Americans and Asylum Policy in the Reagan Era." Migration Information Source, 2006.

Kanstroom, Daniel. *Aftermath: Deportation and the New American Diaspora*. Oxford: Oxford University Press, 2012.

Massey, Douglas S., Joaquin Arango, Graeme Hugo, Adela Pellegrino, and J. Edward Taylor. *Worlds in Motion: Understanding International Migration at the End of the Millennium*. Oxford: Oxford University Press, 2005.

Martínez, Óscar J. *A History of Violence: Living and Dying in Central America*. Translated by John B. Washington, and Daniela Ugaz. New York: Verso Books, 2016.

O'Neill, Onora. "Children's Rights and Children's Lives." *Ethics* 98, no. 3 (1988): 445–463.

———. *Bounds of Justice*. Cambridge: Cambridge University Press, 2000.

Rabe, Stephen G. *The Killing Zone: The United States Wages Cold War in Latin America*. 2nd ed. Oxford: Oxford University Press, 2016.

Rajendra, Tisha M. *Migrants and Citizens: Justice as Responsibility in the Ethics of Immigration*. Grand Rapids, MI: Wm. B. Eerdmans, 2017.

Sassen, Saskia. "The Making of Migrations." In *Living With(out) Borders: Catholic Theological Ethics on the Migration of Peoples*, edited by Agnes M. Brazal, and María Teresa Dávila, 11–21. Maryknoll, NY: Orbis Books, 2016.

———. *Guests and Aliens*. New York: New Press, 1999.

———. *Losing Control? Sovereignty in an Age of Globalization*. New York: Columbia University Press, 1996.

Skeldon, Ronald. *Migration and Development: A Global Perspective*. London: Addison-Wesley Longman Higher Education, 1997.

Taylor, Margaret H., and T. Alexander Aleinikoff. *Deportation of Criminal Aliens: A Geopolitical Perspective*. Washington, DC: The Inter-American Dialogue, 1998.

Walker, Margaret Urban. *Moral Understandings: A Feminist Study in Ethics*. New York: Routledge, 1998.

Young, Iris Marion. *Responsibility for Justice*. Oxford and New York: Oxford University Press, 2011.

Chapter 11

Going It Alone

Political Ethics and the Rights of Unaccompanied Migrant Children

Hille Haker

Thousands and thousands of minors are "unaccompanied alien children," as they are legally named in the United States, or "unaccompanied migrant children," as the UN defines them. In reality, unaccompanied migrant children never go it completely alone. Indeed, they are literally accompanied on their routes from one location to another, demarked by borders between nation-states. They may have been with their parents or relatives and separated during the journey, or by border control agents. They may well be accompanied by other minors and adults, by supporters and shelters that offer them water, meals, comfort, and some rest. They are accompanied by smugglers or so-called coyotes who know ways through the Sonoran desert, and they are also accompanied by the drivers of trains, buses, cars, or those who have the courage to steer a rubber boat across the Mediterranean Sea. They are virtually accompanied by the tears and good wishes of those they leave behind, sometimes their parents, grandparents or other kin, sometimes non-related caretakers who cannot guarantee the children's safety or well-being in their home countries. As research has shown, violence in the home countries, not the 'pull' factor of the destinations, is the common cause of children leaving their countries unaccompanied.[1]

While crossing the border to the United States or the European Union, unaccompanied migrant children are also accompanied by the surveilling border controls, by helicopters over their head, or by the aircraft and other security measures. If they cross the border to the United States, for example, they may be accompanied by the employees of the Office of Refugee Resettlement (ORR); although they are rarely accompanied by lawyers to the hearings of their cases, they are accompanied by social workers, volunteers, and journalists.

Some children reunify with parents in the receiving country and begin the emotional, cultural, and social journey into their new lives. But even when they have made it that far, they may end up in deportation procedures again after months or even years. They may be separated again, when their undocumented parents are deported, sometimes after decades of living in the United States. Unaccompanied migrant children are but one group of migrants, but without question, they deserve the highest priority—and more than any other group of migrants, they are the face of the crisis of responsibility we currently observe regarding migrants and refugees.

Refugees especially have become a pawn in American and European politics, increasingly used to fuel a nationalist populism. According to the increasingly immigrant-hostile political stance, even welcoming an unaccompanied migrant child or minor, we are told, creates a future security problem for the homeland. Those who call for the protection of human rights are accused of romanticizing those who cross the border, prioritizing one group of people to the disadvantage of another group, and ignoring the responsibilities regarding citizens in the United States or in the European Union. The promotion and defense of the so-called *"welcome culture"* (as the response to the refugees was labelled in Germany in 2015), is deemed *irresponsible* because of its strain on the receiving societies. Humanitarian responses only create incentives for more and more migrants and refugees entering the United States or the EU. Citizens of the US and European countries are told that immigrants threaten "our" national identity. "We" need to protect "us" against "them." The trope of migrants and refugees as a threat underlies not only multiple media reports and policies—it increasingly shapes people's perception, especially when they are not encountering the persons behind these condescending narratives.

The following analysis examines the current shifts in the political ethics of migration and the crisis of responsibility that Western societies face. When the fate of children who flee from conditions that threaten their basic security and who are separated from their families is not considered an issue of urgent action, this indifference becomes the most scandalous manifestation of an ongoing and much broader failure of international migration and refugee politics. As most of the authors have done, I will mostly refer to the US context; yet, the underlying political theory and ethics concerns both the United States and Europe.

THE POLITICAL SHIFT FROM POLITICAL REALISM TO A NATIONAL POPULAR POLITICS

At present, three major approaches to the politics of migration can be discerned: political realism, nationalist populism, and cosmopolitism. In this part, I will analyze the shift from political realism to nationalist populism, and turn to cosmopolitanism in the next section. Up to a few years ago, political realism was the predominant approach of US and European politics: refugees, asylum seekers, and migrants, it was held, indeed require some support, and the moral imperatives were easily affirmed as long as and the numbers of refugees or asylum-seekers reaching the borders of the United States or Europe were considerably small or immigration matched national interests economically. Nevertheless, the overall approach to immigrants was more interest-driven and less driven by the obligations to respond to the "rights of others," as Seyla Benhabib has coined it. International Conventions were embraced in national and regional policies, while beginning in the 1990s, the legal rules of asylum were increasingly redefined in almost all Western countries. Currently, almost 70 million people are displaced globally, with 3 million seeking asylum. With the increase of refugees in the United States and in Europe—in part the effect of stricter rules of migration after 9/11 in the United States, the US- and NATO-led wars in Afghanistan and Iraq, and the civil war in Syria—the mask of morality was taken off: politics, political realism claims, is all about trade-offs between conflicting claims, and therefore, pragmatic solutions must be found with respect to the migration and "refuge crisis."

Political realism argues that solutions must, first, balance the international humanitarian obligations with national obligations. Second, it must balance the concerns of migrant persons, including unaccompanied migrant children, with the concerns of law-abiding citizens (or law-abiding migrants). Third, it must take seriously the anxieties raised on a cultural level when citizens fear that immigrants (whether migrants, refugees, or asylees) transform the cultural identity considerably. Finally, however, realists argue, migration never solves the problems in the migrants' home countries. And for children, migration is not in their best interest, because they should not be migrating alone in the first place; to receive them with open arms, provide them with education and the jobs that their families may soon depend on only creates incentives for more families to send their children abroad.

These arguments are certainly not to be easily dismissed. Yet, from an ethical point of view, they easily distort what is at stake, especially when the Weberian distinction between an ethics of purist "conviction" (Gesinnung) and political "responsibility" (Verantwortung) is evoked.[2] The mentioned political solutions push the rights of migrants and/or refugees to the background, but even there, they do not disappear because of a political theory. Moreover, what may sound rational in view of a pragmatic politics of problem-solving, may, in effect, undermine the moral stance of Western cultures. Where, when, and how "unaccompanied" migrant children are accompanied is not only a political or legal question; it is also a moral question. Moral responsibility is not merely a question of weighing actions or policies in view of their consequences; it means, first and foremost, to respond to *others*, and to respond to them *with respect, compassion, and care*, and then to search for the best possible solutions. A political ethics regarding unaccompanied migrant children must critique the realist approach if or when it violates children's rights to protection and well-being.

Over the last years, the realist approach has been criticized by several populist movements who claim that the first responsibility in view of the "refugee crisis" is to defend the values of the United States or Europe. Whereas political realism makes the effort to balance international and national interests as well as ethical and political imperatives, the nationalist politics denies that there can even be a moral claim on a "nation" that is not strictly tied to its national interest.[3] Nationalist populist movements—often with the enthusiastic support of Christian groups and the Catholic Church—define these values along the lines of the so-called "American identity" and the so-called "Europe's Christian heritage," and they argue that these identities are threatened by migrants and refugees.[4] In the United States, the populist narrative is constructed around the broadly repeated and widely amplified assumption that many people yearn for a cultural belonging that is at risk; the identity narrative offers an appealing interpretation, it is said, to those who are disoriented or even uprooted by their experiences of the social transformation the West is undergoing. And indeed, the transformation of industries, the overall globalized economy with its changing labor conditions, the changes of demography, the transformation of social institutions such as the family, and the growing cultural and religious diversity due to immigration have changed Western societies considerably over the last decades. In response to these transformations, populist movements have increasingly won ground politically, and they have been rather successful in shifting the US and European migration policies. Nationalist populism and migration are tied together, because the nativist narrative promotes the social and cultural ideal as an imagery that is under attack from "liberal democracy" as well as from "illegal immigrants." It idealizes a social bond that often does not exist at all;[5] yet, migrants and refugees create a perfect negative platform: *they* do *not* belong; their presence threatens the very identity that must be safeguarded and restored. Like Victor Orban's politics of an "Illiberal Democracy," Donald Trump's "America First" slogan entails a well-known roadmap, echoing the Western nationalist politics of the 19th and 20th century. The US president takes every possible opportunity to communicate the backbone of his political message: foreigners, Muslims, migrants, or refugees are not welcome in the United States. And by now, the Republican Party has almost unanimously departed from its previous approach of political realism (that it shared with many members of the Democratic Party) and embraced a more and more nationalist populist politics. Likewise, in Europe, more and more elections turn in favor of ethno-nationalist parties and, strikingly, the

United States and Hungary have dropped out of the United Nations Global Migration Compact that is up for signature by UN members at the end of 2018. Even the most vulnerable "others," namely unaccompanied migrant children fleeing and/or migrating to the United States or Europe, do not belong—not to "us," and not "here." They are other people's and other peoples' responsibility. This narrative may resonate exactly *because* millions of people in the United States and in Europe can rightly claim that they have enough to deal with already—they have not yet recovered from the overall global economic and financial crisis, they are indeed left behind by a politics that claimed to benefit all while all along, the inequality gap widened dramatically over the last few decades, with no substantial gains of the poor and lower middle class, and they do indeed fear for the future of their children. But while white Americans, and moreover, white Christian Americans, fell in great numbers for Donald Trump's campaign slogans, only a fraction of African Americans and Hispanic or Latino/a Americans did. Poverty and economic stress cannot be the only cause for the broad resonance of populism in many countries: it is also true that it falls on the fertile soil of a racialized, Christian nationalism. Notwithstanding that there are many variations in both approaches, the realist position does agree with the premise of an international or even global moral and political-ethical responsibility, while the nationalist populism does not. The current political shift towards a nationalist identity politics, further fueled by xenophobia and islamophobia, has two important ramifications that are not only politically but also ethically relevant.

First, the moral appeal to empathy or compassion seems to penetrate less and less the thick emotional wall of indifference to any fellow-feeling. In the United States, moral indifference towards migrants is considered the right response to a "crisis" the American people, not the refugees, are facing; US citizens must be protected against migrants and refugees, foreigners, and culturally nonconforming individuals who all threaten the cultural identity of the country. Every public leader knows that political emotions can be easily ignited; as Martha Nussbaum has recently argued from a liberal perspective, they are needed to create the bond between the civil life and the political institutions, including the political representation, the constitution, or the political ideas of the polity.[6] When emotions are, however, exploited and merely used to promote an agenda that pits one group against another or against other groups that live or enter the polity, a moral line is crossed: political demagogy creates two different classes of human beings—one worthy of respect, care, and compassion, and one whose needs, dignity, and rights are dismissed or regarded other people's responsibility. Though empirically the group that is addressed by and that is drawn to nationalist populism does not necessarily profit in practical matters, the message being sent still promises the elevation of their *cultural* identity: a way of life that was denigrated by "liberalism" seems to be finally dignified and attended to "again," whereas it was seen as outdated and ridiculed for a long time—a good example for that in the United States is religion, while in Europe, the evoked "Christianity" of Europe functions more like a racialized ethnic undercurrent. Moral division between different people (and peoples) defines Donald Trump's Republican Party, the Front National in France, Viktor Orban's Fidesz Party, the Law and Justice Party (PiS) in Poland, the Alternative für Deutschland (AfD) in Germany, and all other nationalist populist parties that have emerged in recent years.[7]

Second, for many, the mere appeal to international law, to treaties, to conventions, or human rights is no option in this situation, because it has not brought the changes as promised over the last seven decades, in spite of all the UN human rights efforts and policies. Even where these were transformed into domestic laws, the governments in Europe as well as the Trump administration are pushing hard on legal reforms or appointments of government-friendly judges. Fighting their policies in the courts (as important as it is) comes with the risk that human rights are fully encapsulated in positive law. When human rights are, however, pushed to the background of politics or when they are merely defined along the lines of current laws, the moral meaning of human dignity is reduced to the legality of practices that have multiple other ends beyond moral protections. Moral dignity, I hold, must be explained through the concept of vulnerable agency.[8] And moral agency is rooted in moral convictions, which are necessary to secure the relation between morality and politics. When moral convictions are *merely* tied to claims of a fixed cultural identity, a moral identity that is based on equality erodes. And with it, the respect for the equal rights that is enshrined in the moral concept of human dignity erodes, too.[9] Thus, when human rights interpretations are almost entirely limited to their legal dimension, they become detached from the personal moral identities, the moral stances of societies, and the vision of politics as securing and promoting the rights and well-being of people. The task of political ethics, then, is to contribute to the public discourse by reclaiming the relationship between politics and ethics. This task goes way beyond the topic of this book; yet, the issues discussed in relation to unaccompanied migrant children highlight that it is high time to shape the political debate in broader ethical terms.

IN DEFENSE OF HUMAN DIGNITY AND HUMAN RIGHTS

The alternative to political realism and national popular politics, promoted, fostered, and embraced by the international community over the last 70 years, is a cosmopolitan political approach that transcends the nation states and national interests in the name of universal human dignity and human rights.[10] The question today is whether there is—still—a case to be made for human rights. In the following, I will focus on one right only, namely the right to hospitality, and to one group, namely unaccompanied migrant children; the discussion on the human dignity and human rights, politically defined as cosmopolitanism, must be defended against the nationalist popular scorn.

The Right to Hospitality

The idea of cosmopolitanism emerged as a response to the first wave of globalization in early modernity, the Western, Christian colonization of the "new world" by European powers, and it became tied to the project of enlightenment when Kant evoked it in his famous essay on "Perpetual Peace," arguing for a universal right to hospitality.[11] Kant's concept of hospitality is central to current renewals of cosmopolitanism, most prominently argued for by Seyla Benhabib who combines the universal obligation to hospitality that Kant had argued for with a political theory of human dignity and human rights. Critics of this approach argue, however, that Kant's cosmopolitan vision cannot be separated from the epistemology and context of European and American colonialism from which it stems. Following Francesco di Vitoria and the Salamanca School of Natural Law of the 16th century who fought hard for the recognition of the "humanity" and dignity of the American Indians, Kant does not argue for the hospitality of *European* societies towards immigrants but vice versa: his context was the late 18th century European and American colonialism, and Kant's reasoning about the "right to visit" that he claims is *not* a "right to residence," must be seen in this context. Hence, Kant argues indeed for a universal right to hospitality, though he was clearly addressing European "visitors" of the colonies. To dismiss this historical context, Jasmine K. Gani, among others, holds, results in a distortion and a far too optimistic assessment of the human rights theory.[12] Furthermore, when taken as a blueprint for the duties towards refugees, migrants, and asylum seekers, the negative record of the European or US history of racism and their human rights violations is easily brushed over. This critique must be kept in mind, but regarding Kant's essay, it ignores Kant's own critique of colonialism. This is what Kant says about his fellow Europeans:

> "the *inhospitable* conduct of the civilized states of our continent, especially the commercial states, the injustices which they display in *visiting* foreign countries and peoples (which in their case is the same as *conquering* them) seems appallingly great."[13]

Kant argued politically *and* ethically, establishing a universal hospitality right that combines the humanity of *all* human beings with a political theory that allows for arrangements and contracts between guests and hosts beyond this basic protection right. And this was indeed an important milestone for the establishment of international law that matters up to today. Kant's context also matters in another respect: Europe had no strict borders between nation states; rather, the territory belonged to the sovereigns who treated it (and, often enough the inhabitants) as their property or at least their realm of control and power. Seen from this perspective, Kant's effort to insert a political ethics into the politics of his time is as important as the acknowledgment of his contemporaneity to the European colonialism, which certainly entailed the conviction of the superiority of the European "race" and the higher "development" of its culture and political institutions. Both contexts, this means, matter in an honest reading of Kant's text. In contrast to the colonizers of the African and American continents, today's migrants do not come to the host countries to seize their land and property, as J. Waldron succinctly remarks: "They come not because they want to seize resources; they come because they want to be in the vicinity of, and to associate themselves with, the open economic networks that characterize a prosperous modern society."[14]

Recalling this historical context makes it clear, however, that the ethics of universal human rights, together with the principle of dignity, rests upon the experience of their negation in practice, and it must be wrested from their adversaries at any given time, even when these are masked as their defenders. Yet, as Garrett W. Brown aptly states: "... the fact that history has not lived up to the demands of cosmopolitan hospitality in its purest form does not mean that it is not something we ought to do, or that the theory itself is corrupt and 'perverted'."[15] Rather than giving up on universal human rights and the respective obligations, it is necessary to implement policies that are in line with them.

The idea of cosmopolitanism implicitly drives the idea of universal human rights, which are the centerpiece of the political ethics of the United Nations. They subject any policy to the imperative to create the conditions for every individual—and not just citizens of a polity—to live a life in dignity and decency. This political ethics clashes with the national populist politics but also constrains the political realism's balancing of human rights claims with other interests, instead calling for often necessary prioritizations of the different groups of human rights.[16] In practice, it can certainly be questioned whether any country ever lived up to the vision of the "united nations," as the human rights reports by several non-governmental organizations show on a regular basis. Thus, the difference between the realist approach that Western countries clearly backed over the last decades and an ethno-nationalist approach that is promoted by the right-wing parties in Europe and the United States may easily be overlooked when it comes to migration politics. But it makes a difference whether the human rights regime is watered down by political realism or whether it is abandoned entirely by a nationalist political theory that is centered on the "ethnos" rather than the "demos" (Benhabib). In the United States, for example, immigration policies resulted in the deportation of millions and millions of people already since the 1990s, and the removal of undocumented migrants was a declared policy after the September 11 2001 attacks.[17] Likewise, European countries, including Germany with its profound right to asylum that was untouched in the Basic Law of Germany until it was changed in 1993, tightened the grip on migrants, refugees, and asylum seekers long before 2015 when millions of people fled from the wars in Syria, Afghanistan, and Iraq, adding to the migrants and asylum seekers from African and Eastern European countries. Some argue, therefore, that it is only a gradual transition to the new policies of deterrence that we observe since 2015 and 2016 in Europe, and in the United States since the Trump presidency. When seen, however, from the perspective of the three approaches I have discerned, the recent (re)turn to nationalist policies is revealed as a far more radical break, namely a break with the United Nations' approach promoted since 1948. The Trump administration argues that it only interprets the current laws more strictly than the Obama administration. Yet, it changed Obama's declared deportation policy to look for "felons, not families" to a policy that targets *any* undocumented immigrant. The current administration has increased the interior deportation (of undocumented migrants and refugees) by about 37% in 2017 compared to the numbers of the Obama administration in 2016, and it continuously depicts *all* migrants as criminals, including the youths who come to the United States as unaccompanied children.[18] President Trump may well score a point among his supporters who buy his narrative of America's past glory that must be retrieved, because the overall numbers of removals at the border decreased considerably in the first year of his presidency. But more people—and politicians—take them as what the deterrence, the raids, and the deportations of migrants are: human rights violations. They do not only affect children who are apprehended at the border or are held in detention facilities—they also affect all families with undocumented members who may have lived for quite a while in the United States. Children become "unaccompanied," too, though not in the legal sense of US law, when their parents are deported and their families are torn apart, highlighting the problematic of the term "unaccompanied child" when it really means to be separated from one's parents as child. Regarding the effects of these policies on children merely as the side-effects of national security measures is a moral transgression that departs entirely from the norms of children's rights and human dignity.

The Human Rights of Children

As Mark Rohan has argued,[19] international law changed since the 1948 Universal Declaration of Human Rights, strengthening rather than weakening rights that are relevant for unaccompanied migrant children. The Convention of the Rights of the Child (CRC) states already in its preamble that the family is "the fundamental group of society and the natural environment for the growth and well-being of all its members and particularly children" and that "the child, for the full and harmonious development of his or her personality, should grow up in a family environment."[20] Art. 9 obliges the state to ensure that "a child shall not be separated from his or her parents against their will" unless it is in the child's best interests; and Art. 10 demands applications for reunification to be dealt with in a "positive, humane and expeditious manner," allowing the prohibition of exit or entry only for reasons of "national security, public order[,] public health or morals or the rights and freedoms of others." But when the mere fact that children—or their families—are crossing the border between Mexico and the United States is interpreted as an issue of national security and/or public order, we can see that even Kant's cautious argument for a duty to hospitality is at stake not only politically but also as a moral (and Christian) norm of human conduct. Children *have* the right to be protected against unlawful interference with their families (Art. 16 of the CRC), and regarding refugee children, Article 22 obligates states to "trace the parents or other members of the family of any refugee child in order to obtain information necessary for reunification with his or her family." And, like the CRC, the International Migrant Workers Convention from 1990 is a "Convention on the Protection of the Rights of All Migrant Workers and their Families," also emphasizing the right of the family to be regarded as a unit. Rohan argues that apart from much discretion that is left to nation states, some of the newer obligations to protect children's and families' rights create *positive obligations* for the states that they cannot simply circumvent in a distortion of the legal interpretation:

> A clause requiring positive action on behalf of the state alters the traditional balance between state sovereignty and human rights, placing a higher burden on the state to show that it has a legitimate reason for exclusion.[21]

Despite ongoing debate on the concept of cosmopolitanism, the bottom line of its underlying *ethics* that I am merely concerned with here is that national interests must adhere to the universal principle of human dignity. As a political theory, it is closely tied to a political *ethics* of human rights. This does not mean that all borders must be abolished or that there is an unlimited right to immigration. Rather, it acknowledges that nation states have legitimate interests regarding immigration, that local and regional contexts matter, and that there may be different ways to adhere to the human rights of migrants or the standard of the best interests of children, whether these are refugees or asylees, or migrating for social or economic reasons. How exactly the rights of children will be implemented, this means, depends very much on the contexts and circumstances of different countries. Regarding international law, however, this contextual flexibility does not support a *right to exclude* when this involves the denial of a basic right to security, or the annihilation of children's or families' rights to stay together or to be re-united. A political *ethics* of human rights and responsibilities cannot compromise on this norm. Why is it important to distinguish between the political theory and the political ethics of cosmopolitanism? Jeremy Waldron's thought experiment, reconnecting the political (and institutional or governmental political actors) to the ethics of people (as the enactors of political representatives), is illuminating:

> It is helpful sometimes in legal and political theory to transform a question about the rights of states or sovereigns into a question about the rights of people. Instead of asking whether it is permissible for sovereigns to exclude foreigners, perhaps *sometimes we should ask whether it is permissible for the people of a state to advocate the passage of laws to prohibit migrants (or particular classes of migrants) from entering their territories.*[22]

Like Nussbaum, Waldron points to the necessary coherence between political ethics and social values. Samuel Scheffler, however, elaborates further on the cultural identities in socially and culturally pluralist societies.[23] He makes an important point, acknowledging that moral convictions and values are indeed intertwined with the cultures they originate in—but their moral significance does not stem from the cultural norms as such but rather from the moral validity they entail for the persons. Charles Taylor called this the strong evaluations that shape persons' moral identities. Hence, the debate whether hospitality to immigrants, refugees, and asylum seekers is indeed merely a "charity" option or indeed an obligation, as Kant argued, and what its scope exactly is, points back to the dialectic of a hermeneutical-ethical interpretation of experiences and a normative argumentation regarding their relevance for one's moral identity.[24] Moral norms, translated into guidelines and, ultimately, laws, function as a reminder of the political ethics of a polity, and they are all the more important when empathy or compassion, hospitality and solidarity, a sense of justice as equality, or the political will to at least narrow the gap between the universal rights and national interests are overshadowed by an ethos of an assumed homogeneous cultural and/or national identity, which dismisses the "claims of others" as either invalid or secondary to the cultural identity claims.

The task of ethics is therefore, first, to unfold the histories concealed in the human rights norms and subject them to a thorough and critical analysis. Second, ethics must justify the norms via argumentation and make these arguments transparent in public discourses. In our context, it may suffice to point to the fact that nobody, especially not the defenders of the "cultural identity" of Western civilization, questions that children need their families. The question of unaccompanied migrant children is not a question of this underlying norm; rather, it is a question whether we *perceive* certain children as who they are, namely children who require the care of others, and how we determine who is *responsible* for the necessary measures in order to secure the care for them. If the United States or Europe refuses to take on responsibility for children because "alien children" do not belong to "us," it means that they are, in fact, *morally* excluded from humanity. Looking at migration in the global context shows that the vast majority of migrants are received by the poor and sometimes poorest countries. Thus, the American and European politics of exclusion reveals a moral corruption within the political ethics that claims to accord with universal human rights.

The human rights framework provides moral norms, offering a framework for actions, policies, and laws aimed at securing the dignity and rights of every human being.[25] But these norms are ineffective unless they correspond with the values, cultural and social norms, and the self-understanding of moral agents. Without a basic coherence between social values, moral norms, and policies, the prescriptions remain detached, abstract, and ineffective. Hence, the current shift of policies is much more a symptom of the crisis of responsibility than it is a crisis caused by migrants or refugees.

Children's Rights Interpreted

The Universal Declaration of Human Rights does not determine how exactly the corresponding policies are to be implemented. Some say that this is the biggest weakness of the human rights framework, rendering it a rhetorical bluster that does not matter too much in our policies anyway. But what would be the alternative, given the threats we face today? Furthermore, if understood as political-ethical framework that *requires* being spelled out in the concrete, actual ethical judgments and politically contextualized assessments, it calls for thorough contextual analyses. And this may well be a strength, for two main reasons, as can be seen with respect to the Convention of the Rights of Children: First, it orients the necessary political compromises *within* the limits of human rights; citizens have the responsibility to discern whether the real politics is still in line with the protection and promotion of the rights of children—and what measures are taken, for example, when their human right to stay or reunite with their parents is denied. Such a discernment is obviously often complex and complicated, and experts and citizens may well differ in their judgments. But this is exactly why practical reasoning, exercised in legal cases as well as in ethics must be part of the political process of decision-making.[26] The second reason that contextual interpretation strengthens human rights is related to the first: the abstractness of moral norms reflects but also conceals their own history that can—and must—be unfolded in historical narratives. When we want to explain why human dignity matters, it is not enough to say that it is what human beings deserve, or that it constitutes their status as persons as the natural law and modern tradition of natural rights did. Rather, it is necessary to acknowledge that, among others, the right to migrate, refuge and asylum and the respective duty of hospitality is the result of a very torn history and the struggle for these rights that preceded the signatures and ratification process. Instead of brushing over these histories, we must remember them, and remind ourselves that the human rights always had to be wrested from those who had power and exercised it with violence. The critics of cosmopolitanism are right to point out to the flaws and failure of the conceptual human rights history: the natural law and natural rights tradition were both used as an ideology that, in the very name of human dignity, denied multiple groups the status of being human, of personhood, and human dignity. But as the history of most UN Conventions also shows, the rights that *are* finally being decided upon are usually preceded by long and thoughtful discussions, promoted by those whose rights were at stake.

The Convention on the Rights of the Child, signed forty years after the Universal Declaration of Human Rights, originated in a movement for the commitment to protect children from forced labor and exploitation in the 19th century, and this is but one example of why historical contexts matter as much as the contextual interpretations how to implement them in the multiple areas that are of concern for them.[27] At the beginning, children were mostly taken as the passive addressees of human rights, to be enforced by adults in their treatment of children. The often-invoked "best interests standard" (Article 3), for example—important for the multiple proxy decisions that caretakers, social workers, lawyers, doctors, or political authorities must take for unaccompanied migrant children—is not only part of the CRC but also the standard used in child-related legislation in the United States, which, as the only member of the UN, has not ratified the CRC.

While unaccompanied migrant children fall under the category of the "child" in the CRC, they are mostly children in their adolescent years, often near the threshold of adulthood. Over the course of the 20th century children's own agency has been more and more emphasized. Children are certainly victims of their circumstances, but growing up they become also agents who take their fate into their own hands. Navigating cross-cultural interpretations of what signifies the status as child, youth, or adult easily creates confusion, and sometimes frustration for both children and adults. The perception of a child who needs the care of an adult may easily descend into the reluctance to respect a child's agency, and this is all the more true in the case of adolescents, as every parent knows. But vice versa, the perception of children's agency may also conceal their vulnerability, especially those of migrant adolescents, and even more so when they themselves do not wish to be seen as vulnerable. In the legal context of child protection, the age of 18 determines the end of the protection laid out in the CRC—but also the end of proxy decisions—shifting the emphasis to the general human rights framework or the respective laws. For example, the right not to be discriminated against stays in place, while the right to be reunified with one's parents does not. In the context of migration and asylum for refugees, the shift from the protection under the CRC or related US laws to the protection under adult laws has major ramifications, both for the legal procedures and the social provisions (education, healthcare, placement in foster families) available for youths but not for young adults.[28] Ethically speaking, however, these abrupt changes do not necessarily reflect the young adults' needs.

The Plural Roots of Human Rights: The Case of Religious Ethics

The 20th century's UN declarations, conventions, and overall framework of human rights take up century-long ethical reasonings from multiple cultural, philosophical and theological or religious traditions. The text of the Universal Declaration of Human Rights in 1948 was drafted and discussed, amended and edited by multiple non-Western interlocutors before it was finally signed by *all* Nations.[29] Furthermore, human dignity and human rights are not only embraced by secular ethics but also by religious ethics, providing a particular link between moral values that are embedded in historical experiences and the moral norms corresponding to them. The three largest world religions, Judaism, Christianity, and Islam, all share an ethics that begins with a divine "No" to undignified lives, and a divine "Yes" to every individual human being. The Jewish ethical norm of "love of one's neighbor," for example, is linked to the biblical stories of protections and provisions for members of the community as well as to the hospitality for strangers, creating a particularly "thick" narrative ethics of social justice.[30] The Christian norm of "neighborly love" cannot be understood without recognizing this background. Christianity's own narrative begins with a young Jewish woman who lives under the occupation of a foreign power, poor, engaged but not married, pregnant, and in transit. Like so many before and after her, this woman is being denied shelter, rejected in the most vulnerable state imaginable: ready to give birth.[31] On the level of the narrated story, none of the people who denied her the comfort of a roof over her head could possibly know what would happen next—after all, as the story is told, they all had good reasons for rejecting the young couple. Yet the implied reader of the story is put in the shoes of the young woman; from this perspective, *her* plea for shelter is as necessary as legitimate. The readers of the story know that a rejection of the couple violates a central religious norm of Judaism, namely the norm of hospitality to the stranger. If one only recites the norm of "hospitality," the stories behind it are easily forgotten; the stories of Judaism, Christianity, and Islam not only illustrate the norm; they concretize it in ever-changing contexts. The anti-Judaism that is found in many Christian interpretations of the birth and death of Jesus reiterates the moral division between one group (Christians) against another (Jews) that the Jesuanic ethics exactly strived to overcome. In Christian ethics, the "neighbor" addressed in the norm of neighborly love emerges in and from these narratives: 'others' *become* our neighbor when we become *their* neighbor, and letting them be neighbors to ourselves. Hospitality to the stranger is one dimension of the love of neighbor, and as such links the universal right to universal responsibility. Moreover, the religious norms of love and justice, like the norm of hospitality, too, cannot be separated from the experiences of *denied* responsibility, *refused* love, or *injustice*; together with the norms, these experiences are enshrined as sacred memories in the religious traditions of all three religions, meant to inform the convictions and moral identities as much as the political practices and institutions of their followers.

THE PROJECTION OF CHILDREN AS THREAT TO SECURITY

Since socially and culturally mediated moral values matter for the policies and political representatives citizens legitimize, it matters how they conceive of unaccompanied migrant children. Numerous measures of the Trump Administration are aimed at expelling young people already in the United States or preventing children from crossing the border, either alone or in the company of their parents or other caretakers. Donald Trump ended the Deferred Action for Childhood Arrivals (DACA) legislation; it had been implemented by the Obama administration in order to provide some legal protection for undocumented young people born in the United States, issued as Executive Action after Congress failed to move on an immigration law. Trump reversed it by the same means. But the Trump administration has done much more: it began to redefine the conditions for special protections granted to children crossing the border alone. It has stepped up the prosecution of smugglers who bring children to the United States. It separated children from their parents upon arrival in the United States. It plans to deport unaccompanied migrant children once they turn 18, without any court hearing. Central American minors can no longer apply for asylum from their home country. The restrictions on the time children can be held in shelters are planned to be removed.[32] Although several of these measures are already or will be contested in the courts, the administration is moving fast to fill in the multiple vacancies in federal courts, aiming to secure that the policies it stands for will be secured by case law long after this presidency is over.

The stigmatization of migrant children is regularly fueled by Donald Trump's speeches. In September of 2017, for example, Trump blamed the DACA program for the numbers of unaccompanied migrant children crossing the U.S. border from Mexico. In the 2018 State of the Union address, he claimed that DACA "helped spur a humanitarian crisis—the massive surge of unaccompanied minors from Central America including, in some cases, young people who would become members of violent gangs throughout our country, such as MS-13."[33] The assertion was no longer that victims may *turn into* criminals but rather, that criminals migrating to the United States *pose* as victims.

Lauren Heidbrink has identified three markers of criminality that overdetermine the depiction of unaccompanied migrant youth: the "illegal alien," the "criminal," and the "enemy within."[34] In contrast to the depiction of the secretly border-crossing "illegal alien," the fact is that many unaccompanied migrant children turn themselves in at the border, order to seek asylum. Second, stories of young men of color, depicted as drug dealers or members of gangs are amplified and scandalized for political purposes. "Migrants turning criminals" and "criminals posing as migrants" shape the public perception. Third, the binary of "friend" and "foe" that Heidbrink identifies, creates the narrative of the "the enemy within," which has led at times to "further institutionalizing the criminalization of young men of color, of foreign origin, and of particular faiths."[35] From 2002–2011, the United States implemented the so-called "National Security Entry-Exit Registration System" (NSEERS) for certain international citizens, but also for particular groups of people living in the United States, mostly from predominantly Muslim or Arab countries. In 2017, the Trump administration began to reapply it for immigrants from Muslim countries.[36] The effect of such a criminalization on migrant families, and children's self-esteem in particular, may be devastating.

As a *group*, unaccompanied migrant boys or young men are especially faced with stigmatization; they are depicted as potentially violent and engaged in criminal conduct. Pruitt, Berents, and Munro who have studied the gendered stigmatization call for research that examines how masculinity is constructed around violence, in order to counter the myth that violence is an inherent part of masculinity.[37] But gendered stereotypes also concern migrant girls or young women: the flipside of "male violence" is the "female victim" who experiences sexual violence on the journey.[38] Sexual assaults against girls and adolescent women are always egregious human rights violations, but exposure to sexual violence and exploitation is not an attribute to girls alone; migrant young men, transgender or non-binary individuals are also vulnerable to it—yet they are rarely mentioned in media reports. The particular vulnerable agency of all minors is easily lost in translation when gender stereotypes fuel the stories of migrant adolescents. Understanding the stage of adolescence as the transition from childhood to adulthood, exposing this group to particular vulnerabilities and accompanied with yet unknown possibilities of agency, should be motivation enough to support them in the transition and to counter the projections of fear, rather than feeding them.[39]

CONCLUSION

An ethics of child migration is faced with multiple and complex questions on several levels. Apart from the empirical analyses, legal and ethical reasoning the books provides, are there at least some practical solutions? I can point to some tentative pathways:

First, we must place unaccompanied migrant children at the center of the debate, and let them tell their stories publicly, as Javier Zamora has done so impressively. Several authors of this book have provided empirical studies that offer a glimpse into the realities that unaccompanied migrant children are faced with. Others have turned to the narratives of migrant children and the ethnographic scholarship of the same authors, or turned to historical studies for the legal, theological, and ethical analyses. Experiential knowledge, empirical knowledge, and historical facts together shape the context in which the ethical reasoning takes place, and it is important to be informed of the realities unaccompanied migrant children are confronted with.

Second, we need to attend to the ontological, moral, and structural vulnerability of migrant children, together with their agency, which several authors in this book emphasized. Social work is needed especially for adolescents, as their identity is shaped considerably by the often stigmatizing experiences. Social workers, community networks, and teachers need to be informed about the contexts of migrant children's roots, and they must acknowledge the effect of the dramatic uprootedness that all these children have experienced, and the often traumatic experiences it entails.[40] Gender stereotypes and gender norms are difficult for any child when they do not match a person's self-understanding and identity, and they may have an accelerating effect when combined with social stigmatization that easily exaggerates male agency and female vulnerability. Educational tools must be (further) developed to attend to migrant children's needs and skills, and be implemented in K-12 curricula, vocational schools, and work places, as the example from Germany has shown.[41] Universities should develop practical tools in collaboration with migrant adolescents, social workers, teachers, and labor organizations.

Third, we need to become close observers of the political changes, not only in the United States or in Europe but also in other regions. NGO's and public media are indispensable for this task. Several authors of this book are restlessly working for the public to better understand the political and legal affairs, or are well connected to the Catholic migration networks. The close and transdisciplinary collaboration is a promising approach to respond to the complexity of child migration.

Fourth, the political shift to a national populist politics must be criticized and resisted by all means in the public sphere. Ethnonationalism is not a question of bipartisan politics; it must not be normalized if it entails—as it currently does—the discrimination of groups for reasons of their descent, ethnicity, or religion. Embracing rightwing extremists as part of the normal spectrum is dangerous for any society that aims to embrace universal human rights: xenophobia, islamophobia, anti-Semitism, and white supremacy are not "normal" political positions to be placed side by side to other views—and journalists or scholars should not be fooled to embrace the narrative that masks hate speech as "white victimization." The vision of the "United Nations" is clearly set up against the discriminatory social imagery of first-class and second-class human beings. History shows, however, that often the narrative of the threatened identity is used to pit those who may all be disenfranchised by an economic order that prevents them from flourishing against each other. The political-ethical vision of the "united nations" is indeed cosmo-politian: it rests upon the respect and recognition that people owe each other, acknowledging that every individual "aim[s] for a good life, with and for others, in just institutions," as Ricœur aptly coined it.[42] Adults are, after all, the primary role models for children. If they cannot endure the "otherness" of others they should not expect that adolescents, searching for their own identities and belonging, will react differently. Therefore, social and political programs are needed that address the receptivity of particular populations for the identity politics of the "white, Christian American" or the "white, Judeo-Christian European" heritage, in order to foster a thick virtue ethics that builds upon the sense of justice and compassion, which is, after all, rooted in the very tradition that is evoked by most of the current popular movements.

Fifth, according the US Conference of Catholic Bishops, the Catholic Church is the largest non-governmental refugee settlement agency of the world.[43] The Church has made its position regarding the treatment of migrants and refugees very clear: it cannot and will not be silent when a whole group is discriminated against, a whole religion—Islam—is denigrated, and when children are separated or prevented from being reunited with their parents. In the United States and in Europe, the Catholic Church has been outspoken in its critique. US Bishops lament, for example, the record-low numbers of refugees accepted into the United States, merely approximately 9,600 refugees in the 2018 fiscal year so far, which is less than 25 percent of the (already radically reduced number of) refugees allowed for this year.[44] Yet, the US Catholic Bishops have welcomed Donald Trump's explicit anti-reproductive rights policy, looking the other way with respect to the overall moral division he fosters and promotes. As Susan Terrio has shown, (female) migrant adolescents are not protected against the overreach of those who rather make the decision for the girls than leaving it to them and their doctors. This is a clear misunderstanding of the best interests standard, because it reflects an understanding that disrespects the agency of adolescent girls faced with a pregnancy. The prioritization of abortion and marriage norms over the rights and well-being of adolescent children cannot be justified ethically or theologically, and for now, the US courts have interpreted it in this way, too. Many Catholic ethicists oppose the Vatican's stance on gender, sexual ethics, and abortion that Catholic Bishops are following. While this discussion belongs into the internal forum of the Church, theologians will need to raise their voices even more strongly when these positions are used to inflame the much broader political battle I have described.

Sixth, theologians should continue to align with Jewish and Muslim organizations especially (though not exclusively)—and step up their efforts of interreligious scholarship and programs, because these create the ground for learning experiences that may then be used in education and developing of cultural (and intercultural) competency among the many groups who live together in immigration societies. The religious stories of hospitality, migration, love, and justice in all three religions offer a narrative ethics of migration that fleshes out the religious ethical values and the norms the believers of these religions share as their tradition. Here, the World Parliament of Religions, among others, has a vested role to play. In addition to the scholarship, interfaith initiatives are important means to counter the religious and cultural division on an everyday basis.

Identity politics that builds upon and promotes the denigration of others, especially minorities or affiliates with a particular religion, in order to secure a particular cultural identity is never acceptable ethically. Since the new nationalist popular politics is so often tied to Christianity, Christians must speak out. Ultimately, however, adults who fail to protect children's basic security and fail to foster their development, be it through their actions and omission to act or through their indifference to policies that entail children's rights violations, not only fail these children. They also fail the most basic test of moral decency. The current crisis has not been created by the migrants or refugees. It is a crisis of lacking moral and political responsibility, and while certainly not the only failure regarding migration, refuge, and asylum policies, the failure to care for unaccompanied migrant children is its most scandalous and inexcusable manifestation.

NOTES

1. Cecilia Menjívar, and Krista M. Perreira, "Undocumented and Unaccompanied: Children of Migration in the European Union and the United States," *Journal of Ethnic and Migration Studies*, Special Issue: Undocumented & Unaccompanied: Children of Migration in the European Union and the United States (December 21, 2017), https://doi.org/10.1080/1369183X.2017.1404255.

2. Konrad Ott, *Zuwanderung und Moral* (Stuttgart: reclam, 2016).

3. A demonstration of this shift is the Trump administration's announcement in December 2017 to drop out of the UN Global Migration Compact. Cf. Rick Gladstone, "U.S. Quits Migration Pact, Saying It Infringes on Sovereignty," *New York Times*, December 3, 2017, https://www.nytimes.com/2017/12/03/world/americas/united-nations-migration-pact.html.

4. The current narrative was preceded by a similar battle of Euope's identity during the years of the Lisbon Treaty of the European Union. Cf. Josef Ratzinger, "Europas Identität. Seine geistigen Grundlagen gestern, heute, morgen," in *Werte in Zeiten des Umbruchs. Die Herausforderungen der Zukunft bestehen* (Freiburg: Herder spektrum, 2005), 68–88. For a thorough analysis cf. Christof Mandry, *Europa als Wertegemeinschaft. Eine Theologisch-Ethische Studie zum politischen Selbstverständnis der Europäischen Union* (Saarbrücken: Nomos, 2009).

5. Arlie Hochschild has offered an interesting insight into anger that drove the rise of the Tea Party in the United States; but intended or not, the book *also* depicts the often ill-functioning relationships, marriages, families, communities, and environments that the interviewees described as their social contexts. Cf. Arlie Russell Hochschild, *Strangers in Their Own Land: Anger and Mourning on the American Right* (New York: New Press, 2016).

6. See Martha Craven Nussbaum, *Political Emotions: Why Love Matters for Justice* (Cambridge: The Belknap Press of Harvard University Press, 2013). For a discussion cf. Hille Haker, "Compassion and Justice," *Concilium* 4 (2017): 44–54.

7. Cf. Cas Mudde, and Cristóbal Rovira Kaltwasser, eds., *Populism in Europe and the Americas: Threat or Corrective for Democracy?* (Cambridge: Cambridge University Press, 2012); Walter Lesch, *Christentum und Populismus. Klare Fronten?* (Freiburg:Herder 2017).

8. Hille Haker, "Vulnerable Agency: Human Dignity and Gendered Violence," in *Dignity and Conflict: Contemporary Interfaith Dialogue on the Value and Vulnerability of Human Life*, eds. Jonathan Rothschildt and Matthew Petrusek (Notre Dame: University of Notre Dame Press, 2018, forthcoming), 393–436.

9. Elena Namli and Linde Lindkvist make the same point in their contribution. See Chapter 7 in this volume.

10. Cf., for example, Seyla Benhabib, *The Rights of Others: Aliens, Residents, and Citizens* (Cambridge; New York: Cambridge University Press, 2004); *Another Cosmopolitanism* (Oxford; New York: Oxford University Press, 2006); *Dignity in Adversity: Human Rights in Troubled Times* (Cambridge, UK; Malden, MA: Polity, 2011). A good overview of the discussion in light of recent immigration policies in the United States can be found in Rebecca Sharpless, "Cosmopolitan Democracy and the Detention of Immigrant Families," *New Mexico Law Review* 47, no. 1 (2017): 19–63.

11. Immanuel Kant, "Perpetual Peace: A Philosophical Sketch", in *Kant's Political Writings*, ed. Hans Reiss (Cambridge: Cambridge University Press, 1991), 93–115.

12. Jasmine K. Gani, "The Erasure of Race: Cosmopolitanism and the Illusion of Kantian Hospitality." *Millennium – Journal of International Studies* 45, no. 3 (2017): 425–46.

13. Kant, "Perpetual Peace", 106 (emphasis there). For an analysis cf. Garrett W. Brown, "The Laws of Hospitality, Asylum Seekers and Cosmopolitan Right: A Kantian Response to Jacques Derrida." *European Journal of Political Theory* 9, no. 3 (2010): 308–27.

14. Jeremy Waldron, "Exclusion: Property Analogies in the Immigration Debate." *Theoretical Inquiries in Law* 18, no. 2 (2017): 469–89.

15. Brown, "The Laws of Hospitality", 313. For a discussion of EU policies cf. also Garrett W. Brown, "The European Union and Kant's Idea of Cosmopolitan Right: Why the EU Is Not Cosmopolitan." *European Journal of International Relations* 20, no. 3 (2014): 671–93.

16. Alan Gewirth, *Human Rights: Essays on Justification and Applications* (Chicago: University of Chicago Press, 1982).

17. According to the Institute of Migration Policies, 12 million people were removed from the United States in the two terms of the Clinton administration, counting both border and interior removals; more than 10 million were removed under the Bush administration, and more than 5 million under the Obama administration, of which more than 3 million people were removed at the border. Summarizing Obama's policies, the report states: "While the Obama administration record is characterized by much higher removals than preceding administrations, it also shows less focus on increasing absolute numbers of overall deportations and a higher priority on targeting the removals of recently arrived unauthorized immigrants and criminals. The administration also placed a much lower priority on removing those who had established roots in U.S. communities and had no criminal records." Cf. Muzaffar Chishti, Sarah Pierce, and Jessica Bolter, "The Obama Record on Deportations: Deporter in Chief or Not?" Migration Policy Institute, January 26, 2017, https://www.migrationpolicy.org/article/obama-record-deportations-deporter-chief-or-not.

18. Cf. Julianne Hing, "Why Numbers Alone Obscure the Real Deportation Story," *The Nation*, December 28, 2017, https://www.thenation.com/article/why-numbers-alone-obscure-the-real-deportation-story.

19. Marc Rohan, "Refugee Family Reunification Rights: A Basis in the European Court of Human Rights' Family Reunification Jurisprudence," *Chicago Journal of International Law*, 15, no. 1 (2015): 347–75, http://chicagounbound.uchicago.edu/cjil/vol15/iss1/15.

20. Cf. Katherine Kaufka Walts, Ch 5 in this volume.
21. Rohan, "Refugee Family Reunification Rights," 357–58.
22. Waldron, "Exclusion," 484 (my emphasis).
23. Samuel Scheffler, "Immigration and the Significance of Culture." *Philosophy & Public Affairs* 35, no. 2 (2007): 93–125.
24. Cf. for a thorough argument of the two pillars of ethics Haker, Hille. *Moralische Identität. Literarische Lebensgeschichten als Medium Ethischer Reflexion. Mit einer Interpretation der "Jahrestage" von Uwe Johnson* (Tübingen: Francke, 1999).
25. Cf. Hille Haker: "No Space. Nowhere. Refugees and the Problem of Human Rights in Arendt and Ricœur," *Ricoeur Studies* 8, no. 2 (2017): 21–45.
26. Cf. Ricœur, *The Just* (Chicago: University of Chicago Press, 2000); J. Waldron argues to interpret human dignity strictly as a legal concept, but there is no reason why legal philosophy and political ethics should not inform each other, even though they may overlap practically in many ways. Cf. Jeremy Waldron, *Dignity, Rank, and Rights* (New York; Oxford: Oxford University Press, 2012).
27. Paula S. Fass, "A Historical Context for the United Nations Convention on the Rights of the Child," *The Annals of the American Academy of Political and Social Science* 633 (January 2011): 19. See also Kaufka Walts, Chapter 5 in this volume.
28. See Namli/ Lindkvist, Chapter 7 in this volume.
29. Linda Hogan, *Keeping Faith with Human Rights* (Washington: Georgetown University Press, 2015).
30. Cf. among others Jacques Derrida, *Of Hospitality* (Stanford: Stanford University Press, 2000). Andrew Shepherd, *The Gift of the Other: Levinas, Derrida, and a Theology of Hospitality* (Oregon: Pickwick Publications, 2014). Judith Still, *Derrida and Hospitality Theory and Practice* (Edinburgh: Edinburgh University Press, 2010).
31. See. Cristina Traina, Chapter 8 in this volume.
32. Maria Sacchetti, "DHS proposal would change rules for minors in immigration detention," *Washington Post*, May 9, 2018, https://www.washingtonpost.com/local/immigration/dhs-proposal-would-change-rules-for-minors-in-immigration-detention/2018/05/09/267af486-4f00-11e8-b725-92c89fe3ca4c_story.html?utm_term=.8d9deb87b3ff.
33. Donald J. Trump, "Statement from President Donald Trump," September 5, 2017, https://www.whitehouse.gov/briefings-statements/statement-president-donald-j-trump-7.
34. Lauren Heidbrink, "Criminal Alien or Humanitarian Refugee?: The Social Agency of Migrant Youth." *Children's Legal Rights Journal* 33 (Spring 2013): 162.
35. Ibid.
36. George Joseph, "Draft DHS Report Called for Long-Term Surveillance of Sunni Muslim Immigrants," *Foreign Policy*, February 5, 2018, http://foreignpolicy.com/2018/02/05/draft-dhs-report-surveillance-of-muslim-immigrants.
37. Lesley Pruitt, Helen Berents, and Gayle Munro, "Gender and Age in the Construction of Male Youth in the European Migration 'Crisis'," *Signs: Journal of Women in Culture and Society* 43, no. 3 (2018): 687–709. 697.
38. Office of Refugee Resettlement, "Facts and Data," https://www.acf.hhs.gov/orr/about/ucs/facts-and-data.

39. See Philip M. Anderson, Chapter 4 in this volume who gives an example of how social work can respond to the particular needs of (male) adolescents, while Stephanie Arel, Chapter 3 in this volume, analyzes the emotional and social risks related to the lack of belonging and attachment figures.

40. Cf. Arel, Ch. 3 in this volume.

41. Cf. Anderson, Ch. 4 in this volume.

42. Paul Ricoeur, *Oneself as Another* (Chicago: University of Chicago Press, 1992).

43. http://www.usccb.org/news/2015/15-148.cfm.

44. Catholic News Service, "U.S. Catholic Leaders Concerned by Low Number of Resettled Refugees," March 28, 2018, https://cruxnow.com/church-in-the-usa/2018/03/28/u-s-catholic-leaders-concerned-by-low-number-of-resettled-refugees.

BIBLIOGRAPHY

Benhabib, Seyla. *The Rights of Others: Aliens, Residents, and Citizens*. Cambridge; New York: Cambridge University Press, 2004.

———. *The Rights of Others: Aliens, Residents, and Citizens*. Cambridge; New York: Cambridge University Press, 2004.

———. *Another Cosmopolitanism*. Oxford; New York: Oxford University Press, 2006.

———. *Dignity in Adversity: Human Rights in Troubled Times*. Cambridge, UK; Malden, MA: Polity, 2011.

Bernstein, J. M. *Torture and Dignity: An Essay on Moral Injury*. Chicago; London: The University of Chicago Press, 2015.

Brown Garrett W. "The Laws of Hospitality, Asylum Seekers and Cosmopolitan Right: A Kantian Response to Jacques Derrida." *European Journal of Political Theory* 9, no. 3 (2010): 308–27.

———. "The European Union and Kant's Idea of Cosmopolitan Right: Why the EU Is Not Cosmopolitan." *European Journal of International Relations* 20, no. 3 (2014): 671–93.

Catholic News Service. "U.S. Catholic leaders concerned by low number of resettled refugees." March 28, 2018, https://cruxnow.com/church-in-the-usa/2018/03/28/u-s-catholic-leaders-concerned-by-low-number-of-resettled-refugees.

Chishti, Muzaffar, Sarah Pierce, and Jessica Bolter. "The Obama Record on Deportations: Deporter in Chief or Not?" Migration Policy Institute, January 26, 2017, https://www.migrationpolicy.org/article/obama-record-deportations-deporter-chief-or-not.

Derrida, Jacques. *Of Hospitality*. Stanford: Stanford University Press, 2000.

Fass, Paula S. "A Historical Context for the United Nations Convention on the Rights of the Child." *The Annals of the American Academy of Political and Social Science* 633 (January 2011):17–29.

Forst, Rainer. *The Right to Justification: Elements of a Constructivist Theory of Justice*. Edited by Jeffrey Flynn. New York: Columbia University Press, 2012.

Gani, Jasmine K. "The Erasure of Race: Cosmopolitanism and the Illusion of Kantian Hospitality." *Millennium – Journal of International Studies* 45, no. 3 (2017): 425–46.

Gewirth, Alan. *Human Rights: Essays on Justification and Applications*. Chicago: University of Chicago Press, 1982.

Gladstone, Rick. "U.S. Quits Migration Pact, Saying It Infringes on Sovereignty." *New York Times*, December 3, 2017, https://www.nytimes.com/2017/12/03/world/americas/united-nations-migration-pact.html.

Haker, Hille. "Compassion and Justice." *Concilium*, no. 4 (2017): 44–54.

———. *Moralische Identität. Literarische Lebensgeschichten als Medium Ethischer Reflexion. Mit einer Interpretation der "Jahrestage" von Uwe Johnson*. Tübingen: Francke, 1999.

———. "No Space. Nowhere. Refugees and the Problem of Human Rights in Arendt and Ricœur." *Ricoeur Studies* 8, no. 2 (2017): 21–45.

———. "Vulnerable Agency: Human Dignity and Gendered Violence." In *Dignity and Conflict: Contemporary Interfaith Dialogue on the Value and Vulnerability of Human Life,* edited by Jonathan Rothschildt and Matthew Petrusek, 393–436. Notre Dame: University of Notre Dame Press, 2018, forthcoming.

Heidbrink, Lauren. "Criminal Alien or Humanitarian Refugee?: The Social Agency of Migrant Youth." *Children's Legal Rights Journal* 33 (Spring 2013): 133–90.

Hing, Julianne. "Why Numbers Alone Obscure the Real Deportation Story." *The Nation*, December 28, 2017, https://www.thenation.com/article/why-numbers-alone-obscure-the-real-deportation-story.

Hochschild, Arlie Russell. *Strangers in Their Own Land: Anger and Mourning on the American Right*. New York: New Press, 2016.

Hogan, Linda. *Keeping Faith with Human Rights*. Washington: Georgetown University Press, 2015.

Joseph, George. "Draft DHS Report Called for Long-Term Surveillance of Sunni Muslim Immigrants." *Foreign Policy*, February 5, 2018. http://foreignpolicy.com/2018/02/05/draft-dhs-report-surveillance-of-muslim-immigrants.

Kant, Immanuel. "Perpetual Peace: A Philosophical Sketch." In *Kant's Political Writings,* edited by Hans Reiss, 93–115. Cambridge: Cambridge University Press, 1991.

Lesch, Walter. *Christentum und Populismus. Klare Fronten?* Freiburg: Herder 2017.

Mandry Christof. *Europa als Wertegemeinschaft. Eine Theologisch-Ethische Studie zum politischen Selbstverständnis der Europäischen Union*. Saarbrücken: Nomos, 2009.

Menjívar, Cecilia, and Krista M. Perreira. "Undocumented and Unaccompanied: Children of Migration in the European Union and the United States." *Journal of Ethnic and Migration Studies*, Special Issue: Undocumented & Unaccompanied: Children of Migration in the European Union and the United States (December 21, 2017), https://doi.org/10.1080/1369183X.2017.1404255.

Mudde, Cas, and Cristóbal Rovira Kaltwasser, eds. *Populism in Europe and the Americas: Threat or Corrective for Democracy?* Cambridge: Cambridge University Press, 2012.

Nussbaum, Martha Craven. *Political Emotions: Why Love Matters for Justice*. Cambridge: The Belknap Press of Harvard University Press, 2013.

Office of Refugee Resettlement. "Facts and Data," available at https://www.acf.hhs.gov/orr/about/ucs/facts-and-data.

Ott, Konrad. *Zuwanderung und Moral*. Stuttgart: reclam, 2016.

Pruitt, Lesley, Helen Berents, and Gayle Munro. Gender and Age in the Construction of Male Youth in the European Migration 'Crisis.'" *Signs: Journal of Women in Culture and Society* 43, no. 3 (2018): 687–709.

Ratzinger, Josef. "Europas Identität. Seine geistigen Grundlagen gestern, heute, morgen," in Werte in Zeiten des Umbruchs. Die Herausforderungen der Zukunft bestehen. Freiburg: Herder spektrum, 2005, 68–88.

Ricoeur, Paul. *Oneself as Another*. Chicago: University of Chicago Press, 1992.

———. *The Just*. Chicago: University of Chicago Press, 2000.

Rohan Marc. "Refugee Family Reunification Rights: A Basis in the European Court of Human Rights' Family Reunification Jurisprudence." *Chicago Journal of International Law* 15, no. 1 (2015): 347–375, http://chicagounbound.uchicago.edu/cjil/vol15/iss1/15.

Sacchetti, Maria. "DHS Proposal Would Change Rules for Minors in Immigration Detention." *Washington Post*, May 9, 2018. https://www.washingtonpost.com/local/immigration/dhs-proposal-would-change-rules-for-minors-in-immigration-detention/2018/05/09/267af486–4f00–11e8-b725–92c89fe3ca4c_story.html?utm_term=.8d9deb87b3ff.

Sharpless, Rebecca. "Cosmopolitan Democracy and the Detention of Immigrant Families." *New Mexico Law Review* 47, no. 1 (2017): 19–63.

Scheffler, Samuel. "Immigration and the Significance of Culture." *Philosophy & Public Affairs* 35, no. 2 (2007): 93–125.

Shepherd, Andrew, *The Gift of the Other: Levinas, Derrida, and a Theology of Hospitality*. Oregon: Pickwick Publications, 2014.

Still, Judith. *Derrida and Hospitality Theory and Practice*. Edinburgh: Edinburgh University Press, 2010.

Trump, Donald J. "Statement from President Donald Trump." September 5, 2017. https://www.whitehouse.gov/briefings-statements/statement-president-donald-j-trump-7.

———. "State of the Union Address." January 30, 2018. https://www.whitehouse.gov/briefings-statements/president-donald-j-trumps-state-union-address.

Waldron, Jeremy. *Dignity, Rank, and Rights*. New York; Oxford: Oxford University Press, 2012.

———. "Exclusion: Property Analogies in the Immigration Debate." *Theoretical Inquiries in Law* 18, no. 2 (2017): 469–89.

Index

About the Contributors

Philip M. Anderson is professor for intercultural social work at Regensburg University of Applied Sciences in Bavaria, southern Germany. He is an historian and graduate of York University, United Kingdom, and did his PhD at the Ludwig-Maximilian-University in Munich. He has worked as a migration researcher for many years in Germany and has published extensively, focusing on commissioned studies on migration and integration issues for decision-makers at local authority level and for major charities and NGOs. Topics of research have included the social and human rights of undocumented migrants, access to care services for migrant elders and the specific situation of asylum seekers in Germany, looking in recent years particularly at access to vocational training for refugees. He is currently involved in a nation-wide network of PhD studies coordinated by the University of Hamburg on "Neglected topics of Refugee Research."

Stephanie N. Arel is an Andrew W. Mellon Fellow at the September 11 Memorial and Museum and a visiting researcher at New York University. She is the author of *Affect Theory, Shame and Christian Formation* (2016) and coeditor of *Post-Traumatic Public Theology* (2016). She holds an Integrative Trauma Certificate, a training in trauma modalities for clinical treatment, from the National Institute for the Psychotherapies (NIP), New York, NY. Her work revolves around the interplay of psychology and religion to inform an evaluation of trauma and its impact on human dignity.

Adam Avrushin, JD, PhD, is associate director at the Center for the Human Rights of Children at Loyola University Chicago. He has served in leadership positions at multiple child-serving organizations and worked as an attorney/guardian *ad litem* for children involved with Illinois' state child welfare system. His current research examines the service needs of unaccompanied immigrant children and their families in Illinois, as well as the community assets and services to address these needs.

Molly Greening is pursuing her PhD at Loyola University Chicago in the Integrative Studies in Ethics and Theology (ISET) program. She was the first person to graduate from Loyola's dual MA program in theology and women's studies/gender studies and was a research assistant for the 2015–2016 Faculty Fellowship Program offered by the Center for the Human Rights of Children at Loyola University Chicago. Her research interests focus on feminist ethics and migration ethics. She is currently training to be a facilitator for Soliya, an international nonprofit focused on creating online cross-cultural dialogues with young people from around the world.

Hille Haker, PhD, holds the Richard McCormick S.J. Endowed Chair of Catholic Moral Theology at Loyola University Chicago. Her research focuses on questions of moral identity and narrative ethics, bioethics and social ethics, especially questions of human rights and human security, and feminist ethics. Her books include *Moralische Identität. Literarische Lebensgeschichten als Medium ethischer Reflexion* (1999), *Ethik der genetischen Frühdiagnostik* (2002), and *Hauptsache gesund* (2011). She coedited several books, among them: *The Ethics of Genetics in Human Procreation* (2000), *Ethik-Geschlecht-Wissenschaften* (2006), *Medical Ethics in Health Care Chaplaincy* (2009), and *Religiöser Pluralismus in der Klinikseelsorge* (2014). She has been a codirector of the international journal *Concilium* and served on several Bioethics Committees, including the *European Group on Ethics in Science and New Technologies to the European Commission.* In 2015, she received one of the Faculty Fellowships offered by the Center for the Human Rights of Children at Loyola University Chicago Her present research is a book project on *Recognition and Responsibility.*

Kristin E. Heyer is professor of theological ethics at Boston College. Her books include *Kinship Across Borders: A Christian Ethic of Immigration* (2012) and *Prophetic and Public: the Social Witness of U.S. Catholicism* (2006). She has also published the coedited volumes *Public Theology and the Global Common Good: The Contribution of David Hollenbach* (2016); *Conscience and Catholicism: Rights, Responsibilities and Institutional Responses* (2015); and *Catholics and Politics: Dynamic Tensions between Faith and Power* (2008). Her articles have appeared in such journals as *Theological Studies*, *The Journal of the Society of Christian Ethics, The Journal of Catholic Social Thought, Political Theology, and Asian Horizons.* She is co-chair of the planning committee for Catholic Theological

Ethics in the World Church and she is an editor for Georgetown University Press' Moral Traditions series.

Katherine Kaufka Walts, JD, is director of the Center for the Human Rights of Children at Loyola University Chicago. The center pursues an agenda of interdisciplinary research, outreach and education, and advocacy to address critical and complex issues affecting children and youth, both locally and globally. Prior to joining Loyola, Kaufka Walts was an immigration attorney, representing children and adults in immigration and criminal justice proceedings in the United States. She has published widely on topics including immigration, human trafficking, and children's rights.

Linde Lindkvist, PhD, is senior lecturer in human rights studies at the Stockholm School of Theology. He specializes in questions of human rights history, the right to religious freedom and children's rights. He is the author of *Religious Freedom and the Universal Declaration of Human Rights* (2017), which evolved out of his 2014 thesis from Lund University. His ongoing postdoctoral project concerns the origins of the UN Convention on the Rights of the Child.

Elena Namli is professor of theological ethics at Uppsala University, Sweden. Her research focuses on social ethics with a particular emphasis on human rights in different cultural and ideological settings. Her publications include *Human Rights as Ethics, Politics, and Law* (2014), *Jewish Thought, Utopia, and Revolution* (coedited with Jayne Svenungsson and Alana M. Vincent, 2014), *Mänskliga rättigheter i det offentliga Sverige* (*Human Rights and the Swedish State,* coedited with Anna-Sara Lind, 2017).

Tisha M. Rajendra is associate professor of Christian ethics at Loyola University Chicago. She is the author of *Migrants and Citizens: Justice as Responsibility in the Ethics of Immigration* (2017) and has published in the *Journal for the Society of Christian Ethics*, *Ethical Theory and Moral Practice* and *Political Theology*. Her research areas include the ethics of migration, solidarity, virtue ethics, and philosophical and theological theories of justice. She is currently working on her second book, a volume on solidarity as practiced by fragmented selves in contexts of injustice.

Celeste Sánchez has a BA in sociology and a minor in Spanish from UCLA and an MSW from Loyola University Chicago with an emphasis on mental health and migration studies. Her employment experience includes direct caregiver and youth group facilitator at Nuestros Pequeños Hermanos in Guatemala and Honduras, graduate research assistant at Loyola University

Chicago, National Science Foundation investigation research assistant in Guatemala, and social worker for the Immigrants' Rights Project at the pro bono legal firm Public Counsel of Los Angeles, California. She began her doctoral studies at Loyola in August 2018.

Susan J. Terrio is professor of anthropology and French studies at Georgetown University. Her recent books include *Judging Mohammed: Juvenile Delinquency, Immigration, and Exclusion at the Paris Palace of Justice*, (2009), *Whose Child Am I? Unaccompanied, Undocumented Children in U.S. Immigration Custody* (2015), selected as a Choice Outstanding Academic Title for 2016, and a coedited volume with New York University Press titled, *Illegal Encounters: The Effect of Detention and Deportation on Young People* (2018). She has been awarded fellowships from National Endowment for the Humanities, the Radcliffe Institute at Harvard University, the Russell Sage Foundation, the Institute for Advanced Study at Princeton, and the Woodrow Wilson International Center for Scholars.

Cristina L. H. Traina is professor and chair of religious studies at Northwestern University in Evanston, Illinois. The author of *Feminist Ethics and Natural Law* and *Erotic Attunement: Parenthood and the Ethics of Sensuality between Unequals*, she has focused on method in ethics as well as on ethics of gender, sexuality, economy, and environment. She currently works questions of children's moral agency in situations in which children are "out of place": paid work, solo migration, politics, armed conflict, and other settings.

Maria Vidal de Haymes, PhD, is professor of social work at Loyola University Chicago, where she teaches baccalaureate and graduate level courses in social welfare policy and migration. She is director of the migration studies sub-specialization and coordinates a several migration focused immersion courses and international field internships in the School of Social Work. Her teaching, scholarship and professional service address issues of poverty, inequality, and social exclusion. She is the coeditor of the *Journal of Poverty* and serves on several advisory boards of international and local advocacy and service organizations that accompany immigrant and internally displaced populations.

Javier Zamora was born in La Herradura, El Salvador, in 1990. His father fled El Salvador when Zamora was a year old, as did his mother when he was about to turn five. Both parents' migrations were caused by the US-funded Salvadoran Civil War (1980–1992).

In 1999, Zamora migrated through Guatemala, Mexico, and eventually the Sonoran Desert. Before a coyote abandoned his group in Oaxaca, Zamora managed to make it to Arizona with the aid of other migrants. His first full-length collection, *Unaccompanied* (2017), explores how immigration and the civil war have impacted his family.

Zamora is a 2018–2019 Radcliffe Institute fellow at Harvard University and holds fellowships from CantoMundo, Colgate University, MacDowell, Macondo, The National Endowment for the Arts, Poetry Foundation, Stanford University, and Yaddo. He is the recipient of 2017 Lannan Literary Fellowship, 2017 Narrative Prize, and 2016 Barnes & Noble Writer for Writers Award for his work in the Undocupoets Campaign.

Zamora lives in San Rafael, California.